# The Making
## of a
# Maverick

# Eric Macfarlane

Pen Press Publishers Ltd

First published in Great Britain by
Pen Press Publishers Ltd
The Old School
39 Chesham Road
Brighton BN2 1NB

ISBN: 1-905621-64-7
ISBN13: 978-1-905621-64-4

Printed and bound in the UK

A catalogue record of this book is available from
the British Library

Cover design by Jacqueline Abromeit

From a student to his students

# About the Author

Eric Macfarlane was what is known in education as 'a late developer'. He gained the qualifications for university entry as a mature student, graduating from Birkbeck College, London, with a first class honours degree in English, at the age of 29. Five years later he was appointed to the headship of Letchworth Grammar School and went on to become principal of Queen Mary's College in Basingstoke, one of the country's first and largest sixth-form colleges. His book, *Sixth-Form Colleges*, became a definitive statement on this form of provision for the 16-19 age group. Eric Macfarlane has written regularly for the press, both serious articles on education and lighter pieces for the general reader. *The Making of a Maverick* attempts to bridge the gap between these two forms of writing.

# Acknowledgements

I should like to thank Jill, my wife and best friend, for her unflagging support during the writing of this book and - more particularly - throughout the career that it chronicles. I also owe a debt to the many friends, relations, ex-pupils and ex-colleagues who have helped me recall shared experiences.

1

# Force-feeding at Miss Falkner's

Throughout my childhood years in the 1930s and 1940s I lived with my mother and grandmother in a district called Rushmoor, a nondescript ribbon development midway between the Chiltern villages of Penn and Hazlemere. Apart from having a name, the area lacked any identity: there was no focal point or sense of community. My mother considered the properties jerry-built and their inhabitants working-class – the latter judgement no doubt coloured by the impact on the area of a few high-profile families who produced a seemingly endless supply of snotty-nosed, under-clad street urchins.

The stigma of being a single parent did nothing to under-mine my mother's view that we were a cut above our neigh-bours. Nearly everyone else's employment was local, on the land or in the factories and businesses three miles away in High Wycombe. My mother, however, worked in a distant and prestigious place called 'The City': she was a bookkeeper in Whitbreads' counting-house in Chiswell Street near St Paul's Cathedral. Even in the country, she dressed smartly in town clothes, which she made herself from Vogue patterns. My clothes also differed significantly from those of my companions.

After Sunday lunch, when local families promenaded along the pathways that crossed the fields behind the two rows of houses, I was paraded in my infant years like a little Lord Fauntleroy, in a tailored camel-coloured coat with brown velvet collar. The rest of the time I ran wild, fully integrated into the Rushmoor riff-raff. This freedom stemmed partly from the strength of my mother's belief in the open-air life, which outweighed her concern at the company I kept, and partly from the fact that she wasn't around most of the time to keep an eye on me. My grandmother brought me up, but exercised a very light control.

Money was tight and the maintenance of our public image had to be paid for by a contrasting frugality within the home. We grew vegetables and had a plentiful supply of eggs from our own chickens (both my responsibility as I grew older), but meat and groceries were less readily available. We made one or two purchases at a time, comparing prices carefully in the surrounding villages. There was an emphasis on 'filling' foods, such as dumplings and porridge (made with water). Puddings were my grandmother's speciality: a rotation of rice, sago, semolina, tapioca and macaroni, relieved by the occasional baked apple or plum duff. Quantities tended to be small and, when war broke out and rationing was introduced, we didn't notice much difference.

The ground floor of our rented house was dimly lit by fragile and flickering gas mantles; the upstairs by dripping candles carried in Wee Willie Winkie metal holders. The only heating was in the living room, from a small open fire fuelled with wood that I collected locally. The rest of the house was freezing – literally so for long periods in the winter, as the temperatures indoors matched those outside on the top of the Chiltern Hills. Every year the water froze solid in the exposed plumbing, expanding and splitting the pipes in the process. I was never unduly concerned at the loss of washing facilities, but use of the unflushable WC wasn't a particularly pleasant experience. When the thaw came, there was a constant battle to stem the flow of water from the burst pipes until repairs could be carried out. The various bodged soldering jobs gave the pipework a gnarled and carbuncled appearance from which one could determine the history of the winter repairs. Bedclothes were in short supply and, although I was privileged to have the most generous allocation of covers, I was always cold at night during the winter months. My grandmother, who inclined naturally and cheerfully to self-sacrifice, huddled under her outdoor coat.

There were a few token patches of old lino in the downstairs rooms, but rough boards elsewhere. Furniture was limited to the bare essentials, except in the front room, which contained one or two nice pieces, testimony to my dead grandfather's skills when he'd worked as a furniture designer for one of the High Wycombe chair manufacturers. This room was unused for 364 days a year but came into its own on Christmas Day when our small family of three took up residence for an afternoon and evening of reading and board games.

Keeping up appearances necessitated no-one's seeing how we lived indoors and people were never invited into the house. By contrast, several of our neighbours kept an open door and I was intrigued to observe how the other, supposedly poorer, half of the world lived. I envied my friends the kitchens in which they spent so much of their time cocooned in a stale fug of warmth generated by their cooking ranges. I was a particularly early caller at one friend's house where the family periodically enjoyed a fried breakfast accompanied by lashings of Daddie's (sic) sauce.

Much of my waking life was spent as a member of the Rushmoor gang, an assorted, all-age company of adventurers which I joined as a very young initiate and captained some years later. We spent whole days together out in the Bucks countryside, building tree houses in the beech woods, scrumping from the abundant plum and cherry orchards, snaring rabbits on the perimeter of a nearby estate owned by the gentleman racing driver, Earl Howe. No Rushmoorite was denied membership of the gang, although there were individuals who were tolerated rather than welcomed. There was, in particular, a gawky, skeletal youth known as Gandhi whose pumping elbows and bony knees created havoc in our frequent games of street football. He employed the tackling strategy perfected years later by England's Nobby Styles who, on the way to Wembley World Cup glory in 1966, negated foreign flair by climbing all over opponents with flailing arms and legs. There was, however, another more persistent problem with Gandhi in the form of a vicarious vocational hazard. His father worked on the 'Dirty Denis' cesspit lorries, assembling and disconnecting the slime-coated hosepipes that sucked up the raw sewage from the brick tanks that were sunk into rural gardens. Some of the all-pervasive pong that his dad brought home with him each evening transferred itself to the unfortunate Gandhi, who was consequently required to keep his distance in our company. Perhaps the close contact that he sought on the football pitch was some kind of compensatory or retaliatory psychological urge.

Gang warfare was rife in the area and we were constantly engaged in armed conflict with marauding bands from one or other of the neighbouring villages. I was often a particular target on these occasions, the circumstances of my birth apparently being circulated with more interest elsewhere than in Rushmoor. Sticks were used for close combat, but most engagements were conducted at a distance, with stones as the main weapon – thrown or propelled by catapult. The catapults were roughly-hewn DIY jobs, except one: maintaining our image of privilege, my mother bought mine from Hamleys of Regent Street. It had a straight-sided metal prong, thick thongs of elastic and a pouch of high quality leather. What she thought she was doing, I have no idea. She could hardly have been unaware of the purpose to which I put this expensive purchase, at least not after I returned home one evening with a duck egg protruding from the side of my head as a result of a direct hit by one of the enemy.

There was another privileged boy in the street who enjoyed less freedom than I did but shared my favoured situation as the recipient of expensive toys and weapons of destruction. He was given an air rifle for a birthday and wasted no time in trying it out on the temptingly-raised posterior of a contemporary who was examining a cowpat in a local meadow. The next day the rifle appeared in two pieces sticking out of the dustbin at the gate of his house. I was impressed by this unequivocal demonstration of peremptory paternal discipline and realised vaguely that there was, for good or ill, something lacking in my own upbringing.

The search for campsites was a recurring challenge to the Rushmoor gang. One of our most elaborate and ingenious efforts was at the base of a neglected haystack. Over a period of days we burrowed into the stack and right through to the other side, then proceeded to dig out subsidiary passages and spaces until we had excavated a whole labyrinth of tunnels and rooms. The material we were working on was more rotting compost than hay and we emerged after each day's labours looking like Bevin boys returning from the pits. Gandhi was excused the usual obligation to keep his distance, on the grounds that we all stank so powerfully that he was indistinguishable from the rest of us. The distinct possibility that our haystack home might collapse and bury us all alive appeared not to occur to anyone. Such hazards were part of everyday life.

One day, having set our rabbit snares, we penetrated the Earl Howe Estate more deeply than previously and discovered a substantial gamekeepers' hut where equipment of all kinds was being stored. The door was heavily padlocked but we forced a window to gain access. However, before anyone could scramble inside, we sighted, and were simultaneously sighted by, a gamut of gamekeepers approaching in the distance, guns in the crook of their arms. We turned and fled with the posse in pursuit, shooting as they came. Since no-one was hit, I assume they fired in the air or deliberately over our heads, but that possibility obviously wasn't acknowledged when we later regaled absent friends with an account of the incident. I was one of the youngest on this occasion and lagged at the back of the fleeing pack. Rounding a corner in the plantation trackway, which momentarily put us out of the gamekeepers' view, I veered sideways, crashed through a hedge and flattened myself in a slight hollow beyond. I was convinced that my thumping heart would give me away, but Earl Howe's men all pounded past, leaving me to wend my way to safety by a circuitous route.

Scary as this incident was, I think we were, as a rule, more in fear of Farmer Brant than the Earl Howe gamekeepers. Brant was a fierce bull of a man, florid, foul-mouthed and infuriated by any sign of trespassers. He gave chase instantly when he saw us on his land and we were in no doubt that the thick stick that he always brandished would be put to good use if we were ever caught. For a big man he had a surprising turn of speed. There was an occasion when we were having an innocent cowpat fight in one of his fields, flicking the juicier green deposits at each other with sticks, when he vaulted a five-bar gate and came at us full tilt. I still bear the scar from a deep gash in my upper leg that I sustained on this particular occasion when scrambling over a barbed wire fence.

There were other potentially more dangerous situations. During the early part of the Second World War, when I was eight years old, three of us were wandering along a road on the outskirts of High Wycombe some three miles from my home, when we became aware of unusual happenings well above our heads. It was a dogfight – British and German planes swooping, diving, firing on one another. We stood, hands on hips and heads arched backwards, observing what was going on, until an air-raid warden came rushing along the road, whistle blowing and rattle clacking, to usher us into one of the nearby houses.

I was accustomed to straying miles from my home, usually with friends but occasionally alone. I never minded my own company and for some activities preferred to operate solo. Each year I kept a record of the birds' nests that I found, identifying their owners and making a note of their location, the number of eggs, the dates on which they hatched and whether the babies survived. I had 87 entries one year, including details of a number of rare specimens and unusual nesting sites. There was a beautifully-made yellow hammer's nest precariously balanced in the fork of a dead fern that was abandoned when it collapsed after a storm. I grieved when a favourite nest and its contents were damaged or destroyed and came to realise how precarious life was in the natural world.

I ought, perhaps, also to have been aware of my own vulnerability, wandering alone along remote rural footpaths and trackways, but my mother's encouragement to 'get out into the fresh air' was never qualified by warnings not to speak to strangers. The current view seems to be that the dreadful things that now happen to unaccompanied children didn't occur 60 or so years ago, but that isn't true. As a teenager I did a substantial early morning paper round. There were two adjoining cottages on my route with families that both included ten-year-old girls, one dark-eyed and dark-haired, the other sunny blonde. They were inseparable, the happiest of companions. One day they disappeared, their bodies found a week later in a wood some miles away. Subsequently, a soldier was charged and convicted of their abduction and murder. Perhaps the difference then was that the harrowing details of such events weren't zoomed into every home in the country, terrifying parents and making them afraid to let their children out of their sight.

My formal education began at a dame school in 1937. My mother wanted 'the best' for me and, like many parents today, suffered from the delusion that this necessarily meant self-sacrifice in order to pay private school fees. The school, known as Miss Falkner's, was co-educational and catered for the full age range of compulsory schooling, 5-14. The number on roll was restricted to eight or nine pupils, the maximum that could be seated round the table that occupied most of the front room in Miss Falkner's poky little house. Remaining floor space, such as it was, accommodated an upright piano, assorted boxes of craft materials and teetering piles of books, papers and piano music. A modern-day health and safety inspector would not have been impressed.

Access to the schoolroom was via a narrow hallway that ran from the front door to the rear of the house. On the right, as one entered the building, there was a small table displaying homemade preserves and chocolate fudge, which Miss Falkner made and sold to parents to supplement her income as a schoolteacher. At the beginning and end of morning and afternoon school our teacher stationed herself opposite this table, ostensibly to receive and release her young charges, but also clearly to encourage parents to buy her wares. To enter and leave school we had to squeeze through the restricted space between Miss Falkner's ample girth and the preserves table. I can still recall the passageway's unique odour – a musky blend of freshly-made marmalade and warm woollen underwear well past its washday.

All teachers seem larger than life to young children and Miss Falkner was no exception. She was short, but solid and brawny, with a concentration of weight in the rump. Exuding rude health and heartiness, she belonged to that breed of woman that one expects to encounter in a farmyard, sleeves rolled up in all weathers and wielding a pitchfork or man-sized shovel. In fact, she invariably bustled to the door in the mornings adjusting her sleeves or skirt straight from some manual chore. With her hoarse masculine voice and throaty laugh she was closer to a panto dame than a school-ma'am.

Parents only saw Miss Falkner in a jovial mood, but her cheeriness wasn't always maintained in the classroom, where she suffered acute bouts of exasperation in the face of her pupils' habitual ignorance and stupidity. Miss Falkner's bête-noir was the senior scholar, George Randell, a ruddy-faced rustic who, having failed both the 11+ and 13+ examinations (for the local grammar school and technical school respect-ively), was a daily reminder that the school didn't always succeed in fulfilling its primary function. George was a frequent target for what would now be termed child abuse. Arithmetic lessons were regularly accompanied by the rhythmic tattoo of our teacher's clenched fists pounding on his bowed back as she attempted – almost literally – to ram home the rules that his poor brain could never fully grasp, let alone apply. One day, a particularly savage onslaught convinced a hushed school that it was about to witness a truly traumatic event, none other than the demise of its senior member. As the blows rained down, George's contorted features were ground more and more painfully into the table. His face was always red, but it now turned an alarming puce, his breathing becoming increasingly desperate as he fought agonisingly for air. To everyone's relief – not least, I imagine, Miss Falkner's – he survived, to endure many more arithmetical and physical torments.

Chastisement of female and more junior pupils was verbal, although an exception was made for one young lad called Micky Sutton, who was Miss Falkner's great-nephew. Micky believed, with some justification, that this family connection worked to his disadvantage and that his great-aunt lost no opportunity to demonstrate to the rest of the school that her young relative could expect no favours. One day, when several of us were walking to school, Micky, with my encouragement, snatched Laurence Weedon's cap and threw it over someone's garden hedge. Laurence retrieved it but, being a somewhat mollycoddled child, reported the incident as soon as we got to school. Anticipating Miss Falkner's wrath and its inevitable direction, Micky made for the staircase, closely followed by auntie's flailing fists. As the sounds of the bedroom pursuit reverberated above, I suffered an anguish of anticipation awaiting my turn for retribution in the hall below. Fortunately, Miss Falkner wasn't built for such energetic physical exercise and was a spent force when she eventually descended.

Micky had the benefit of extra-curricular tuition from his great-aunt by staying at school for lunch, and occasionally overnight, when he was taught to play the piano and to eat his greens. As a piano teacher, Miss Falkner employed the sharp-edge-of-a-ruler-across-the-knuckles method of instruction. Her way of dealing with food fads was similarly direct: pinch the nose, pull the head back and insert the food that had been declined. If only she could have found an equally effective way of force-feeding children with knowledge she would have experienced far less frustration in the classroom.

For most of the time at dame school I managed to avoid censure: I was no star, but, either by accident or innate cunning, I was reasonably successful at concealing the full extent of my ignorance. This facility sometimes deserted me, a specific instance occurring during one of our regular vocabulary lessons. The English paper in the 11+ exam contained frequent questions on word pairs such as opposites and masculines/ feminines. We were well drilled in these exam 'bankers' and subjected to regular spot checks to test our retention of them. During an oral session, I was called upon to name the female equivalent of 'dog'. My automatic response, when becoming the sudden focus of pedagogic attention, was always panic and on this occasion my mind went completely blank. Miss Falkner cajoled and hectored but it was no use: I simply couldn't dredge the word up from the depths of my storage system. In one of those classic situations in which adults mistake children's ignorance or forgetfulness for insolence or stubbornness, I think Miss Falkner was convinced that I knew the answer, but that I was either too squeamish or too well-bred to voice what I felt was an obscenity. Never one to give up, she continued to harangue and castigate, but eventually had to admit defeat. I felt that I had been found wanting in a number of ways that I didn't fully understand.

A more regular humiliation occurred every time we had a music lesson. Music meant singing, and from time to time the school gathered round the piano for stirring renditions of such classics as *Yankee Doodle Dandy* and *The Grand Old Duke of York*. My participation in these convivial occasions was prematurely curtailed as, early in my school career, I was identified as a 'groaner' and made to stand in the corner away from the rest of the school, a silent observer and listener. This exclusion from music-making has unfortunately proved to be a defining moment in my life.

Our other practical activities consisted of various forms of craftwork of the kind traditionally associated with girls' finishing schools: knitting, sewing, embroidery, appliqué. The winter term was a powerhouse of production with everyone sweating on deadlines to complete fondly-produced items in time for their presentation to parents for Christmas. Some of the tasks set for us were surprisingly ambitious. When I cleared my mother's house after her death I discovered a sizeable tablecloth embroidered in coloured silks, still in pristine condition; it had clearly never been used but stored away as a piece of nostalgia. There were also some more modest examples of my needleman's skills in leather and felt.

11

Miss Falkner lived with her elder sister whom she called in from time to time to admire our craftwork and occasionally to appraise more academic achievements. Millie was a little bird-like lady, as quiet and introspective as Miss Falkner was raucous and overpowering. Unlike her sister, Millie was said to have an academic qualification. She had been a headmistress and, notwithstanding her slight stature and calm manner, there was a presence about her that would undoubtedly have commanded her pupils' respect. How much Millie could see of our work I don't know, for she was almost blind. When I started school I was rather frightened of her whenever she emerged from the dark inner recesses of the house to fulfil her inspectorial duties.

Our Miss Falkner was really too familiar to us to be frightening, but we always had to be watchful for her changing moods. She dominated the classroom and there was never any opportunity for levity or tomfoolery. It wasn't, however, an unduly oppressive environment. There was a cosy familial feeling about the schoolroom and we received a lot of individual attention. There was no blackboard and little class instruction: Miss Falkner spent her time manoeuvring her buttocks round the table and conscientiously helping each pupil in turn. As we progressed up the school, the secondary selection procedure loomed ever more threateningly over us, but we never experienced the competitive stresses of the 'good' prep school, partly of course because the wide age range meant that our progress was measured, as it should be, against our own ability, not that of others.

At the end of each school year every pupil, even George Randell, was presented with a new book as a reward for progress. My first-ever prize was a lightweight volume intriguingly entitled *The Digger Gnome Earns a Pippity Pebble*, but I quickly graduated to more substantial literary works – R M Ballantyne's *The Young Fur Traders*, James

12

Fenimore's *The Last of the Mohicans* and a full-length version of Defoe's *Robinson Crusoe*. My pride in winning these prizes was undiminished by the knowledge that everyone else was also a winner. I valued the books and enjoyed the colourful illustrations depicting dramatic scenes from the narratives. Unfortunately, despite Miss Falkner's efforts to extend our vocabulary, I found the texts themselves disappointingly inaccessible. Nor was I ever drawn to come back to them in later life, although I did dutifully read *Robinson Crusoe* many years later when it was a prescribed text on my English Honours degree course.

2

# Gradgrind's Legacy

The grammar school that I attended for eight years was no
ordinary run-of-the-mill selective school, having received a
Royal Charter in 1562 from Elizabeth I. The Royal Grammar
School, High Wycombe, was steeped in tradition, although
by the time I arrived in 1942 only the headmaster sported a
mortar-board, headgear that in an earlier stage of the school's
history had been obligatory for masters and boys alike.

E R Tucker, the headmaster, was an Oxford classicist.
Appointed in 1933 at the callow age of 31, he had set out
with youthful vigour to expand the sixth form and establish
strong links with Oxford and Cambridge. These aims were
impressively realised and a year after I entered the school
– although in no way connected with that event – Mr Tucker
was elected to the Headmasters' Conference, an exclusive
club whose members mostly represented prestigious public
schools. The Royal Grammar School marked this significant
rise in its status by replacing football with rugby as the main
winter sport.

To gain admission to the Royal Grammar School, boys

from the High Wycombe area competed in the 11+. Once in the school they quickly realised that competition for academic distinction was to be their daily preoccupation. The routine was dominated by tests and form rankings. Fortnightly reports were produced, giving marks and positions in each subject together with an overall form position. Regular exams produced further sets of marks which, combined with those awarded in class and for homework, gave a definitive statistical statement on each boy's academic standing and potential. The ghost of Dickens' Thomas Gradgrind stalked the corridors 'ready to weigh and measure any parcel of human nature, and tell you exactly what it comes to.' It has always been a challenge to educationists to find a way of encapsulating all one needs to know about a child in a set of figures. Today we have carried this process a stage further by seeking to reduce the complex character and achievements of a whole school to a position in a league table.

In the obscure nomenclature favoured by the RGS, the first and second years were termed third forms, Lower III and Upper III (the Roman numerals were important). At the end of the lower third year a boy's overall form position determined the route that he would take to School Certificate (the equivalent of today's GCSE). The most academically successful boys were selected for an 'express' course, designed to prepare them for School Certificate examination entry at 15; the remainder worked at a normal rate and took their certificate at 16, the age for which it was intended. The two express forms recognised just two categories of scholar – linguists (U IIIA) and scientists (U IIIS). These forms were smaller than the two non-express forms, the assumption being that those pupils who most easily coped with academic work merited more advantageous teaching and learning conditions than those who found it more difficult.

There were 35 boys in my lower third form and my overall

end-of-year position of 16th meant that I would probably just miss the cut for an express course. However, when the choice was made, precisely 16 express places were awarded to my form (with slightly fewer to each of the other lower thirds). With little variation between subjects in my year's results, there was nothing to indicate whether my academic potential – if any – lay in languages or the sciences. When the coin landed I found myself boarding the A-express, to study Latin, German and French. I had been a very young entrant to the secondary school; thus my academic specialism (and likely career direction) were chosen for me while I was still only 11. Selection for the express route to School Certificate meant that I would take the exam at 14, rather than 16. However, this early exam entry proved conjectural for I didn't complete the express course. I struggled from the outset in the fast stream and by my third year was ensconced near the bottom of form IVA. This was an unpleasant experience at the time but it proved useful years later when, as a teacher, I had a natural empathy with pupils caught in a system that told them they were academically gifted and then proceeded to destroy their confidence and self-esteem by confronting them with daily failure.

My escape from this situation came about in this way. One of the minor idiosyncrasies of the rail system in the area in which I live is that the 17.30 Waterloo to Exeter express stops at Basingstoke each evening to enable people to board, but not to alight. The RGS express forms functioned in the opposite way: ejections but no replacements. When the occasion arose for my express form to offload some of its passengers I sensed an opportunity. The boys occupying the bottom two positions in form IVA were to transfer to a lower stream. I persuaded my mother to come up to the school – a brave move by a parent in those days – to ask if I might accompany them. This initiative may have been a rare example of mature judgement on my part, an astute awareness of the benefits of travelling more slowly and arriving at one's destination unharmed. I suspect, however, that it had more to do with the fact that the departing boys were my special mates. The prospect of being separated from them – even perhaps losing my place in their team for playground matches of tennis-ball soccer – would have been bleak indeed.

I quickly adjusted to the slower pace of the M stream, settling for what the football pundits refer to as mid-table mediocrity. I was quite conscientious and conformist and belonged to that section of the class that did its own homework, rather than copying someone else's on the bus or train. On the other hand, the course never aroused in me the sort of interest or enthusiasm that might have produced noteworthy results. The M in 'M stream' stood for 'modern', a term that, with the introduction of secondary modern schools following the 1944 Education Act, was soon to be applied to another grouping of less able students. To me it was a misnomer: I never saw the relevance of what we did in school to the world in which we were actually living. There must have been boys that got an adrenaline rush from reading Stevenson's *Travels with a Donkey* or Addison and Steele's *de Coverley Papers*, but I wasn't one of them. Maths was another mystery. Our problem solving focused on a crazy world of fanatical roadmen, repeatedly digging holes and filling them in again, and dim-witted householders attempting to fill their Saturday night bath tubs with both taps fully on but no plug in.

The more influence that exams exert over teaching, the more tedious and repetitive the classroom experience. I studied the same period of history for five years because the staff thought that pupils would do better in the subject in Higher Certificate (the equivalent of GCE A-level) if the sixth form work covered the same ground as the School Certificate course. In the years immediately prior to School Certificate we were continually drilled in the specific routines we would encounter in the exam papers. In English language the same four tasks were repeated week after week and we concentrated on these to the exclusion of the dozens of other activities in which we might have engaged to improve our use of language. One lesson each week was devoted to the précis question, in which Latinate prose passages had to be reduced to a third or a quarter of their length, in accordance with a long list of rules governing such technicalities as verb tenses, the case of personal pronouns and direct and indirect speech forms. I never properly understood the passages, the mechanical processes involved or the purpose of the exercise. A few years later, when I was starting to take an interest in the English language, I realised that these précis lessons had had a practical application: that they were merely an academic and formalised version of a natural process in which human beings constantly engage, that of summarising something they have heard or read. Our English master was presumably unaware of this or surely he would have tapped into boys' everyday experiences, asking them to give oral and written résumés and summaries of books and articles read, films seen, radio programmes listened to, instructions received, conversations overheard.

Précis lessons may have failed to excite me, but the fifth form English course did notch up one significant success: I enjoyed a literary work for the first time. The dramatic opening of Thomas Hardy's *Mayor of Casterbridge*, in which the drunken Michael Henchard sells his wife and young daughter in the furmity tent at Weydon Priors' fair, grabbed my immediate attention and I read the book at two or three sittings. With unobtrusive sketching in of background detail, skilful changes of narrative pace and steady building of tension, Hardy makes this bizarre incident entirely credible. The point at which a buyer unexpectedly presents himself, thereby turning a mock auction into a startling reality, is one of the great heart-stopping moments in English literature. Meanwhile, back in the classroom, we were busy filling successive exercise books with dictated extracts from a book of Hardy criticism.

It was in the sixth form that dictation really came into its own: the masters talked and we wrote down what they said. In the absence of any guidance on note-taking procedures, and lacking the wit to devise any strategy for ourselves, most of us attempted to get everything down verbatim. It was an exhausting and un-edifying process entailing writing down one statement whilst trying to listen to and remember the next. History lessons, in particular, kept uncompromisingly to this pattern: the two masters who shared responsibility for the Higher Certificate course each came in, opened his file at the point reached the previous lesson and read and talked his way through the next part of the syllabus. Both were intelligent and knowledgeable scholars with, it appeared, a genuine desire to communicate their subject to their pupils. Why, then, were they so mind-blowingly unimaginative in the way in which they set about their task?

There were numerous possibilities. They had received no professional training and had little understanding of the learning process. Insofar as they gave any thought to how to teach, they adopted the methods that they themselves had experienced as pupils and students. Confident in their academic achievements as a suitable qualification for teaching, they inclined to the view that the processes of learning and teaching were just matters of common sense. Being themselves academically gifted and successful, they had little experience of the kind of study problems encountered by mere mortals. Above all, they were teaching unimaginative syllabuses, preparing pupils for unimaginative examinations and working in a very unimaginative and traditional institution that rarely questioned its policies and procedures: they simply absorbed and became part of the prevailing culture. If one were to analyse why so many of the staff in our most revered universities currently use the 1940s' RGS sixth form history model of teaching, one would probably come to much the same conclusions.

Given the prevailing culture, it was perhaps not surprising that memorable learning experiences were a bit thin on the ground during my secondary schooling. However, one day in a lower third history lesson the master let us loose in the school grounds to look for flints that one could shape, by painstakingly chipping and scraping them against other stones, into objects that bore some resemblance to Stone Age implements. It was my only school experience of fieldwork, but one that helped condition my positive response, many years later, to the Nuffield Science Project with its Chinese proverb watchwords 'to hear is to forget, to see is to remember, to do is to understand'.

The mid-20th century grammar school curriculum included only a limited range of practical and creative subjects and the majority of pupils didn't study these beyond the junior forms. However, as a lower stream pupil (following my voluntary transfer from the express form) I was able to continue with art to School Certificate level. The assumptions about learning and teaching remained the same as for the academic subjects: pupils were expected to pick up the requisite skills by a process of osmosis. There was no systematic instruction or guidance in how to draw or paint. The master interpreted his rôle minimally: to keep order, set the boys to work and mark the outcome of their efforts. He rarely descended from the pedagogic rostrum to observe work in progress, make suggestions or offer words of encouragement. I believed that I was rather a dab hand at art, but was probably deceived by the subtlety of the master's marking system. Work received one of three marks – 10, 11 or 12 out of 10. Occasionally someone was distressed to receive an abysmal 9 and, at the other end of the scale, outstanding work had been known to earn 13.

A few months before the School Certificate exam, the art

master suffered a prolonged illness and arrangements were made for us to receive a weekly art lesson at the town's technical school. Here we entered a new world in which serried ranks of desks gave way to a semi-circular furniture arrangement providing everyone with an equally clear view of the teacher and any object that we had to draw. More significantly, we were instructed in some of the basic skills of the subject, such as how to hold a pencil in a way that combined control with flexibility and free flowing movement. We had been conditioned to think of the 'tech' as a very inferior institution, but from that point on I began to question the assumption that the Royal Grammar School held all the answers as a place of learning.

In the sixth form a trip was organised to London to a schools' conference at which the speakers included Dr Bronowski, rising mathematics and science star, and Sir Hartley Shawcross, Attorney General in the post-war Labour Government and later Chief British Prosecutor at the Nuremberg Trials. It was my first encounter with people of this stature and I was impressed that such eminent professionals from the outside world should deign to give up their time to speak to schoolboys. It made one feel worthwhile, grown-up, even important. It was a good experience and both Bronowski's subsequent television series, *The Ascent of Man*, and the Nuremberg Trials meant more to me as a result.

An experience of this kind may not, in itself, constitute an educational epiphany, but it can provide a spark that fires pupils' intellectual curiosity and enthusiasm for learning – which is, of course, the teacher's chief task. Unfortunately, such flashes of enlightenment were isolated occurrences at the RGS, welcome breaks in routine, but not an integral part of the school's educational thinking, which was focused elsewhere.

Michael Parkinson once said that his grammar school accomplished for its pupils what myxomatosis did for rabbits. Perhaps this was an exaggeration, but any school that emphasises academic competition to the extent that many post-war grammar schools did is bound to produce as many failures as successes. The process of separating the sheep from the goats begins with streaming and then, within this system, each form has its regularly-published lists of winners and losers in the form of subject and form league tables. The system builds up the confidence and self-esteem of those who are doing well and undermines those who are doing badly. The gap between those at the top of the league and those at the bottom widens as pupils perform to their teachers' expectations.

In the middle of any form ranking there will be a number of floaters drifting in and out of the two halves of the form and defying precise classification as out-and-out successes or failures. Except during my time in the express stream, this was the territory that I inhabited: the 16th position that I gained in form L III D defined my academic status for most of my secondary schooling. On the debit side, I dropped out of the A form, needed two attempts to obtain School Certificate – plus a further English language retake to confirm a provisional place in the sixth form – and gained an undistinguished Higher Certificate that didn't reach the standard required for university entrance. On the other hand, whereas many of my contemporaries left after School Certificate or just one year in the sixth form, I plodded on and eventually obtained what many would have considered respectable results. From the school's viewpoint, my masters persevered with what they must have regarded as modest academic material, allowing me to make a number of fresh starts. They would have felt poorly rewarded for their efforts had they known the extent to which my subsequent career would be spent in promoting educational priorities and policies diametrically opposite to those of the Royal Grammar School.

3

## Schoolboys Anonymous

There was a maths teacher at the Royal Grammar School whose lessons were considered lively and enjoyable. He joined the staff from a 7-14 village elementary school where he had had a reputation as a friendly and very dedicated teacher. He was professionally trained but, having no degree, was considered unfit to teach any but the most junior forms and lower streams. He arrived at the RGS as I started the express course and I therefore never came under his influence. However, I remember his cheery smile around the school.

Smiling wasn't much in vogue with our masters. They were a pretty austere and humourless bunch who made little attempt to get to know us as human beings. To many we were only names – surnames – on a list. There was a house system, but this was merely a structure for sporting and musical competition, not a means of providing pastoral care. The concept of responding to individual educational needs would have seemed as laughable as offering a menu choice for lunch in an 18th century workhouse. My flirtation with a foreign languages course left me with gaps on the science side, but there was no mechanism for providing support to help me deal with this problem: the response was the same as Miss Falkner's to my groaning in singing lessons – exclusion. At some stage I was permanently banished to one of the laboratory prep rooms, with a textbook, to prepare for a School Certificate exam in combined physics and chemistry, in theory an easier option than the separate subjects but, in practice, beyond my attainment without any tuition.

The lack of personal contact between masters and boys led to insensitivity on both sides. Masters were frequently harsh and uncompromising in their judgement of their pupils. One of my classmates in form IVA was a Polish boy whose conscientiousness and success at his work did nothing to diminish his popularity among his peers. One morning he arrived at school contorted with excitement at a composition he'd completed for his English homework. We crowded round in response to his bubbling enthusiasm, clamouring to savour and then to acclaim his magnus opus. Acquainted with the essay's contents, we were full of admiration for what was clearly a literary masterpiece. If ever a homework merited 13 out of 10, this was surely it. The set topic had been *A Sports Event* and our Polish classmate had described a farcical football match in which all the players were woefully lacking in the requisite ball skills. Key characters were given names like Snot Rag and Big Bum, which we all thought a particular stroke of comic genius. The composition was handed in and we waited impatiently for its assessment. It was returned, unmarked, with a diagonal red line across each page and, underneath, a terse command: 'See me!' In the ensuing one-to-one it was made clear that the composition was both stupid and offensive. Our literary champion was devastated. We were dumbfounded, quite unable to comprehend this total rejection of our collective judgement. It was another of those childhood experiences that left one utterly perplexed at the ways of the world.

24

The process of growing up involves a painful coming to terms with the difference between adult and child perceptions. What is important to one is often inconsequential to the other; where one sees cleverness or reasonableness, the other may assume stupidity or perversity. The conventions of language use provide numerous examples. Children and adults have very different views on formal and informal usage, polite and impolite forms, what is linguistically amusing, witty or unfunny. From an early age children have to learn that context is all-important in language usage: the vocabulary of the home doesn't necessarily transfer to other situations; much of the language of the playground will not be acceptable in the classroom; the way one speaks isn't the way one writes.

An awareness of the different uses of language and the conventions surrounding them comes only gradually. As usual, the learning process entails making mistakes and false judgements. The sensitive teacher, instead of bawling pupils out when they get things wrong, will build on their efforts – good or bad – to develop a fuller understanding. There were qualities to commend in the football farce composition: the writer's exuberance; his instinctive sense of the comic potential of situations in which human beings are hopelessly clumsy and unco-ordinated; even his juvenile delight in rude language. As contemporaries, we had responded instinctively to these features. Teachers need to do the same: to accept that sometimes children will write, and indeed should be allowed to write, as children, not as aspirants to adulthood. As a piece of free writing, our classmate's composition had been a genuine response to the subject set – *A Sports Event*. He hadn't been asked to produce an article in the style of a newspaper reporter or to provide a match report suitable for the school magazine, or to write in any other specific mode. As an attempt at comic writing the essay had, of course, serious failings and the ways in which it fell short of maturity in that difficult art form could have provided a fund of material for subsequent English lessons. Our masters, however, were no more likely to see opportunities of that kind than to dance the hokey-cokey or teach the Karma Sutra.

A few of the staff were not merely insensitive but vindictive. We had a French teacher who was widely loathed for the ways in which he flaunted his power over pupils. His speciality was the open-ended, after-school detention which caused particular anxiety to boys who had long and awkward journeys to the remoter rural parts of the school's catchment area. Having set the detention task, he'd inform us that he was going home for a bath and would be back later. Detentions normally offered boys a small grain of comfort from the knowledge that the instigator was being inconvenienced as well as the pupils: our French master's ploy not only denied us this limited satisfaction but was peculiarly effective in highlighting the contrast between his leisured state and our extended working day. His choice of activity for whiling away his time accorded neatly with his frequently-declared disgust at the obnoxious odour of young males: his first words upon entering a classroom were invariably 'smelly boys, smelly boys', accompanied by an impresarial flapping of his hands to direct the raising of lower window sashes to dispel the putrid air. His claims that he took a twice-daily bath to decontaminate himself might well have been true, for his skin was as white and luminous as the underbelly of a shark.

Saturday morning school was one of the distinctive features of the RGS in those days and on one such occasion a mate of mine was questioned by this French master about his unusually spruce appearance. He was going to London after school, Wilson naively explained, to see his first professional football match. 'We'll see about that,' was the master's pleasant rejoinder. Predictably, Wilson was found wanting during the lesson and numbered among those detained for additional

French exercises after morning school. He missed train and match. I knew how much my friend had been looking forward to his outing and have never forgotten the sensation of disgust that I felt at his maltreatment. Trivial as this incident was in the general picture of Man's inhumanity to Man, it afforded an early insight into the sadistic pleasure that authority figures can derive from victimising those within their control. It was an important lesson in mean and gratuitous abuse of power.

Different masters were associated with specific forms of bullying. Doggie Scott could bounce a heavy wooden-backed board rubber off a boy's head from 20 feet. Bulldog Clark punished inattentiveness by opening an offender's desk, forcing his head forward and bringing the lid down hard. Piljy Jones seared weak mathematicians' olfactory organs with a thick rubber band cut into a single length. Placing one end just behind a boy's ear, he would extend the rubber different distances, according to the degree of mathematical incompetence, and then let fly. One sum wrong merited a mere six-inch stretch of the rubber; two wrong, nine inches; three wrong, 12 inches; and so on. Had George Randell been unfortunate enough to pass the 11+, he would have had permanently swollen and inflamed ears.

The deputy headmaster, S A Morgan, taught us geography. His inevitable moniker 'Sam' did him an injustice, conjuring up, as it does, a picture of boyish curls and a sunny disposition. Sam Morgan was lean and hungry as an SS officer, with slicked-back hair and a skin-taut, florid face that gave the impression he was just managing to keep in check a raging desire to inflict physical violence. In fact, Sam eschewed corporal punishment in favour of humiliation, an instrument with which he maintained exemplary class discipline. He had a marked aversion to boys fidgeting or fiddling with things on their desk. One offender was required to crawl out to the front of the classroom, tip the waste-paper basket over his head and spend the rest of the lesson sitting on the floor amidst apple cores and pencil shavings. Another – a very meek and inoffensive lad – was instructed to drop his expensive-looking wooden pencil box out of the first floor window onto the JTC parade ground below, where it shattered into pieces.

Sam had a unique method of marking that enabled him to deal with a pile of exercise books at the speed of a post office counter assistant stamping a pile of licences. While we were busy ogling pictures of topless tribeswomen in copies of the *Geographical Magazine*, he would open a set of books at the work to be marked and then proceed to transfer them one by one from the right-hand side of his desk to the left, somehow managing to tick and insert a single-digit mark en route. To facilitate this process, geography homeworks consisted of a single-page drawing of a map, with most of one's time being spent on careful shading of the coastline with a blue crayon. Sam's discipline was such that he was able to arrive for lessons late and depart early without detriment to class order, a procedure that enabled him to spend several ten-minute sessions each day on the playing field with his golf clubs.

Despite his threatening appearance and iron discipline, there was, once a term, an assembly ritual that provided a hint that, inconceivable as it seemed, Sam might have a sense of humour. Morning Prayers followed a familiar and unvarying pattern consisting of hymn, prefect's biblical reading, notices and an occasional homily from the headmaster. Masters did not demean themselves by assuming policing rôles like crowd control and so we were shepherded into the school hall by prefects and packed into pens formed by rows of dining tables. Somewhat surprisingly, we were then allowed to talk – which we did, all 700 of us simultaneously. Then suddenly one of the rear doors was flung open and Sam Morgan burst into the hall. Taking six giant strides down the side aisle, he gave a single ferocious roar – WHARRP! Whether this sound was originally a recognisable command (Quiet!? Hark!?) was never clear, but there was no mistaking the nature of the order. The silence was immediate and total. Daily repetition never diminished the effect of this impressive demonstration of authority. It was in the final assembly of each term that the wayward thought occurred to us concerning Sam's sense of humour. There was a ritual on these occasions whereby the boys were called upon to give a series of 'three cheers' for the school and various leadership groups within it: the staff, the officers of the JTC, the officers of the ATC, etc. Different masters led each round of 'hoorays', culminating in Sam's striding down the side of the hall and, in his severest back-of-the-throat voice, rasping, 'School! Three cheers for the holidays!' The roof was replaced during the vacation.

Our PT master was half anthropoid, half sergeant-major. The cardinal sin in his rigorous gym routine was 'idleness' and the tone was set at the beginning of each lesson with a ritual beating of the last two boys to get changed and start running on the spot in their lines in the gym. Our flimsy PT shorts provided scant protection against the strap-like sole of a well-worn gym 'slipper'. Thus our keenly-honed competitive instincts were seen at their sharpest in the changing room stampede to avoid the consequences of tardiness. A similar incentive to keep moving was applied on the rugby field, enjoyment of the game being enhanced by the application of a hazel switch to the back of the knees.

The school attached considerable importance to boys conducting themselves in a gentlemanly way, but apparently saw nothing incongruous in masters bullying those within their control. Not surprisingly, given the example set by some of their elders and betters, boys indulged in a good deal of aggressive macho behaviour towards each other. After PT lessons, a popular form of horseplay in the gym changing room, while boys were still naked after their cold shower, was to whiplash each other's genitals with wet knotted towels. Anyone who considers this simply an innocuous boyish wheeze should try it out some time.

Predictably such behaviour usually took the form of the strong victimising the weak, as in the master/boy model that was readily available. There was a plump short-sighted boy in the lower third whose likeness to the Owl of the Remove would probably in itself have been sufficient to qualify him for playground persecution. In addition, though, he was of a very nervous disposition, the result it was said of a bad experience in the blitz before he was evacuated from London to the High Wycombe area. In response to any physical pain, he emitted a long drawn-out animal squeal, which was obviously irresistible to those who took pleasure in others' suffering. In an odd conformity to the school's insistence on the outward trappings of civilised behaviour, the bullyboys formed an orderly queue while they waited their turn to pinch, punch or otherwise torment this unfortunate individual.

An even more orderly queue formed each day outside the headmaster's study but in this instance the physical punishment was administered to, rather than by, those waiting for their part in the action. E R Tucker's study resounded throughout the day to the unmistakable sound of cane contacting taut buttocks. All breaches of school discipline received the same form of treatment, although there was a rough scale of charges according to the seriousness of the transgression. The worst offence was 'bringing the school into disrepute'. On one memorable occasion, two boys who had been caught pilfering sweets in Woolworth's were thrashed in front of the whole school during Morning Prayers. Around about this time another young gentleman made a personal statement on the school by defecating copiously in one of the washbasins in the boys' loos. I was consumed with curiosity concerning the punishment that he would receive if he were caught. Mercifully, perhaps, he wasn't.

The physical ill-treatment of the weak by the strong was condoned by the RGS not least by its system of "prefects' meetings". These were kangaroo courts thinly veneered with formal procedures. Prefects brought younger boys to the meetings to charge them with a range of out-of-class offences: failing to wear a cap on the way to school, pushing in the bus queue, running in the corridor – that sort of thing. If pronounced guilty, the evil-doers were beaten by the head boy, with the senior prefects lounging around watching. The outcome of my first prefects' meeting was not in doubt as my offence – not standing to attention when addressed by a prefect – had been committed against none other than the head boy himself. How naïve can you get? Wickens was a willowy, aristocratic youth who, like his name, seemed straight out of *Tom Brown's Schooldays*. To compensate for his lack of body weight, he took a run with each whirl of the cane and struck with surprising force. The school could well have cited me as an example of the effectiveness of the prefects' meeting system as I never put in a second court appearance.

Another popular form of victimisation was the ill-treatment of weak staff by the boys. Religious knowledge (RK) was taken by a wizened old clergyman known as 'Pop' Shaw, incumbent of a barren and almost congregationless church close to the school. He was the most timid of men with a toneless voice and absolutely no classroom control. During his lessons the mild and meek made an early start on their evening's homework while the rest created mayhem. Improvised bands were a popular activity, featuring Jews' harps, cazoos and percussion instruments ingeniously fashioned out of combs, paper, rubber bands, pencils, protractors and rubbers. One day a bonfire was lit in the middle of the room.

Free milk was provided at school during the morning break. The crates were deposited on the school field where we helped ourselves to our third of a pint and, if the prefects weren't watchful, to someone else's as well. Pop Shaw was unfortunate to teach form IVA immediately after break. He would arrive to an empty room and, after a carefully-judged delay, a single scholar would put in an appearance, enter the room, bang the door loudly and apologise politely for being late. A second member of the form would then come in following precisely the same routine, and so on till the whole class had assembled. At this point, in response to a pre-arranged signal, we would raise our hands simultaneously and chorus, 'Please sir, may we have another milk?' Whereupon, without waiting for a reply, we fought our way to the door and made for the field. Another delay and the whole process would begin again. Most of a lesson could be taken up in this way.

An attractive young lady appeared one day as a temporary teacher of English. She was far too feminine and nice for the RGS's harsh male environment and must have suffered agonies of embarrassment at some of the classroom innuendos and barely-concealed asides. Before her classes, some of the young fifth form machos adjusted the furniture to provide a phalanx of desks across the back of the room behind which they stimulated their sexual fantasies during the lesson. Inevitably, these sessions degenerated into unseemly competitions.

Some of the crudeness and harshness of school life receded when we entered the sixth form. Sam Morgan remained a feature and made few concessions to senior pupils, but several of the masters I encountered on the Higher Certificate course were scholarly and humane gentlemen who, if not exactly inspiring or imaginative, were earnest and conscientious, and worthy of pupils' respect. The boys' pretence of gentle-manliness also carried slightly more conviction. My personal fortunes took a turn for the better with the award of a prize for my work in geography, admittedly a low status, under subscribed subject beneath the notice of genuine RGS scholars. A bigger boost to my confidence and self-esteem came with membership of the school cross-country VIII and cricket 1st XI, and particularly with the award of cricket colours, which entitled me to wear a variant of the maroon school blazer with custard-yellow piping round the edges. I was six feet one-and-a-half inches at the time and, with my blazer set off by a tri-coloured cap in maroon, green and blue, must have cut a colourful and imposing figure. Later, at Borough Road Teachers' Training College, I was to wear this outfit, to great public acclaim, in a rag day fancy dress parade.

Sport at the RGS, like academic work, was fiercely competitive and school teams were expected to win. We had an indifferent season in 1950 when I was a member of the 1st XI and the member of staff in charge castigated us in his end-of-season report in the *Wycombiensian*, the school magazine: 'few of the batsmen were capable of staying at the crease', 'the bowling lacked fire' and the whole side was 'lazy and unintelligent in the field'. In these written reports opposing school teams were referred to as 'the enemy' and, although lip-service was paid to principles of fair play and sportsmanship, no-one was fooled.

Our cross-country course started on the games field and entailed an opening sprint to a small gate which, because of a broken hinge, only partially opened, allowing just one person through at a time. Larger double-gates nearby, which gave vehicular access to the grounds, could have been thrown wide to provide free passage for the runners, but the restricted exit gave us an advantage when competing against other schools for, knowing the problem, we set such a scorching pace at the start of every race that we were invariably queuing to get through the gateway ahead of the whole opposing team. By the time the opposition's leading runner was able to get through, our first man was 200 yards away. We were on the receiving end of a piece of even sharper gamesmanship in a cricket match at Slough Grammar School. Put into bat first, we found boundaries hard to acquire on account of an overgrown outfield. Coming out to field after tea, which had been taken between innings, we observed that the outfield had been trimly mown in readiness for the home side's batsmen.

One of the undoubted perks of seniority at the RGS was that the sixth form common room was situated on the wing of the building nearest the playing fields of the High Wycombe Girls' High School. It was fortunate that the fields themselves were not visible, for the sights afforded would have been more than an incarcerated male community could have borne. However, on their games afternoon, some of the senior girls would use a bus stop near the RGS and pass within viewing distance of the common room. The most popular and disturbing of these sightings was of a remarkably sweet and demure young lady whose slight hint of coquettishness was irresistible. 'It's Jill Tucker!' was a cry that produced a stampede for the windows where first comers could obtain a prime position by standing on the sills and clinging to the sashes. My status rose 500% when it became known that, back in the village where Miss Tucker and I lived, we were 'walking out' together. Jill was no relation to Headmaster Tucker, but the kudos of the attachment could hardly have been greater had she been his daughter.

These were heady times for me, but recognition among my peers had been a long time coming and, as far as the school as an institution was concerned, I believe I retained my anonymity to the end. When I left, the headmaster's single paragraph testimonial covered half a small piece of notepaper and, apart from a statement about my Higher Certificate performance, simply noted that I was 'a capable, practical (where this came from I cannot think), all-round fellow', 'big and strong' and 'a very accurate and reliable fast bowler' (the latter being, I suspect, a happy consequence of my claiming the headmaster's wicket in the annual school v masters cricket match). I doubt if many of the school's other testimonials were any more

34

revealing, for the institution's concentration on statistical details of performance left it in no position to provide genuine character references or meaningful comments on pupils' response to learning.

There were undoubtedly times when anonymity worked to one's advantage. Thursday afternoons in the senior school were set aside for military training in either the Junior Training Corps or the Air Training Corps. My early years in the JTC had not been a particularly satisfying experience and, when I entered the sixth form, the prospect of a further two years of square-bashing and crawling through the Buckinghamshire countryside disguised as a tree was not appealing. I cut the first parade of the new school year, observed that my absence passed undetected, and took Thursday afternoon off for the rest of my time in the school. During this two-year period, I noted with mild surprise that, according to periodic lists posted on the sixth form common room notice-board, I gained steady promotion to the rank of sergeant.

A somewhat more bizarre instance of individual anonymity and the names-on-a-list culture was the strange case of A Pillock. Frequent notices appeared in the common room requiring or inviting sixth formers' signatures for various purposes. Waggish young men would sometimes add fictitious names to the ensuing lists and, over a period of time, A Pillock became an automatic insertion. Much to our delight, the day arrived when Pillock's name appeared on a list produced by the school. Having gained recognition as a bona fide member of the sixth form, Pillock became a familiar name on official lists. He may still be going strong.

4

## Barrack Room Ballads

National service provided a rare opportunity for young
members of the country's different social classes not only
to meet each other but to live and work together. The Army,
in particular, recruited from a complete cross-section of
backgrounds. The Royal Artillery, the regiment to which I
was assigned when I left school, obviously appreciated that
this situation would be a considerable culture shock for some
recruits and separated each new intake into footballers, rugby
players and those who performed with neither round nor oval
ball. This cunning strategy effectively segregated the ex-public
schoolboys from the hoi polloi for the duration of their basic
training, after which they moved off for their predestined short-
service commissions. Their brief contact with mere mortals
was thus confined to a few commoners from rugby-playing
grammar schools, like the RGS.

My familiarity with both footballing codes created a slight
initial problem, which was quickly resolved in favour of the
Hooray-Henries' barrack room, where I shared a corner with
several Wykehamists and Harrovians. Our squad proved to be

rather over-endowed with barrack-room lawyers whose fathers' army rank was considered sufficient justification for telling the rest of us what to do. However, the relaxed public school self-assurance of most of my new acquaintances generally made for congenial companionship. One of my immediate neighbours was the son of the Sheriff of London, an unpretentious and unassertive young man who went on to distinguish himself at Sandhurst where he received the Sword of Honour at the Royal Artillery Officers' Passing-out Parade.

Once the officer class had departed we were arbitrarily regrouped. My next-door neighbour this time was a leading exponent of estuary, or effluent, English whose verbal dexterity included the use of the f-word to qualify both components of double-barrelled nouns such as 'sergeant-major' and 'parade-ground'. His descriptions of 1950s' football matches, with their centre-forwards, inside-rights and outside-lefts, would have made a Jamie effing-Oliver cookery demonstration seem like a Wednesday afternoon lecture at the WI.

I was probably better prepared for the Army's social mix than most of my contemporaries. A variety of teenage sports activities had brought me into contact with a wide range of people: I was on good terms with members of the back street clubs in the High Wycombe snooker league, but also knew how to conduct myself with the minor gentry who turned out for the town cricket club's select Wednesday XI. In contrast to my plodding academic progress, I appear to have learnt quickly in these experiential situations and was, I believe, regarded as a somewhat sociable fellow, able to relate to most people. This stood me in good stead in the Army.

My sporting activities also helped me to meet the Army's physical demands: being reasonably fit, I was untroubled by having to live life at the double and quite enjoyed the daily, sometimes twice-daily, PT sessions, drill periods and endurance tests. Those recruits unused to regular exercise took

37

a while to adjust to five-mile runs with bricks in their packs and 100-yard dashes carrying a fellow soldier and his kit on their shoulders. The sheer pace of the day, with its constant changes of activity and associated clothing, was exhausting.

Whilst not the world's most well co-ordinated person, I was also fortunate enough to be able to avoid extremes of ineptitude on the drill square. Anyone who found the Army's square-bashing routine really difficult was given a hard time. There was an archetypal odd-man-out in the squad to which I belonged, a quiet and inoffensive chap called Henshaw whose arms persisted in swinging in time with their adjacent, rather than opposite, legs. The drill sergeant's apoplectic attempts to rectify this abnormality were hindered by Henshaw's apparent uncertainty over which was his left and right side. The abuse and invective flowed freely and were directed not only at the disfunctionalist himself but also his parents and an assumed girlfriend of whom the sergeant appeared to have a discon- certingly intimate sexual knowledge. It was all to no avail and, much as it pained the Army to acknowledge defeat in its efforts to achieve absolute conformity, Gunner Henshaw was given special dispensation to observe his squad's passing-out parade through the NAAFI window.

It is the memories of bullshit that most national servicemen carry to the grave with them: the burning and bulling of boots, the buffing of brasses, the blancoing of belts. Officially our working day didn't start until 6.00 am and was over by 11.00 pm. However, in order to complete all our preparations for the daily inspection of kit, weaponry, bed and barrack room, we invariably had to rise early and retire late. The term 'bullshit' has two definitions – 'spit and polish' and 'nonsense'. The connection between the two became all too clear as each evening we worked through a myriad of mind-numbing tasks, polishing the studs in the soles of our boots, 'squaring-off' tubes of toothpaste, ensuring that the backs of brass buttons gleamed as brightly as their fronts, shining the rough wooden floor of the barrack room. One of the most bizarre rituals was the Brasso polishing of the inside as well as the outside of our mess tins, a procedure that would have prostrated us with food poisoning had we used the utensils for the purpose for which they were designed. Fortunately, the taxpayer stumped up for duplicate sets, one for meals, the other for display.

Much of what we had to do in the cause of cleanliness and smartness was little more than a means of demonstrating the power that the system and its enforcers had over us. The extent to which this message was driven home depended entirely on the whim of the NCOs who controlled our lives. Demands varied greatly from one sergeant and bombardier team to another, and occasionally from one NCO to another within a team. Some NCOs had quite a friendly, bantering relationship with their squad; others had us grovelling with servility from reveille to lights-out. The frequent movement of service personnel meant that routines and requirements were always changing.

A new sergeant arrived and immediately sought to stamp his authority on the squad. He inherited a situation in which we had been granted weekend leave – a 36-hour pass as a reward for good turn-out and effort. However, the new arrival's policy, he informed us, was never to grant leave other than on compassionate grounds: our passes were cancelled. The young troop officer intervened, ordering the passes to be re-issued. The sergeant had to comply, but then introduced a ploy familiar from RGS days whereby he kept us working well beyond the normal Saturday dismissal time so that most of us missed our trains. Conflict of this kind between a hardened and inflexible 'old-soldier' NCO and a newly-commissioned national serviceman was not uncommon, with the raw recruits uncomfortably caught in the cross-fire. The bullying NCOs were no worse than their schoolmaster equivalents, but had a more debilitating effect

39

as they could persecute around the clock. Officers were quite watchful, but NCOs who wanted to abuse their power had plenty of opportunity to do so.

As a basic training centre, the Royal Artillery at Oswestry acted as a clearing house for army recruits, most of whom moved on, after ten weeks, to other regiments or corps. A few weeks into our time at Oswestry we were interviewed by an army careers officer to discuss the branch of the Army in which we would like to spend the rest of our national service. Most of the ex-grammar school boys, conditioned as they were to regard themselves as intelligent and well-educated, selected the Intelligence Corps and the Education Corps as their first and second options. Both destinations offered an assured route to non-commissioned officer status and, with little means of making a more informed choice, I duly put my intelligence and education at His Majesty's Service. As a result of this consultation process, I was selected for the Royal Corps of Military Police. It was my first experience of how the exercising of choice usually operated in the Army.

After our initial training there was a hiatus as the regiment undertook the seemingly difficult task of processing its decisions over our destinations. We were assigned to 'holdings' and a daily round of 'fatigues' – scrubbing urinals and WCs, shovelling coke, whitening stone markers round the guardroom garden and washing greasy cooking pans. The compensation for this somewhat restricted lifestyle was a significant increase in our leisure time: the working day was comparatively short and, as our time was spent in denim overalls, there was no kit cleaning in the evenings. I took the opportunity to do some reading – Priestley's 'time plays', Dickens' *Oliver Twist*, John Masefield's autobiographical account of life *In The Mill* and, most appropriately, Kipling's *Barrack Room Ballads*. It was a somewhat idiosyncratic entry point to my voluntary reading of English literature, an occupation that was to become one of the most significant, possibly *the* most significant, of my national service experiences.

After three weeks in holdings, I was transferred to the Military Police HQ in Woking. Inkerman Barracks consisted of a forbidding collection of penitentiary-like buildings forming the perimeter of a formidable parade ground that was to become very familiar over the ensuing weeks. If first impressions left any doubts about the regime that I was entering, these were quickly dispelled by the initial briefing. The aim of the 18-week period of further training was to turn out a unique breed of soldier, smarter and better drilled than the guards, fitter than the commandos, more intrepid than the SAS. Our earlier training began to look like a mild version of the Boy Scouts.

We were assigned to one of three squads – tall, very tall and exceptionally tall. (Size was clearly an important factor in the selection procedure for the RMP.) Our three instructors were highly focused, ultra-efficient and very demanding. Their rôle required them to act the tyrant, but there was no victimisation or vindictiveness. Although we would not have admitted it, we rather liked our instructor, a corporal who was younger and less experienced than his two sergeant colleagues and therefore always struggling to emulate their standards. We felt a bit sorry for Corporal Humphrey and worked hard to meet his demands. The common enemy was the Company Sergeant-Major and the instructors were just as likely to incur his wrath as the rest of us. On one occasion Corporal Humphrey paraded us slightly wide of our designated spot on the drill square and received a prolonged rollicking in front of the three squads and two other instructors. For good measure, the squad itself was confined to barracks for two weekends, a gratuitous punishment presumably designed to stamp out any sympathy that we might have felt for our Corporal. CSM Cook clearly measured his man-management success in terms of the degree of loathing he was able to generate.

I was personally called to account on two occasions by the incomparable Cook, once for a relatively minor matter and the other time for a serious offence. The first incident concerned a gratuitous and infinitesimal mark on one of my leather gaiter straps, which the CSM had to get down on all fours to verify as an unacceptable aberration in my turnout. I was roundly berated for sloth and idleness. A few weeks later, whilst dressing for the first parade and inspection of the day, I had the misfortune to break one of my leather bootlaces. There was no spare and no time to obtain a replacement, so I did the only thing possible: knotted the broken ends and laced the boot up so that the knot was concealed behind one of the eyelets. With the boot uppers forced together over the knot, only the slightest swelling indicated anything untoward. This time, however, CSM Cook required no ground-level scrutiny to detect a serious breach of military discipline. 'TWO STEPS FORWARD, MARCH!' Thunderous command. 'FALL IN TWO MEN! QUICK MARCH! LEFT, RIGHT! LEFT, RIGHT! LEFT, RIGHT!' Cell door opens. Clangs shut. Incarcerated for invisible (almost) bootlace knot.

Considering how assiduously CSM Cook worked at making himself unpopular, it was interesting that many of those he persecuted subsequently vied with each other to request a recording of his stentorian parade-ground voice on the long-running radio programme *Forces Favourites*. Nostalgia knows no boundaries, as another group of radio listeners will know from the number of public school old boys who, in interviews and magazine programmes, enthusiastically recall the way they were bullied, buggered and abused at school. The rose-coloured spectacles view of unpleasant past experiences was once explained to me as a defence mechanism against having to write off a negative part of one's life and therefore of oneself. It's probably simpler than that. In recalling adverse experiences we tend to present ourselves as heroes who have faced hardship, even danger, and survived to tell the tale. More importantly, the sharing of adversity with others produces a memorable camaraderie and intensity of human relationships. At least, this was how I interpreted the pang of regret that I felt when I eventually passed under the arch of the Inkerman Barracks gateway for the last time, on my way to my next posting.

Each evening at Woking a wartime spirit was engendered in the barrack room as we recalled the day's rantings and humiliations and prepared for the following morning's parade and inspection. The cheerfulness of the jokers kept everyone's spirits up and the group pooled its expertise and wisdom to help those who were at risk of being overwhelmed by their difficulties. There was a knack to the spit and polish routine and ways of speeding up the process were readily passed on. There was a strong sense of purpose in which group success was more important than individual achievement. The squad was as good as its weakest member and we shared the instructor's aim to bring everyone up to standard. In the various tests we faced – in the gym, on the firing range, on the route marches and cross-country runs – there was a basic target that all trainees had to achieve. Everyone, for example, had to run a mile – in boots and battle-dress – in six minutes: interest focused not on the first man home but the last, and those of us who were used to receiving athletics accolades found an alternative satisfaction from running with weaker squad members, pacing them and encouraging them across the finishing line in the allotted time. It was a very different experience from that at the RGS where the group identity was always subordinate to the constant need to compete with each other for marks and positions. In the school situation one's ability to succeed usually depended on others' propensity to fail. There were, of course, times in the RMP when individuals were pitted against each other, but the group effort was always predominant. A feature of major inspections was the 'stick man' competition, in which the smartest man on parade was identified and awarded a weekend leave or remission of duty. Each squad put forward a contender, helped him to prepare his kit, and then carried him, like a piece of crystal glass, onto the drill square for inspection.

The importance of team effort was most obvious in the drill routines. Everyone's movements had to be synchronised and, as in a choir or orchestra where a single discordant voice or over-dominant instrument mars the performance, so one individual's mistimed movement could completely spoil the effect of a sequence on the parade ground. Gradually we became more precise and co-ordinated, until the day arrived when the entire squad's studded boots hit the parade ground in perfect unison and the single pistol shot sent a shiver of excitement up everyone's spine. Even when this achievement became commonplace, it never failed to produce a *frisson* of elation.

The need for precisely co-ordinated teamwork is abundantly obvious in the Army, but it is of course just as relevant to many civilian occupations. Fire-fighters, medical staff in an operating theatre, actors and dancers, university research units and project teams in industry are a few examples. At a slightly less demanding level, most people's working lives, and many of their leisure activities, involve co-operating with others, yet strangely the crucial skills involved in this process receive scant attention in our school system beyond the primary stage. The closest we come to developing teamwork in secondary, further and higher education is usually in sporting activities. In the classroom and lecture theatre the conventions foster competition and individual success at the expense of co-operation and mutual support. Our education system grossly undervalues the contribution that pupil and student collaboration and interaction can make to the learning situation. Paradoxically, as teamwork has become increasingly important in industry, commerce and the public services (including teaching), so the growing obsession with tests, exams, marks and grades makes it more and more difficult for schools to devote significant time to co-operative group work.

My recollections of Woking's harsh training regime are always tempered by thoughts of how the trainees learnt to work together and support each other. There are other positive memories, not least the surprisingly conscientious care system run by the medical officers. There was an occasion during the winter of 1950-51 when I ran a temperature and was confined to bed on the Medical Officer's orders. A corporal from the guardroom was detailed to ensure that the barrack room fire was kept well stoked up and that my meals were brought to me from the canteen. I had no more than a heavy cold, but the special treatment made me feel like a celebrity in intensive care. It was an interesting example of the Inkerman MO's attention to detail. He carried out his own independent inspections of the barrack room to ensure an absence of germ-carrying dust, the presence of ample coal supplies for the fire, and strict adherence to the rule that the rows of men should sleep alternately head to wall and head to the centre of the room – presumably to reduce the risk of passing on any infection. During an excessively cold spell he badgered our instructors to take care that, during outdoor activities, there were no hypothermia-inducing periods of inactivity, a precaution about as necessary as a voice check on CSM Cook to ensure that his orders were loud enough to be picked up by everyone on the drill square.

During our training at Woking another careers-officer consultation took place – this time to ascertain where we would like to be posted upon completion of our training. Since RMPs were deployed wherever British military personnel were serving in the world, there was no shortage of choice. Old soldier that I was, I knew the name of the game by now and applied for a home posting. A few weeks later I was gratified to be informed that I would be going to Singapore: I'd wanted to get abroad at the Army's expense and had hoped for some exotic part that would be too distant to feature as a future holiday destination.

5

# Redcapping and Reading

Empire Windrush set sail for Singapore on June 13th, 1951. White and spotless, the 14,000-ton troopship was a symbol of promise for its young passengers – transport to an exciting new world. The rôle was a familiar one for the Windrush: three years previously, almost to the day, the ship had docked in Tilbury with 500 Jamaican immigrants, the first contingent of West Indians encouraged by our Government to leave their homeland to settle in Britain. They, too, were on a voyage of discovery, with high hopes of a new life of opportunity and prosperity. Many, however, were to be sadly disillusioned by the hostility, prejudice and discrimination that they encountered in this country. The majority of the teenage troops on the 1951 summer voyage to the Far East were bound for active service in the Malayan jungle where they would engage in one of the most debilitating forms of warfare. Some would never return.

The RMP contingent had a pleasanter destination – Gillman Barracks on Singapore Island, home of the 200 Provost

47

Company, a unit of some 70 officers and NCOs responsible for policing the island's military personnel. The barracks consisted of two fine three-storey buildings with wide verandahs and large open doorways and window spaces that provided welcome draughts during the day, a cool breeze at night and, during storms, a gale that threatened to sweep every loose article out of the building. There were extensive and attractive grounds incorporating a sports field and splendid swimming pool, used by both troops and families of the regular soldiers.

There was a basic routine at Gillman aimed at maintaining our fitness, drill sharpness and general awareness of MP procedures; but most of our time was occupied with round-the-clock policing duties. Crime detection was the responsibility of the Special Investigation Branch, but we did everything else associated with a police force. Some routines required little initiative: we simply followed well-documented procedures that appeared to date back to the Keystone Cops era. Speed checks fell into this category. Cops 1 and 2 hid in a ditch 220 yards apart and, communicating by field telephone (one stage up from two tins and a piece of string), timed War Department vehicles with primitive stop-watches. If the driver was speeding, which he normally was, Cop 2 waved frenetically to Cop 3, cunningly concealed behind a tree further down the road. Cop 3 then stepped smartly out into the road to stop the vehicle. Cops 4 and 5, waiting in their jeep in a side road, emerged triumphantly to demonstrate the overwhelming force of the law and charge the driver with his offence.

Most duties were a little more exacting than this, entailing a response to situations as they arose, a rapid assessment of their seriousness and an equally quick decision on appropriate action. Many of our activities centred on the RMP Headquarters in the centre of Singapore from which we undertook routine patrols and responded to call-outs. Off-duty soldiers in Singapore were inclined to part with their week's wages in one evening and a combination of strong beer and high temperatures ensured plenty of police activity. Major events on the Island involved working closely with the civilian police – stewarding at the Island's grand prix meeting, controlling crowds at the 1951 celebrations that marked Singapore's newly-acquired city status, directing traffic at the City Governor's Proclamation on the occasion of George VI's death in 1952.

We also joined forces with the civilian police on some of their call-outs. A memorable example was a visit to the Happy World Stadium to quell an over-boisterous crowd at a wrestling match that had deviated slightly from its script. The contest involved the 26-stone King Kong and a 22-stone stripling called Chief Little Wolf, resplendent in full North American Indian head-dress. Kong was thrown out of the ring three times, Little Wolf twice. The referee tolerated these violent evictions until he himself was used as a human projectile. Extricating himself from the front row of the audience, he clambered back into the ring to stop the fight, only to be felled with a rabbit punch by Kong and carried out unconscious. A local wrestler, Wong Buck Lee, was persuaded to assume 'control', but incensed a volatile crowd by immediately disqualifying their favourite, King Kong. It was at this point that our presence was requested.

The media's stock-in-trade being sensation, it invariably portrays officers of the law in scenes of strong-arm action, pinning offenders to a wall, dragging bleeding protesters along the street, manhandling captives into the back of a Black Maria. And the soldier's image of Redcaps is a good deal more lurid than this. Yet most policemen, whether civilian or military, seek to avoid brawls and to achieve their objectives without using too much force. Unbelievable as it may seem, they spend much of their time quietly correcting wrongdoers, explaining why their behaviour is unacceptable and, when arrests have to be made, trying to cajole people into coming along quietly.

One of my first lessons in the art of gentle persuasion came when a UK-bound troop ship from Hong Kong docked briefly at Singapore, allowing its military passengers a few hours' shore leave. As usual on such occasions, 200 Provost Company had a busy time later in the day rounding up those revellers who would not otherwise have found their way back to the ship in time to resume their homeward journey. On this particular occasion, the boat was ready to depart, but, just as two of the crew moved to raise the gangplank, I arrived with the very last, and very inebriated, straggler. I had managed to keep on friendly terms with my companion during the jeep journey from the city centre and now coaxed him gently towards the boarding point. All seemed to be going well, if a trifle meanderingly, until it began to dawn on him that he had an audience. Thrown by this unexpected discovery, he swayed to a halt and contemplated the 2500 soldiers hanging over the side of the ship loudly cheering his every unco-ordinated movement. Deciding that a cigarette might help him reflect on this situation, he fumbled extravagantly in the breast pocket of his battle-dress jacket, produced a crumpled pack of Lucky Strike and, amiable to the last, offered me a smoke. Something snapped and with a King-Kong-inspired armlock I propelled him up the gangplank and onto the ship. Just another case of Redcap brutality. But, unfortunately, witnessed by rather a lot of people.

The demands on 200 Provost Company varied considerably, periods of intense activity alternating with significant lulls, a feature of Army life already encountered in the Royal Artillery at Oswestry. As our routine could change without warning, we learnt to expect the unexpected. No-one, however, was prepared for the detailing of a small section of our company to join the Royal West Kent Regiment on active service on the Malayan mainland. Following the liberation of Malaya from Japanese occupation after World War II, Communist supporters, mainly Chinese, began a protracted guerrilla war against the British rulers of the country. The West Kents were operating in Kuala Kuhru Bahru, north of Kuala Lumpur, where jungle-based guerrilla bands were particularly active, ambushing military vehicles, derailing trains, killing white civilians and executing Malayan villagers suspected of supplying British patrols with information on Communist whereabouts. The military presence in the area was being stepped up and, after two weeks' intensive training in jungle warfare, we were attached to a company of West Kents that had lost a quarter of its men in engagements with the enemy. I joined a very young platoon of national servicemen led by an officer who looked about 17. Our main task was to undertake a series of three-day probes into the jungle.

For some reason I expected jungle terrain to be uniformly lie lowing, flat and waterlogged but, although there was some spectacular swamp-wading to be done, much of our time seemed to be spent toiling up steep hillsides and scrambling down the other side. We were heavily armed – rifles, bren-guns, grenades, knives – and, of course, laden with provisions sufficient for the time we were to be away from base-camp. The physical demands were matched by a need for intense mental concentration: we moved with hyper-caution, trigger-ready and alert to every sound and movement. Each bend in the track dried the mouth and thumped the heart. The stillness was disconcerting: we saw few animals, although they could be heard fleeing our path and thereby warning the enemy of our approach. It was only when we rested that we became fully aware of the jungle's activity, the skeltering columns of giant ants, the furrily repulsive spiders, the leeches so persistently intent on breeching our defences to gorge on our blood.

The young West Kent national servicemen impressed us by

their cheerfulness and the calm, almost matter-of-fact way in which they performed their duties. The strain they were under was rarely mentioned, but we did hear one cautionary tale that served as a vivid illustration. A patrol had penetrated the jungle too deeply and lost its way. As the platoon awaited the outcome of a third anxious consultation between second-lieutenant and sergeant, one of the men suddenly went berserk, shouting and screaming and then turning his gun on the officer and NCO, killing the former. As a national serviceman's period of service neared an end, his stress levels rose, reaching a climax when he entered the jungle for the last time. It was customary, when a soldier's departure date drew very close, for his name to be omitted from his final patrol, a nice touch but an ineffectual one as, once the practice was established, the final test of nerve simply transferred to the penultimate patrol.

Contact with the enemy on the Royal West Kent Regiment's sorties was actually quite rare. The pattern of engagement was that a Communist band would attack a civilian target or ambush a military convoy and, after a brief exchange of fire, fade away through the rubber plantations into the jungle, where it could remain concealed for as long as food and water lasted. During my few weeks with the West Kents, the nearest I came to actual fighting was hearing firing by another platoon and subsequently seeing one or two casualties and guerrilla captives brought into camp. It was somewhat alarming to realise that my relief at escaping so lightly was tinged with just a hint of disappointment.

From the West Kents my RMP unit moved off to a coastal camp and the prospect of a few days' break in a picture-postcard setting. However, before we could get down to the beach, we were urgently recalled to Singapore: following a spate of road accidents involving WD vehicles, the Commanding Officer for the Island had imposed a 20 mph speed limit on all Army drivers. 200 Provost Company were to suspend all other operations and provide round-the-clock speed checks for three months. This kind of decision, peremptorily issued from above, made one realise how limited our CO's area of discretion was: his policing experience and expertise counted for nothing if Higher Authority made an arbitrary decision on how he was to deploy his troops. One of our COs – we had several during my time in Singapore – reacted very badly to such reminders of his impotence and was inclined to vent his frustration by a proverbial kicking of the dog, in the form of 200 Company. We were always smartly turned out for our duties in immaculately-pressed shorts and shirts, spotless white webbing and brightly-shining brasses. However, most of the more eccentric bullshitting procedures had been left behind in Woking and we were usually confident that the soles of our boots, the backs of our brasses and the insides of our belts would not be scrutinised when we went on parade. Occasionally, however, and without warning, the CO would decide that things had got slack and that an example had to be made. On one of these occasions three of our number were severely disciplined, one being demoted, dismissed from the corps and designated for posting back to his original army unit. His offence had been inadvertently to leave a cleaning cloth tucked underneath the spare wheel in the back of his inspected MOD vehicle.

The CO's sudden burst of zeal rebounded in spectacular fashion on this occasion, for the disgraced driver responded to his dismissal from the Military Police by requesting discharge from the Army, on the grounds that he was not actually under contract. Having completed his national service a few weeks previously, he had then elected to become a regular soldier. However, the slow grinding of the Army's administrative machine had not produced the relevant paperwork and he was still waiting for confirmation of his change of status. Technically he was a civilian and, by virtue of that fact, entitled to financial compensation for not having been demobbed when his statutory two years of national service had been completed. While he awaited his requested discharge, he enjoyed himself as a free man, threatening to sue the Army if he was required to undertake any further duties or conform to military regulations. On this occasion the customary Army tardiness over implementing postings was conspicuously absent: within a few days our man of independent action was on his way back to the UK and civilian life. We took considerable pleasure in this unusual victory by an individual against the Establishment.

Non-conformity was not really an option in the Army, but there were occasions during national service when I exercised my own judgement in ways that probably seemed incomprehensible to my companions. These weren't wilful acts of bravado or overt attention-seeking challenges to authority; it was simply that, when independent action seemed to inconvenience no-one, I was inclined to do my own thing. Not long after our arrival in Oswestry, we were given a series of injections, following which we were excused duties for the remainder of the day, but confined to barracks because of possible ill effects. Feeling quite normal after my jabs, I took myself off to the town for the evening. On board Empire Windrush the intense heat and airlessness below deck in the Indian Ocean made our confined bunk spaces almost intolerable and I spent several nights on deck, sleeping under the stars with a heavenly breeze from the boat's movement fanning my face.

Loss of sleep was an occupational hazard in the Army and one that I rather resented. Singapore patrols could last well into the early hours of the morning and there were a number of all-night duties, including manning the reception desk at Gillman Barracks and the Singapore RMP HQ in Bras Basa Road. All-night duties earned a rest day, but sleeping during the day never appealed much to me, so I usually tried to get some kip while on night duty. Armoury guard afforded the best opportunity. This was a largely static and uneventful duty, partnering the lance-corporal on the Gillman Barracks reception desk and maintaining watch over the armoury in an adjoining room. There were two periods of brief activity, issuing weapons and ammunition to the night patrols and checking them back in when the men returned. There was a dead period from 2.00 or 3.00 am to dawn during which, with one's desk-duty colleague's acquiescence, one might catnap. I introduced a variation to this arrangement by carrying my mattress down from the barrack room above the reception area and bedding down for two or three hours on the armoury floor.

One night on armoury duty I decided to go up to the barrack room and sleep, fully clothed, on my bed. However, a young and over-conscientious duty officer, finding himself under-employed in Singapore, chose this evening to take the unusual step of driving out to the barracks seven miles away. When he arrived he not unnaturally enquired where the armoury guard was, to which the quick-thinking lance-corporal on reception replied that I was checking the kitchen fire at the rear of the main building. This was a legitimate night-time task for either the reception desk lance-corporal or armoury guard and the second-lieutenant departed to verify my precise whereabouts. Desk lance-corporal set off at somewhat greater speed in the opposite direction, took the stairs to the barrack room three at a time and dragged me off my bed. We were both back just in time to be at our posts when the officer returned. He was mightily suspicious but, young and unsure of himself, kept his thoughts to himself. I reflected that a few miles away on the Malayan mainland, where the British Army was on active service, my offence would have carried the death penalty.

By foregoing rest-day sleep I added considerably to the opportunities for exploring my little corner of South East

Asia. Singapore was a fine city with wide streets, spacious gardens, elegant air-conditioned departmental stores and many imposing public buildings, their grandeur enhanced by their surrounding lawns. Notable landmarks were the City Hall, the Law Courts and St Andrew's Cathedral with its stunning white exterior painted with a concoction of shell, lime, egg white and sugar. Then, of course, there was the famous Raffles Hotel, named after Sir Stamford Raffles who, in 1819, established a station of the British East India Company in Singapore, which led to the city's development as the most important British trading centre in South East Asia.

Like most cities, Singapore had a less salubrious side – a vast, overcrowded labyrinth of mean but vibrant streets where the senses were assailed by the jostling crowds, spicy foods and ubiquitous wailing of over-amplified recordings of Chinese pop stars. Overhanging the conglomeration of eating houses, bars, brothels, opium dens and gambling rooms was the overpowering stench of the Rochore Canal, which passed sluggishly through this part of the city. Notwithstanding, or perhaps because of, its out-of-bounds status, down-town Singapore was a honey-pot for off duty Army personnel and consequently a focus for 200 Company's night-time patrols. Our jeeps and landrovers nosed through the crowds of pedestrians and jinrickshaw drivers, stopping occasionally for us to exchange pleasantries with painted prostitutes or make enquiries of obsequious club owners concerning their white clientele.

We were well received by the local inhabitants, but the courtesies were sadly one-way: in pursuing our duties we showed scant consideration for people's feelings. As we navigated the narrower alleyways, householders had to move speedily to remove domestic articles from our path and many an outdoor sleeper was rudely awakened by the sound of a revving engine, to find his flimsy folding bed rocking rhythmically in the full glare of headlights. We were no more considerate on foot and moved through the brothels like a monsoon wind, flinging the cubicle doors wide open to ascertain the nationality of the heaving buttocks thus exposed. Brown and yellow activists were free, of course, to continue, but British servicemen barely had time to grab their trousers before being ignominiously transferred from one very small room to another.

Somewhere between down-town Singapore and the respectable sector of the city, I discovered a cavernous, candle-lit bookshop, which provided me with a regular supply of second-hand reading material. Literature had become a source of pleasure during my first year of national service and in Singapore, with more time at my disposal, I was becoming something of an enthusiast. My taste was catholic or, more accurately, I was uncritical and indiscriminate in my choice of books, ranging across the centuries and mixing the best-known classics with what would have been regarded as lesser works. The only common factors in the books that I read were the poor quality paper and the eye-strainingly small print. The size of the volume was immaterial: Mrs Gaskell's compact little *Cranford* was sandwiched between the weighty *Pickwick Papers* and a complete set of Guy de Maupassant's short stories (in translation). Plays featured as much as novels – Shakespeare (tragedies and comedies), Ben Jonson, Congreve, Sheridan, Oscar Wilde, George Bernard Shaw and Emlyn Williams.

I was largely ignorant of the writers' backgrounds, the periods in which they wrote and their standing in the history of literature. Contemporary writing was an unknown phen-omenon: the fact that living people were writing novels, plays and poetry had not been mentioned at school. My second-hand back street bookshop maintained the image of literature as something belonging to the past. I did, however, eventually stumble across some modern works and recall being very surprised by aspects of *Operation Heartbreak*, a novel by a contemporary historian, Duff Cooper, that told of an Army officer whose thwarted ambition to fight for his country in the front line was mirrored by his unsuccessful love life. What impressed me were the economy of style and unpredictability of the narrative, features of the novel that I had not previously encountered. This whole world in which I was becoming immersed was full of surprises and it was somewhat puzzling to me how I became involved in it.

As a schoolboy, I wasn't exactly a non-reader: I grew up in the era of the 'penny dreadfuls' (actually priced tuppence) and few boys remained immune from the lure of these much-maligned but not very pernicious escapist story magazines. Temptations faced me daily as I eyed each new edition whilst 'putting up' my early morning paper round. I was a big-earner in those days, progressing from a five-bob-a-week round to a stage when I was pocketing the astronomical weekly sum of 12/6 (62p) – or not exactly pocketing it, as most of my wage went straight back to the newsagent in exchange for the latest teenage periodicals. There were nearly a dozen of these publications, my favourites being the Rover, Wizard, Hotspur, Adventure and Champion. There was no significant difference between them: all featured stereotypical heroes – cowboys on white horses, fearless flying aces, intrepid explorers, amazing robots, phenomenal footballers and pugilists, and a range of good guys in the Robin Hood or Tarzan mould whose capacity for extricating themselves from impossible situations ensured their availability for another adventure the following week.

Neither I nor my companions ever connected these narratives and the pleasure we gained from reading them with the texts presented for tedious dissection in Eng Lit lessons at school. For me, only *The Mayor of Casterbridge* and some of John Donne's more accessible metaphysical love poems survived the classroom critical appreciation process, but it may well be that the former, at least, provided some sort of catalyst for my gradual realisation that the reading of literature could be an enjoyable experience. Certainly by the time I left the Army I was familiar with most of Hardy's novels, shedding a tear not only for Tess and Jude, but for Lady Constantine and Swithin in the much less well-known *Two on a Tower*.

There were other stimuli. Although my mother had little time or energy for reading in middle age and had very few books in the home, she had enjoyed poetry as a girl and occasionally hinted at a dream world created for herself from her reading of real and fictional lives more glamorous than her own. Girlfriend Jill had enthused about some of her school literature and I have no doubt that my reading of Goldsmith's *She Stoops to Conquer* had something to do with her charming portrayal of Kate Hardcastle in her school play. I read Terence Rattigan's *Winslow Boy* having listened to a radio version. The fact that my book purchases included as many plays as novels probably owed something to the influence of Sam Price, a bachelor priest who ran the village youth club to which my social group had all belonged. Sam's blatant attempts to befriend selected young men and inveigle them into the priesthood via cosy vicarage tête-à-têtes would raise serious questions in today's climate, but, an occasional smutty joke apart, nothing untoward occurred on any of my visits to the vicarage or on the occasional trips that Sam and I made to the Theatre Royal at Windsor.

These various flickers may well have combined to ignite a flame of literary desire, but there were certain pragmatic factors that also played an important part in encouraging my new interest. During my latter teen years, when I might reasonably have been expected to make some tentative connections between the classroom and the real world, I was preoccupied with sport and my membership of village, town and school teams. Although I represented 200 Company at both soccer and rugby, my sporting activities occupied far less time in Singapore than they had done during my teenage years. With time on my hands, I could reflect on wasted opportunity and, more importantly, do something about it. However, what I did was not to resume study, but to begin reading literature for pleasure. Naturally, I formed opinions on the books that I read, but I didn't subject them, as at school, to detailed analysis over a three-month period. Moreover, although my choice of books was often indiscriminate and uninformed, I was sole arbiter of what I read and not required to share some Oxbridge don's arcane enthusiasm for Spenser's *Faerie Queene* or Milton's *Areopagitica*.

Readers of fiction are rarely lonely, as their lives are peopled by the characters they meet in their books. Nevertheless, I did wish occasionally that there was someone with whom I could discuss my reading. The only person I found at Gillman to share my interest was an Indian bearer, employed as a sort of universal batman to do some of our more basic kit-cleaning tasks. His education under the Raj had left him with an impressive facility in quoting extensively from the classics but not, it must be said, a great insight into the works about which he enthused. None of my British companions were book readers – a few looked at newspapers or comics – and, not wishing to appear an oddball, I pursued my hobby clandestinely. A secondary school for forces families shared the Gillman site and, although its building was locked out of school hours, the high window spaces were unshuttered and it was easy to scale the walls and to jump down into a classroom where I could read uninterrupted.

Towards the end of my time abroad I injured myself in a football training session: a complicated ligament tear which put me into hospital and plaster. As on my previous encounter with the Army's medical service, I made an immediate transition in status from number to human being, only this time the VIP treatment lasted ten weeks. Doctors and nurses were admirably attentive, food parcels started arriving from Army wives, 200 Company's 2 i/c brought my weekly wage packet up to the hospital in person and a despatch rider regularly delivered my mail. And I sat in bed day after day, bug-eyed and surrounded by books. The ward sister provided an endless supply of new reading material on which we happily exchanged views. This was my Trollope, Thackeray, Jane Austen, George Eliot, Bronte sisters and Mark Twain period.

One day a badly-wounded Fijian soldier was brought in from the mainland to the bed next to mine. Manly, mature and intellectual, he was one of the most impressive and interesting people I've ever met. Clearly in great pain, he nevertheless talked lucidly and profoundly on a range of subjects. As a reader, he preferred autobiography and biography to fiction and was part way through Churchill's Memoirs during the week that he died.

At some stage during my time in Singapore I began to make tentative plans for the future. No-one had ever suggested the possibility of my continuing to study beyond the sixth form and neither my own estimation of my scholastic ability nor my Higher Certificate results had pointed in that direction. Yet the RGS had given me only one model of success in life – the academic one. Thus, when the reading of literature became a pleasurable experience, it occurred to me that I should like to continue with my study of English.

Some teacher training colleges offered a poor man's alternative route to graduation alongside professional training, and I wrote off to enquire whether my modest exam results would qualify me for entry to a college BA course. As a result, I learnt why Latin was an integral part of the curriculum for the RGS A stream: a basic qualification in this subject was an entry requirement for a BA degree course. The system was paying me back for my waywardness as a 13-year-old in dropping out of the express form. However, Borough Road College in Isleworth, Middlesex sent me a scholarly-looking prospectus and suggested that I might like to consider applying for its two-year teacher's certificate course, which included further academic study, albeit not to degree standard. Reference was made to the college's many sporting activities and the leading position its teams occupied in 'the Sports World of London University'. My future career was decided.

# 6

## Learning from Mistakes

Teacher training colleges were financed by the Ministry of Education, but usually governed by the religious societies and foundations that owned their buildings and grounds. Borough Road belonged to the British and Foreign School Society, which formed the college from a school in Borough Road, Southwark, founded at the beginning of the 19th century 'to promote education of a Christian nature on broad, non-sectarian lines'. The school had trained its senior pupils to become 'monitors' or assistant teachers, and it was from this idea that Borough Road's teacher-training rôle developed. The college relocated to Isleworth in 1890 but in 1952, the year of my admission, still retained its original name and Christian character. All students were expected to attend morning prayers.

The Borough Road management were particularly proud of the college's degree work and the highly-qualified academic staff that this apparently attracted. However, once a member of the college, one noticed that undergraduates were distinctly thin on the ground, in fact non-existent in most subjects.

BA undergraduates totalled one or two in each year; BSc students, whose admission did not depend on their having a Latin qualification, were slightly more numerous. Only two-thirds of this small group completed their three-year course and a number of those failed their finals. However, some of the results were very good, as they ought to have been, for the very small numbers meant that students had the benefit of individual tuition. The downside of this situation was that a disproportionate amount of time was devoted to a small percentage of the student population – a not uncommon situation in educational institutions. The bulk of the students, just over 200, followed the two-year teaching certificate course, which provided professional training for potential primary and secondary modern schoolteachers. Grammar school staff at that time were expected to have a degree but not required to undergo any professional training; however, there were, in 1952, eight graduates at Borough Road bucking the system by following a one-year postgraduate teacher-training course.

Alongside their professional training the certificate students studied one or two academic subjects. 'Alongside' was the operative word, for there was no connection between the professional and academic components. The syllabuses that I followed in geography and English covered few geographical topics or aspects of English that would be relevant to the schoolchildren that I was destined to teach. The lecturers made no reference to their subject in the school setting – its place in the curriculum, how it might be taught, current developments in syllabuses and examining. The purpose of our subject-specialist courses was simply to extend our experience and understanding of the academic approach to study.

Academic study for its own sake is a perfectly laudable aim. However, the opportunity that was missed in the teacher-training colleges was to design courses that weren't determined by the aspiration that governs so many university syllabuses: the desire to produce an élite group of postgraduate researchers practised in analysing the minutiae of their specialism. Our special studies were simply diluted versions of very traditional esoteric university courses. As prospective teachers, rather than researchers, we would have benefited from more general, broadly-based courses. In English, for example, we spent an inordinate amount of time dissecting a small number of classics in great detail, when it would have been much more appropriate to have studied a wide range of authors. Rather than devoting all our time to Chaucer, Shakespeare and other greats, we could have been encouraged to read a little modern literature. We might, perhaps, have studied one or two foreign novelists writing in English, read a poetry anthology that included work by a female poet, considered film as a valid form of story-telling, attempted some creative writing or improvised drama. We might profitably have spent some time studying language as well as literature.

My lifelong dissatisfaction with narrow, over-specialised university courses and their pernicious influence on curricula, syllabuses and teaching methods throughout the education system probably began at Borough Road. The seeds, however, were sown at school. Although I rarely experienced genuine enthusiasm for schoolwork, there were aspects of subjects that interested me. In geography and history, for example, I enjoyed learning about other people's lives – present and past, home and abroad. This was perverse of me for human geography and social history were low priority parts of the geography and history syllabuses. The Higher Certificate geography course, for example, was more concerned with teaching us how to construct a Sanson-Flamstead sinusoidal modified conical map projection than in developing our understanding of some of the crucial cultural, economic, and political differences between the world's peoples.

In guarding the intellectual rigour and academic purity of their specialist subject, university departments are often sceptical of any syllabus content that can be too readily understood, and therefore become common currency. This pedantic stance has had a stultifying effect, not only on school syllabuses, but on many courses elsewhere in the higher education system where there is no justification for adopting the more extreme academic practices. The training colleges were, of course, never likely to consider anything other than a traditional approach to their students' specialist studies: in striving to establish the teacher's certificate as a respectable qualification, the last thing they wanted was to invite critical questions from their validating university about the credibility of the academic component of the course.

The conflict that I encountered between my topic preferences and the conventional priorities manifested itself most clearly at Borough Road in English. I was beginning to take a belated interest in my native language and, through my own reading, had succeeded in demystifying some aspects of English usage that had meant nothing to me at school. The Borough Road English course was, typically, concerned only with literature – for decades the study of the way we use language ceased in this country at the age of 16, even for those going on to specialise in English. However, part of the assessed work was a dissertation on a topic of the student's own choosing. This was normally a re-working of scholarly commentary on some aspect of a recognised author's work, but my proposed topic was an analysis of key features of journalese as manifest in the popular press. I wasn't setting out to be eccentric or to test the system: the subject was simply one that interested me and I did not at the time realise how far I was deviating from the norm by choosing a study that was not only linguistic – when it should have been literary – but popular instead of exclusive, and current rather than historical. I did not fully appreciate how accommodating the head of department was in allowing me to proceed. I doubt, however, if his leniency did me any favours with the examiners.

The professional training component of the teacher's certificate consisted of two distinct parts, the practice and the theory of education, for which separate grades were awarded. It was the practical element – the school teaching practice and observation – that justified places like Borough Road being designated 'training' colleges. We had four three-week school placements, during which we could compare and contrast our own embryonic pedagogical skills with those of skilled practitioners. The gulf between the two recalled my first visit, as a teenager and burgeoning young snooker enthusiast, to the Leicester Square Snooker Hall to marvel at the unbelievable expertise of Joe Davis and his brother Fred, mid-20th century predecessors of Messrs O'Sullivan, Hendry, Higgins and company.

One of the most impressive features of the Davis brothers' play was the way in which they avoided getting themselves into positions that would make their next move difficult. The importance of this principle is one of the first things you have to learn in snooker. It's also important in teaching. You do not, for example, give classes or individual pupils an ultimatum that you cannot, or would not wish to, implement. Thus a warning that 'the next person to speak will be sent out of the room (be given a detention, be boiled in oil)' is courting trouble, leading, in accordance with Sod's Law, to a situation in which you have to punish a normally model pupil who has broken the silence to ask to borrow a neighbour's ruler.

Silence is an interesting issue in teaching. Most of the experienced practitioners that I observed on my school placements could command it at will, but used their skill quite sparingly. I was particularly impressed by a geographer who was my mentor in an Acton central school during my second teaching practice. Each morning I made my way to his classroom and waited expectantly with his form for his arrival – in absolute silence. As soon as he had entered the room and greeted the pupils, they relaxed and began to chatter quietly among themselves. It was an impressive display of teacher power – idiosyncratic, yet not without a rationale. A classroom of over 30 unsupervised teenagers can quickly become rowdy and it is particularly unhelpful for youngsters to start the day in that mood. However, with a teacher in the room to moderate the noise level, children can reasonably be given a few moments before registration to satisfy their natural desire to talk to each other at the beginning of the day. The usual strategy is for the teacher to be in the form room ahead of the class.

The Acton geographer was an ex-serviceman, 'emergency trained' on a one-year crash course, a government initiative to help cope with a post-war staffing crisis in schools. He was a loose cannon with few of the characteristics of the conventional teacher, but he had a natural rapport and easy relationship with his pupils, speaking a language they understood and commanding their respect. I was impressed and unwittingly began to adopt his tone and even to use some of his vocabulary. One day on the football field during a training session I found myself issuing instructions to 'keep the ball on the deck' and 'make it count', and being mimicked by some of the teenage boys in my charge. The expressions were not my own and the boys knew it. You have to establish your own persona as a teacher.

My first teaching practice had been in a primary school in Hounslow and one of the staff there ran the Acton teacher close for achieving silence against the odds. Mr Jones was a spare, phlegmatic character with a lifetime of classroom experience behind him. One afternoon a week he attempted to inculcate some art and craft skills into 60 seven-to-eight-year-old boys, while the girls in the same year engaged in mass cookery. Christmas was imminent and the boys were to make an envelope for a card they'd produced the previous week. Before my observation of this process, I was briefed on the aims of the lesson. There were just two: silence when Mr Jones was giving instructions, and no boy to do anyone an injury with the scissors. These were not perhaps the highest of educational ideals, yet, given the class size, not unambitious. The afternoon proceeded in the manner of an animated Giles cartoon: a seething mass of urchin humanity jockeyed for positions at the craft tables and battled its way to the teacher's desk to obtain approval for mutilated pieces of A4.

Mr Jones remained calm and stoical throughout, stilling and silencing the multitude at regular intervals in order to issue instructions on the next stage of the construction process. With the lethal potential of the scissors blunted by dire warnings against misuse, the glue pots took over as the major hazard and, as the afternoon wore on, the nature of pupils' requests for re-assurance changed, with successive craftsmen holding up sodden balls of *papier-maché* for Mr Jones' inspection and critical comment on the amount of adhesive applied. The teaching method was clearly 'learning from mistakes' and, with 60 assorted characters requiring attention, there was no lack of opportunity. Fortunately, Mr Jones had a never-ending supply of paper for re-starts and by the end of the session a commendable proportion of the class had completed the task. Some of the results, grubby and mis-shapen as they were, actually bore a resemblance to a Christmas card envelope.

All the college lecturers were involved in supervising school practice and we had a different supervisor for each of our placements. It was our responsibility to leave a copy of our teaching programme for each week in our supervisor's pigeonhole. The member of staff supervising my primary school practice was the college's head of English and one of my lecturers, an enigmatic character called Johnston who

69

combined a very powerful and dominant personality with liberal ideas on students and study. It was he who was later to accept my deviant dissertation topic. Heavily-built, bald and with an aggressively manipulated gammy leg, Johnston was a forbidding presence. He was, by repute, very red politically and made it clear that he wouldn't be exercising his authority to exact work from us. If we wished to further our education and complete the set assignments, he would be delighted to mark our work. However, if we didn't hand essays in, that would be fine by him: he wouldn't be chasing us for them. I wasn't sure how to respond to such progressive thinking but, bearing in mind the way Johnston's gimlet gaze penetrated each one of us in the lecture room, I played safe and opted for conventional conformity.

Some students misjudged Johnston, believing that his attempt to transfer responsibility for the completion of written work from lecturer to student was simply an excuse for idleness. I presumably shared this view, at least initially, for I seem to have assumed, when I learnt that Johnston was to be my primary school practice supervisor, that I would see little or nothing of him. I was timetabled one afternoon to introduce a class of 10 and 11-year-olds to Browning's *Pied Piper of Hamelin*. However, the class teacher, a young lady with whom I had developed a rather friendly relationship, had registered the fact that I was not feeling particularly well-prepared for this challenge and was tacitly colluding in a reduction of my day's teaching load by allowing the work she was doing with the class to over-run into my timetabled literature lesson. The inevitable happened: Johnston came into our vision, pounding his gammy leg up the school path and clearly heading for my classroom (via the headteacher's study). The class was galvanised into action, abruptly terminating what it had been doing and re-grouping for a belated start to its poetry lesson. By the time Johnston entered the room

I was underway, although it may have seemed slightly odd that 20 minutes into the lesson my rendering of the *Pied Piper* had not progressed beyond line 6. It was not one of my more impressive performances. Johnston let me down lightly with a few constructive comments, but he wasn't fooled.

With the enthusiasm of the beginner I prepared elaborate and immaculately presented lesson plans. Johnston was mildly dismissive: 'These are for your benefit, you know, not mine. Only brief notes are required.' I made the suggested adjustment. Then – another practice, another supervisor, and a request for 'fuller, more professional lesson plans'. Later in my career I shadowed a secondary school child for three days to get a flavour of what the classroom experience was like for a pupil in the school of which I was head. My main purpose was to quantify the amount of time that pupils spent listening to teachers transmitting information (and, depressingly, it was even greater than expected), but one of the incidental revelations of the pupil experience that I observed was how adaptable secondary school children had to be in adjusting to the different, and sometimes contradictory, demands of their various teachers.

Most of our supervisors were charitable and understanding in their criticism, but it was often their sharper comments that remained in the mind. On one of my practices my teaching timetable included two periods of geography per week with several different classes and I was a long way off knowing the name of every child that I taught. During a supervised lesson I referred to a number of children in the rather patronising manner adopted by David Dimbleby on BBC television, when calling on members of a Question Time audience to put their question to the panel: 'the woman in the mauve sweater', 'the man with the ring in his nose'. I was lectured on the importance of being able to address every child by name. It was a good point: children hate being anonymous, and that is how they feel if defined as 'the girl in the corner' or 'the boy by the window'.

Our situation on school practice was similar to that of Mr Jones' 60 little craftsmen: it was understood that we would make mistakes, but hoped that, in the process, we wouldn't do anyone any serious harm. For our part, we were obviously keen that our most glaring inadequacies could be rectified before we started teaching 'for real'. The school placements were hard work, but rewarding. The general view was that this part of our professional training was invaluable. By contrast, the college-based component, the study of the theory of education, was considered by many to be, in polite paraphrase, 'a waste of time'. There was nothing surprising in this. Students undergoing any form of professional training tend to be impatient to acquire the skills they need as quickly as possible. Consequently, they value most highly the direct routes to that end: hands-on experience and the opportunity to observe accomplished practitioners at work. By comparison, reading books and listening to lectures are bound to be seen as slower and less interesting ways of learning.

Most students learn best from the particular and practical; teachers have to resist the temptation to start at the opposite end, the general and theoretical. Theoretical and practical components of learning do not have to be alternatives: they should be complementary and closely linked. There were insufficient opportunities created at Borough Road for students to share their school experiences and to draw conclusions from them, or for lecturers to compare and contrast students' observations with the views of experts and the findings of researchers. Consequently, students often failed to appreciate the relevance of the educational theory lectures that they were required to attend or of the books they were recommended to read.

A basic problem was that none of our lecturers had

themselves received any teacher training and, although most had had some experience of working in schools, these had been independent or grammar schools, not the kind of places in which we would be working. Given this situation, much greater use should have been made of visiting experts, particularly successful teachers who could draw on their current experiences to illustrate educational theories. Theory divorced from practice becomes meaningless, particularly when it is dressed up in the jargon of academe, as in the following extract on 'natural selection' from a text of the time:

Natural selection is not now generally held to have brought about evolution: it occupies rather 'the more modest position of simply accelerating, retarding or terminating the process of otherwise determined change.' Neo-Darwinism is an impossible creed for the idealist in education. A choice between this and some form of Lamarckism is, for us, one 'ultimately between the Herodian and the Magian view and treatment of the child'.

James Ross:
*Groundwork of Educational Psychology*

Faced with this kind of pretentious gobbledegook, students naturally prefer to trust to their own judgements, based on a world that they can understand. They were wise to do so with respect to some of the theories to which we were introduced at Borough Road. The most frequently cited and revered academic authority on our educational theory course was Sir Cyril Burt, a UCL professor of psychology whose work on intelligence and aptitude testing emphasised the hereditary influences in human development. His findings had played a significant part in persuading mid-20th century educationists to accept a secondary school system that segregated those children who would follow a course of academic study leading to a professional career from those destined for occupations requiring no academic qualifications.

Shortly after I left Borough Road, Professor Burt's influential research findings on intelligence began to be questioned by researchers whose work indicated that environmental factors could modify hereditary characteristics to an extent not allowed for by Burt and his fellow 'hereditarians' – in short, we were not stuck for ever with the precise IQ with which we were born. Some of these academics suggested that Professor Burt's work was flawed and that he had succumbed to a familiar temptation facing researchers, that of selecting the data that supports their case and conveniently ignoring that which doesn't. Burt and his supporters retaliated in kind, accusing his detractors of the very malpractice they were levelling at him – the selective use of evidence to prove a case. The unseemly academic debate that ensued began to attract newspaper coverage and public interest after Professor Burt revealed, in response to a challenge to produce the data on which his theories were based, that key papers had been thrown away and others destroyed in a fire. Research assistants who had allegedly worked for Burt had mysteriously disappeared. These revelations fuelled suspicions that Burt had not merely been unscrupulously selective in his collection of data, but that he had actually fabricated evidence to support his theories.

The case against Burt gathered momentum after his death in 1971 and in April 1980 the Council of the British Psychological Society finally accepted that 'the father of British psychology' and leading figure in the world of education was 'guilty of gross scientific fraud'. It was the academic equivalent of the General Synod admitting that the Archbishop of Canterbury had been helping himself to cathedral collection money to finance a drug habit – except that Burt's dishonesty was more serious, as his pronouncements on intelligence had been a crucial factor in denying generations of children an opportunity to study for appropriate educational qualifications. Indeed, Burt's theories remain a legacy today in many parts of the country that are still committed to segregation of secondary school pupils on the basis of a premature assessment of their intellectual potential.

'The Burt Scandal' had rumbled on for nearly a quarter of a century and academics still debate whether he was consciously fraudulent or merely misguided and incompetent. Those attempting an objective assessment have concluded that he did indeed fabricate data but that some of his detractors used dishonest arguments to suggest that the corruption was greater than it really was. What isn't in any doubt is that the seamy side of the academic community's methods was exposed to lengthy public scrutiny so that many of us developed a healthy scepticism concerning the validity and value of much so-called research. The Burt saga remains a dire warning on what can happen when theory becomes detached from reality, feeding on itself independently of the context that was its starting point.

There were some good learning situations at Borough Road, the more memorable for their being, as at the RGS, isolated occasions. One of our geography lecturers took us off down the Great West Road for a day in the country. The auspices were not good: Mr Hill was a landform enthusiast and one feared that the fieldwork would be mainly measuring the depth of topsoil and similar geological practices. However, our destination proved to be Sonning, a picturesque Thames-side village between Reading and Henley, and the survey we conducted was a pleasingly holistic one, combining physical, historical, geological, economic and sociological aspects of geography. We looked at the soil and land forms that had favoured a bridge settlement in the area in early times and the factors affecting the village's more recent growth, also the current economy of the area and character of the village, the developing tourist interest and its effect on the inhabitants. The day's fieldwork was an excellent example of the way in which different aspects of geography relate to each other and showed how the more technical and, for me, more boring elements have an important contribution to make to one's understanding and appreciation of a human situation.

On another occasion we were bussed out to a tough boys' secondary modern school for a demonstration lesson given by Johnston to a class of disenchanted 15-year-olds. It was a tour de force in pupil involvement. Despite his bulk and physical handicap, Johnson was constantly on the move, firing off a stream of questions and controlling the class by his direct eye contact. Edward Blishen, writer and broadcaster, who was emergency trained at the Islington Teacher Training Centre immediately after the war, recalled a member of staff named Jepp who constantly berated his squad of trainees on the need to develop the 'teacher's eye'. 'Your eyes are your number one weapon. Most of you have mild little eyes. Learn to rotate 'em! Swivel 'em! Stare! Glare! Come on, try it.' And then, in despair, 'You'll be torn to pieces if you go into a classroom with such ladylike eyes.' Jepp would have been impressed by Borough Road's Mr Johnston.

Jepp-like teaching tips played very little part in our training at Borough Road, but right at the end of our two-year course one of the education lecturers acted out a series of classroom management scenarios and rituals that had us all on the edge of our seats. We learnt more about the craft of teaching in that one hour than in all our other education lectures put together. The experience left us wondering why a place hadn't been found on the course for more systematic treatment of such practical issues.

# 7

## Freedom and Responsibility

College students had to provide most of their own entertainment and social life in the post-war years. The students'
union at Borough Road organised a series of balls, dances,
socials and reviews and was responsible for the smooth
running of 26 clubs and societies. Participation rates were
very high; for example, a third of the students belonged to
one or the other of the two religious societies. The drama
society was particularly active, with productions not only of
Shakespeare but Gilbert and Sullivan and Noel Coward, not
to mention Pirandello. Most students were involved in a range
of activities and my membership of six of the 12 sports clubs
wasn't exceptional.

University and college sports activities can be a shambles.
The Borough Road clubs were, however, mostly quite well-run
by their student officers, many of whom, because of national
service, were somewhat older than today's students. In most
sports we had regular weekly fixtures culminating in major
inter-college tournaments at the end of the season. Considering
the good reputation of the college's specialist PE course,

facilities were poor: there was no games hall, swimming pool or proper running track. The big disappointment, however, was that the PE instructor was idle and, when he did turn up, concentrated solely on the gymwork; there was no input into games activities. Whilst the responsibility of organising our own training sessions and fixtures was a good learning experience, the absence of basic instruction in techniques and any coaching for either teams or individuals meant that, despite the college's prospectus claims, standards were rather low. Our fixtures, played mainly against what appeared to be other untrained and uncoached college teams, were somewhat scrappy affairs, high on effort and enthusiasm, but significantly lacking in the skills department. Against non-college opposition we were sadly exposed: the first time we played a London YMCA basketball side we thought the Harlem Globetrotters had turned up by mistake.

Our technical deficiencies were most obvious in athletics field events. The day before the 1954 Inter-Collegiate Athletics Championships at Motspur Park our high jumper injured himself and a last-minute replacement was required. I was competing in the mile event, but was dispensable, being second string to a dedicated middle-distance runner. It was suggested that I tried the high jump. I had long legs but no experience of even a simple scissors jump; as for the western roll, Fosbury flop and eastern cut-off, they could have been exotic desserts for all I knew. Nevertheless, I tried a few modest hopovers and, in the absence of any other contenders, agreed to deputise for our injured specialist. I won the event with what was, even in those days, a derisory height of 5 feet 6 inches. I had it on good authority, however, that, as a scissors jump, it was something special. Had the Guinness Book of Records been in existence, who knows?

Very few members of staff showed any interest in students' extra-curricular activities but a notable exception was Mr Kent, a drama and speech enthusiast who offered assistance to the student directors of drama society plays. Mr Kent also entered a verse-speaking team each year in the English Festival of Spoken Poetry and I was persuaded, along with some other members of the specialist English course, to join one or two genuinely interested oddballs to form a 12-man team for the 1954 event. All teams were given the same set pieces to learn – WR Rodgers' *Europa the Bull* and the Chorus Sacerdotum from *Mustapha*, by the 16th century poet, Sir Fulke Greville. Neither poem was particularly memorable or indeed suited to choral presentation. During rehearsals we acquired a certain affection for *Europa*, but were consistent in our dislike of the Chorus Sacerdotum and were not at all surprised to learn that its author had been murdered by one of his servants. The only pleasure we ever gained from the Fulke Greville piece was from loudly declaiming the first line, 'Oh Wearisome Condition of Humanity', at appropriate moments during the college day.

Mr Kent's lecturing, like that of his colleagues, was largely didactic, but he was quite open to student suggestions during spoken poetry rehearsals: no doubt he was as puzzled by the two poems as we were. Our strenuous efforts to make some sense of our set pieces led to constantly-changing decisions over how to speak the lines. Every attention-seeking ploy was tried out: solo lines, duets, alternating light and deep voices, exaggerated dynamics with striking juxtapositions of ultra-slow quiet sections and great bursts of sound and speed. On the day of the festival we were still making minor changes during a final outdoor rehearsal.

We were placed fourth of 12 teams and felt somewhat deflated, the previous year's college team having walked off with the trophy. In the customary losers' search for excuses, we decided that our performance had been undermined by some of the female opposition who had tittered when we'd ascended the stage for our performance. Borough Road students were known as 'Bees' (presumably B for 'Borough', but also perhaps for 'busy') and no opportunity was missed in college for apiarian terminology: the rag mag was entitled *Sting* and the main college magazine – clever stuff this – *Bees' Hum*. We had entered the choral speaking festival as *The Pollenators* and, when we were thus announced and trooped onto the stage like a rugby league team, some of the young ladies present had had naughty thoughts and given mild expression to their mirth. The elderly and distinguished adjudicating panel clearly disapproved of this levity, and no doubt the indiscretion that caused it, and remained po-faced as we took up our positions.

In the college's wide spectrum of extra-curricular activities the opposite extreme to a devout rendering of the Chorus Sacerdotum was the annual rag. Student rags are one of those English traditions which, like cricket and the Royal family, are extremely difficult to explain to foreigners or visitors from outer space: the more detail you give, the more perplexed the listener becomes. Ostensibly, their purpose is to raise money for charity; in reality they are often an excuse for a prolonged period of extremely silly behaviour. The problem for the organisers is to ensure that the fund-raising is sufficiently robust not only to produce a respectable donation to the chosen good cause, but also to cover the cost of repairing the damage caused by student over-exuberance and self-indulgence during the week of the rag. The Borough Road students' union had rather a 'good boy' image in both respects. The sums raised were large and the expenses relatively small: the amount donated to charity in 1953 and 1954 was not far short of £400 in each year. This equalled my first year's teaching salary when I left college, the equivalent of something approaching £20,000 in 21st century terms. The rag was a two-day event and, as well as a foot and float carnival procession, included pub entertainments (samba band, old-time musical) and a public variety show held in the Dominion cinema, for which students had to audition before a formidable selection committee consisting of the principal, two members of staff, the cinema manager and the chief cinematograph operator. There was also a house-to-house collection, an auction and a rag ball. Each year's rag had a celebrity guest (Peter Sellers in 1953, when the Goon Show was very popular) and a theme for the carnival procession that had to ensure adequate scope for traditional features such as scanty dress, false boobs and large quantities of water dispensed with squirters, stirrup pumps and buckets. The water pranks were a great favourite and entailed frequent impromptu practice sessions in the days leading up to the rag. The 1954 theme was *Life with the Romans*, which resulted in such entries as *Nero's Chariot* (pulled by appropriately disrobed slave girls from our sister college in Stockwell), *Roman Orgy* (more undressing), *The Roman Baths* (and again), *The Roman Pub* and, inexplicably, *Girls of St Trinian's*.

There was a perpetual rag mentality among some students, who exploited any excuse for fancy dress and celebration. In 1954 Dr Hamilton, the college principal, received a CBE in the New Year's Honours List and the staff gathered to see him off to Buckingham Palace. What he didn't know was that the whole college would turn out to welcome him back. As his chauffeur-driven limousine swept into the drive and drew up at the main entrance, the band struck up and students with two-foot long toppers in college colours stepped forward to shower him and his family party with confetti. Pete Turner, the president of the Students' Union, gave a little speech and we all joined in 'three cheers'. Prinny was visibly moved. The occasion reflected the strong community spirit at Borough Road: it was a very small college and its members felt a genuine sense of belonging, something we have lost in today's much larger HE institutions.

One bitter winter's day the supporters of three endurance-test contestants marched to the accompaniment of an ad hoc jazz group down to the Thames, about a mile from the college. The intention was to break the ice at a point where there was gentle access to the river and for the three stalwarts, clothed only in bathers and appropriate headgear, to wade in up to their necks. There they were to stand, spurred on by words of encouragement from their various supporters, until a winner was declared, presumably at the point at which two of the three had collapsed from hypothermia. Messrs Redfern, Nicholson and Moorhouse had stripped off and finished their warm-up when Dr Page, the deputy principal, arrived, minus his usual smile, to announce that the college could not condone such foolhardy behaviour, in fact would send the three students down if they persisted in their folly.

With a face-saving show of reluctance, but no doubt some private feelings of relief, the three heroes dressed and we all trekked back to college, there to find that the national press had arrived in the form of a conventional ferrety-looking reporter from the *Daily Mirror*. Having missed all the excitement, his interest lay less in the details of the intended stunt than in the thinking behind it. Had any thinking actually been taking place, it is doubtful whether the aborted contest would have got as far as it did, but our Fleet Street sleuth wanted a better motive than the natural stupidity of students. His explanation was that we were protesting about something, our inadequately-heated accommodation perhaps? Given the Spartan conditions in the dormitories, this was quite astute – but wrong. He interviewed a succession of students in the common room, casting around, Burt-like, for any comment that might support his hypothesis, but the more aggressive his questioning, the more tight-lipped and unhelpful the students became in their loyalty to the college. Finally, having lectured us on the iniquities of trying to thwart the media in its altruistic search for information in the public interest, he departed to write his article. A single paragraph appeared the following day. One detail had been altered – in the reporter's version the students' intention was to *sit* in the water not stand. This little piece of journalistic licence enabled him just to hint at his suggested political motive in his choice of title to the piece – *The Sitters-in*. Otherwise, the bland accuracy of the report was rather an anti-climax.

Among its wide-ranging responsibilities, the students' union was expected to collaborate with the principal and his deputy to maintain student discipline or, as the union constitution put it, assume responsibility for 'the guidance of student conduct and the restraint of activities contrary to the welfare of the college.' The student council, and more specifically the president and his officers, bore the brunt of this responsibility. Pete Turner, who came to college after a short-term commission in the Fleet Air Arm, was president in my second year and I was his fall guy, the vice-president. Episodes such as the Thames endurance test provided me with my first insight into why student pranks and stunts of all kinds are viewed very differently by those who initiate them and those who are responsible for the participants' safety and welfare.

At the time of the 1954 rag Pete was living it up in Moscow, as a member of the first student delegation from this country to be invited behind the iron curtain after the war. The highlight of the trip was apparently a visit to the Kremlin, where he marvelled at the Fabergé jewellery and tried to persuade one of the female members of his party to go to bed with him in an opulent four-poster – strictly, of course, to provide a conversation stopper for their return. She apparently declined but did agree to dance a Charleston with him on one of the larger Kremlin tables. Meanwhile, back in the more modest surroundings of Borough Road, rag weekend was approaching and excitement and water levels were both rising. It fell to me to calm things down, if possible without being too much of a party pooper. It was an uncomfortably ambivalent position, but I made a brief after-dinner speech wishing everyone well for the various events we were organising and requesting a little moderation in the water sports, which were already getting out of hand. The mutterings of 'rhubarb, rhubarb' were reasonably mooted, which I took to be a sign that I'd perhaps got the balance of what I said more or less right.

I deputised for the president on another occasion. One of the more obvious council responsibilities was to represent student opinion to the principal. Like all its predecessors, no doubt, the 1954 student body sought a relaxation in the regulation that guests had to vacate students' study rooms by 8.00 pm. 'Guests' of course meant 'girlfriends' and, as Pete was spending a good deal of his leisure time with the principal's younger daughter at the time, he considered it prudent not to be the person who raised this issue with Dr Hamilton. I planned my presentation of the students' case carefully, having decided on a circumspect approach. The principal had, however, been here many times before and knew the agenda: 'I fully appreciate that if a student wants to get a young lady in the family way he's just as likely to do so at 5 o'clock as 9 pm. Nevertheless....' And Dr Hamilton proceeded to deliver a little homily on the need for the college to take, and to be seen to take, its care rôle seriously.

A number of possible ripostes flashed through my mind: 'Dr Hamilton, if one considers the very cramped spaces that serve as studies in the college, would you not agree that it would take a remarkably athletic and innovative couple to find a way of starting a family in one of them?' Or: 'Come off it, Prinny, don't try that *in loco parentis* guff with me.' But of course I listened politely, thanked Dr Hamilton for giving me so generously of his time and, within a remarkably short while, was on my way back to report to the president. Pete took it philosophically, as indeed he could well afford to do, at least at a personal level: his assignations with the young Miss Hamilton took place in her flat in the college lodge and were unaffected by the 'visitors out' rule.

It was a moot point whether a change in the time for Borough Road guests to leave students' study rooms would have actually made much difference to college levels of sexual activity – not for the reasons that the principal gave, but simply because most girlfriends were students from the women's training colleges and their rules required them to be safely indoors at the time our student body was fondly imagining it might be intensifying its enjoyment of their company in Borough Road. There was one Catholic training college where the inmates had to be in by 7.00 pm, that is at the weekends – they weren't allowed out during the week.

Most of the women's colleges, however, were beginning to lose their convent image and to recognise the natural, if regrettable, desire for the male and female of the species to get together. Borough Road musical and dramatic activities were often joint ventures with Maria Grey, the Froebel training college in Richmond, and rag carnival processions were much enhanced by nubile contingents from more than one women's college. From time to time a coach was hired for a mass exodus from college to one of the more distant female establishments. During the summer months, Easthamstead near Bracknell was a popular venue, as its extensive gardens and parkland minimised the inconvenience of not being allowed into the students' rooms. A slight drawback was the protracted first stage of the homeward journey, caused by frequent stops along the lengthy college driveway to pick up dishevelled members of the coach party emerging from their amorous leave-takings in the undergrowth.

Notwithstanding these occasional sorties, sexual liaisons were, for the majority of students, largely a figment of the imagination, which may help to explain the nature of a practical joke played on the new intake during my second year. There was a tradition for the first year to be subjected to some innocuous prank or trick soon after their arrival and my year had been informed that Dr Page, the deputy principal, attached considerable importance to getting to know the new arrivals and appreciated their passing the time of day with him if they encountered him in the corridor. This wasn't quite as fatuous as it might seem, as Dr Page wore a perpetual grin on his face to which it was difficult not to respond. For a day or two at least we obligingly beamed back with apparent delight whenever we met him.

We decided on a more ambitious although equally daft stunt for our freshers. Notices were posted early in their first week informing them that they were required to attend an evening address by a Dr Lucas on the subject of *Relations with Women's Colleges,* the 'Dr Lucas' in question being one of our number on whom we had conferred an honorary doctorate for the occasion. He was a rather studious, elderly-looking young man with considerable experience in amateur dramatics and strongly recommended by his friends for our purpose. His talk began with some gratuitous observations on the nature of the female of the species and particular characteristics of the young ladies who attended the nearby Maria Grey College in Richmond. General advice followed on how students should conduct themselves in their relations with students of the opposite sex. The content of Lucas's address was a complete giveaway, but the professorial seriousness with which he delivered it, blinking short-sightedly over his spectacles, kept the audience puzzled and uncertain. Until, that is, lack of self-control among the perpetrators in the back row gave the game away. We were easily amused in those days. Each weekday after lunch we would gather in the common room for *Listen with Mother* on the radio. 'Is everyone sitting comfortably?' We assured the presenter that we were and answered all the subsequent questions just as dutifully.

Our sleeping accommodation consisted of two long dormitories on the second and third floors of the main college building. Each bed was partitioned off with 7' high flimsy wooden panels to form small cubicles on either side of a central corridor. Light bulbs ran the length of the ceiling and were switched off at 11.00 pm. Anyone wanting to go to sleep before that time had to put up with the lights being on; those who came up to bed after 'lights out' groped their way along the corridor in the dark to find their cubicle. At some time a joker had transferred a full-size shot from the athletics store cupboard to one of the dormitories and at regular intervals this object was rolled along the bare boards of the corridor: the ominous prolonged rumble that resulted is one of the abiding memories that Old Bees of the fifties have of the college. The entertainment value of course varied according to one's situation: it was greatest for the rollers, less for those violently woken from their sleep, and least for anyone unfortunate enough to be shuffling his way along the pitch black corridor just as the shot was released. One could never be quite sure which of the two floors the lethal projectile was actually travelling along: immediate evasive action was therefore required on both corridors.

With sophisticated entertainment of this kind readily available in college we had no need to go further afield for our nightlife. Nevertheless, I occasionally took advantage of Borough Road's proximity to the Osterley tube station to travel a few stops down the Piccadilly line to the theatre, usually with Pete Turner. We alternated between the Chiswick Empire, with its Sunday night variety shows, and the Lyric Hammersmith, where the fare was a little more sophisticated – Greek tragedy, Ibsen and a new play by T S Eliot, *The Confidential Clerk*. I saw my first professionally-performed Shakespearian play at the Lyric – *King Lear* with Donald Wolfit magnificent in the title rôle. Wolfit, later Sir Donald, was a showman and, in a wonderfully theatrical extension of his part, he remained in character throughout the ovation at the end of the play. Finally, clinging exhaustedly to the stage curtain, he came forward to address the audience: 'After the sublime language that I have been privileged to utter, any words of my own must seem redundant...' and then proceeded to declaim at length on the subject of the play and the production. Shakespeare texts acquired an added dimension after that.

Many of the famous actors and actresses of the time appeared at the Lyric and there were some memorable productions, including one of the great revivals of Congreve's *Way of the World*, starring Margaret Rutherford (later Dame Margaret), Paul Scofield and Sir John Gielgud. I couldn't help wondering why the Lyric productions had never impinged on my consciousness before: the theatre was little further from High Wycombe than most of the Thames Valley towns to which, as a teenager, I had travelled each Saturday with the Wycombe Wanderers' youth team.

My pocket money was £3 a month and came from home in instalments of £1 one week and 10 shillings the next. During my affluent weeks I sometimes splashed out and paid the fare to go all the way down the Piccadilly line to the centre of London with its overwhelming cultural riches. The capital had a romantic appeal and occasionally on a Sunday I walked the streets and squares and parks and became familiar with their famous buildings and monuments.

Once or twice after evening trips to the bright lights I only just got back to college by the 11.00 pm curfew time, and on one occasion I failed. The duty lecturer for the night was standing by the signing out book scrutinising my signature and jangling his jailer's keys conspicuously. Inevitably, it was Mr Johnston, with whom my relations invariably seemed to be embarrassing. He expressed disappointment that someone in my position on the student council should let himself down so badly. It was one of those situations that leave one feeling aggrieved at having done the right thing. Less law-abiding citizens simply asked a friend to sign them in before 11.00 and, when they eventually returned to college, gained access via an unlatched window at the rear of the building – an arrangement usually, but not always, connived at by the duty lecturers.

A number of formalities were observed in college. The midday and evening meals began with a lengthy grace, which Pete or I recited in Latin. The lecturers sat either side of the principal at High Table. Any students arriving late had to mount the rostrum and stand in front of Dr Hamilton until he deigned to acknowledge their presence with a nod of permission for them to take their place at the students' table that ran the length of the dining hall. These rituals were not only accepted, but rather enjoyed: they helped to make the college a bit special. Despite our occasional pranks and sillinesses we were a very formal and law-abiding community. We wore a self-inflicted uniform of blazer or tweed jacket, plus collar, tie and sleeveless knitted pullover. A few non-conformists sported grey suits. There were never any protests or political demonstrations – although we did have a Communist who scaled a large tree to enable the college to mark Elizabeth II's coronation by flying the skull and crossbones. It was said that the Communist Party had a policy of targeting the teacher training colleges to recruit members. Our representative was as dedicated – and about as popular – as a Jehovah's Witness.

The staff also had its maverick. Albert Perry, 'the world's most rejected artist', was a familiar figure, hirsute and scruffy in ginger jacket, tartan scarf and shirt, the latter open to reveal a none-too-savoury woollen vest. He joined his besuited colleagues at High Table but rarely shared their meal, preferring bread, cheese and onion from a newspaper wrapping. Albert's art students were allowed complete freedom to draw or paint whatever they liked: 'Some people like fish and chips, dear friends; others like sausage and mash. Do your own thing.' He undertook little teaching, but occasionally offered advice: 'Turn it upside down, dear friend, for better effect.' Albert had a favourite spot by the Thames for students' sketching and painting sessions, which he liked to observe from the public bar of the London Apprentice. He lived in Tooting where apparently he once stood as a candidate in the Borough elections. He told his students that the two main planks of his campaign had been that children should be given sweets in class to stop them talking and that the size of bricks should be doubled to enable houses to be built in half the time.

On one occasion, Albert's art students lent support to his ongoing campaign for recognition by the Royal Academy by accompanying him to London, where they assembled for press photographs in the Academy forecourt with Albert displaying his latest work, a modern sculpture consisting of a tennis ball attached by wires to a bright green football. The supporting group wore different national costumes to demonstrate the worldwide nature of Albert's fan club. The art students obviously gained vicarious pleasure from Albert's non-conformity and irresponsibility and were remarkably tolerant of their lack of proper art tuition.

Tolerance was a strong characteristic of the Borough Road students in general and drew an interesting comment from inspectors who, in my second year, visited the college on behalf of the Council of the British and Foreign School Society. Having listed some of the deficiencies of the dormitories – worn-out beds and bedding, absence of any heating, no provision of wash basins and so on – the inspectors observed: 'The students, who were most conscious of the pleasure of sharing intimately in college life by living at college, did not complain, but this acquiescence is in its way as disturbing as the conditions themselves.'

This comment provided a different perspective on our

loyalty on the occasion that we were questioned by the *Daily Mirror* reporter. We were shortly to go out into the nation's schools where many of us would be beginning a lifetime's service to education. Throughout our careers we would continue to be noted for the qualities of patience, tolerance and understanding that have come to be expected from those who work with children. But those qualities, admirable as they are, can actually do a disservice to the schools in which teachers work. Teachers' tendency to get on uncomplainingly with their job, to be reluctant to get involved in any union action, to put up with poor facilities, inadequate equipment and generally sub-standard working conditions have paradoxically let children down by contributing to the low priority that our society attaches to educational provision.

The state schools that we now build are, of course, generally a great improvement on those of 50 years ago, but the updating remains piecemeal and the standard of the facilities and, more particularly, the cleanliness and quality of maintenance lag further and further behind that which we expect from most of the other buildings we erect – office blocks, shopping centres, local government buildings, entertainment complexes. The negative message sent out by this ordering of priorities does nothing to help us persuade children to respect their school and value the education it provides.

8

## Education by Deselection

High View County Secondary Modern School, Wallington, where I obtained my first teaching post, was a good place to learn about the secondary school system of the 1950s, being a prime example of the deselection process at work. It was a co-educational 11-15 school situated in one of the streets adjacent to the now defunct Croydon Airport. The catchment area had no discernible centre or sense of community, yet the school had a distinctly familial character, due in part, no doubt, to the high number of siblings among its pupils. The year I joined the staff there were 14 sets of twins on roll. Several very large families provided a steady stream of entrants, so that each new intake seemed reassuringly familiar. There was nothing to explain these phenomena: one awaited definitive research on the breeding habits of those living on airport flight paths.

The pupils' background was extremely varied. The middle-class children were smartly turned out in full grammar school-type uniform, including caps (peaked and tassel-less for boys, tasseled and peakless for girls). A significant number of children, however, came from poor homes and the first absence note I received, written on the back of paper torn from the kitchen wall, aptly demonstrated why it wasn't possible to enforce uniform requirements throughout the school. There were no funds available specifically to help families in need, but the school was sensitive to the marked differences of home circumstances and did its best to provide support where it was needed. Two sportsmen from a single parent family who were chosen to represent Surrey in the All-England Athletics Championships were presented with tracksuits for their big day, not as an act of charity but as a special sports award.

Prominent as the social differences were, the ability range was even more striking. The top streams were bright, alert and eager to learn. The bottom streams, however, contained some pupils who were wholly illiterate and innumerate, some of them also with severe emotional and behavioural problems, children who today would be taught in small groups in special schools or learning support units, not in classes of 30+ in mainstream education.

The stark dichotomy created by the 11+ selection/deselection system was all too clear at High View. Despite the obvious ability of many of the children, there was, in 1954, no provision for them to acquire educational qualifications. They followed a basic non-examined course before seeking employment at 15. None of the classes was set any homework. Meanwhile, their ex-classmates who had passed for one of the two grammar schools, were preparing to take eight or nine GCE O-levels (GCSE A-C grades, in current terminology), followed by the opportunity for further academic study leading to A-levels, higher education and professional careers.

You didn't have to be one of Dr Burt's professorial adversaries to deduce that something was wrong here. The yawning gap between the ways in which selected and deselected pupils were treated was not only manifestly absurd but grossly unfair. The 11+ has always been a lottery: the difference between success and failure is, for many children, only a matter of a few marks, which on another day would be distributed differently. Had one exchanged the brightest 30 children in High View's intake for a comparable number of those who narrowly qualified for a grammar school place, it is unlikely that anyone would have detected a difference.

If this seems an extravagant claim, consider a 1944 educational phenomenon when a national initiative to avert a post-war staffing crisis in schools led to the two grammar schools in High Wycombe each admitting a one-off intake of 11+ failures. Elementary school children who did well in a 13+ exam were offered a belated grammar school place, on condition that their parents pledged that their sons or daughters would pursue a career in teaching. Most of the 13-year-olds in the area suddenly discovered, under parental guidance, that they had never really wanted to be engine-drivers or nurses, but schoolteachers, and two classes, one of boys and one of girls, were duly despatched to re-join their former classmates. The RGS contingent was designated 'Shell', which may conceivably have been a rare stroke of imagination and foresight on the part of the school's management, for, from the moment this class was formed, it took off like an Exocet missile. Seizing their unexpected opportunity to join the privileged classes, the members of Shell left many of the resident scholars, gifted sportsmen and potential leaders behind: their exam results were very good, they packed the school teams and they occupied far more than their fair share of positions of responsibility. Two of their number became the school's first national sportsmen, one, Ted Woodward, captaining the English Schools' Rugby XV on the way to the senior national team. The parallel class in the Girls' High School manifested very similar characteristics – although their sportswomen were athletes and hockey players rather than rugby enthusiasts.

No such second chance of a grammar school place presented itself to High View children: the 11+ deselection was final. The only escape route from the stigma of academic failure was a slender (3-4%) possibility of a technical school place at 13. Clearly the denial of educational opportunities to so many children was untenable and other secondary modern schools in Wallington had already begun to develop examination courses for some of their brightest pupils. We started down this road very tentatively at High View, eventually entering a small number of the top stream for the Royal Society of Arts Stage 1 exams in English, maths and commercial subjects. One or two pupils progressed to Stage 2, a standard a little below GCE O level. In the academic year 1958-9 17 pupils stayed on for a fifth year and were entered for an RSA Certificate exam in a specified group of subjects. One pupil was entered for and passed O level English language. This achievement was paraded at the climax of the school's autumn prize-giving ceremony, but was put in perspective by the parent who, when the single O level certificate had been given out, asked incredulously 'Is that it?' It was indeed a very small beginning, but an academic course had been started in 1957, complete with syllabus and homework timetable, and in 1960 a whole class sat a number of O levels.

The wide range of pupils at High View provided an excellent training ground for a new entrant to the teaching profession and the headteacher's policy of sharing the top and bottom stream work round the staff meant that each day's teaching entailed frequent shifts of approach and management style. I was designated 'form teacher' for 2A, a particularly bright-eyed and bushy-tailed bunch of 13-year-olds. Predictably – since I was the new kid on the block and six feet two and three-quarter inches tall to boot – my bottom stream pupils were the fourth-year leavers, the school's ultimate challenge.

The start of any career is a testing time, but particularly

so in teaching, where one's every move is watched by 30 pairs of eyes or more. The early challenges at High View were heightened by my being hard of hearing at the time: all sounds seemed to be coming from afar and muffled by fog. The problem turned out to be nothing more than ear-wax, aggravated by a summer's swimming, but, not having registered with a doctor in my new town of residence, I experienced a delay in receiving the necessary syringing. There must also have been something wrong with my eyesight for at my first calling of the register I misread a girl's name, referring to Elizabeth De Winne as 'Elizabeth We Winne'. The class hooted with glee and Elizabeth never forgave me. Gaffs accumulated throughout the first day and included the cardinal error of allowing the pupils in my first teaching class to sit where they chose and thus to score an early point in the subtle manoeuvrings that determine who is in control of the classroom. In teaching you don't need to create your own problems in this way: they'll come at you thick and fast anyway.

All beginnings are crucial in the classroom: the start of an academic year or term, the introduction of a new topic, the first few minutes of a lesson. The start of lessons at High View was potentially chaotic. Few children possessed much in the way of equipment: pens, pencils, rulers, blotting paper, exercise paper, textbooks, all had to be distributed at the start of each lesson and then collected in again at the end. I sought to ensure that all this paraphernalia was out on the desks before a class came in. As soon as pupils were seated, they were expected, without waiting for direction, to start writing and reading: heading any blank paper with name and date, noting comments on returned written work and correcting any mistakes, and then reading the library book that they brought to every lesson. Thus with the more responsive classes, and sometimes on good days with others, each lesson began industriously, with no time wasted waiting for latecomers. Sometimes when the concentration was tangible, I was loath to intrude and the class carried on reading for five or ten minutes at the start of the lesson. Developing the reading habit was a high priority.

Most secondary modern teachers learnt to respect the scouts' motto and my preparation wasn't confined simply to knowing the subject matter, but extended to all aspects of classroom management. For example, any extensive board work was completed before school, in the morning break or during the lunch-hour. This time-consuming practice stemmed from my acceptance of the deputy head's advice never to turn one's back on the class ('don't have your head in a cupboard and your bum in the air'), coupled with my failure to master her technique of maintaining this precept whilst writing on the board. Miss Clarke was a leading exponent of the 'teacher's eye' described by Edward Blishen's Mr Jepp, and even the toughest of roughnecks wilted before her glare. She received her classes standing, predator-like, just inside the door, fixing each pupil in turn with her gimlet gaze, as if to say, 'You just as much blink and I'll have you!' Miss Clarke had a caustic tongue and was mistress of the one-line put down. 'What are you doing?' she snapped to some innocent in the corridor. 'Nothing, Miss Clarke.' 'That's right, wasting your time as usual!'

Miss Clarke had no problems with discipline but there were other teachers with 'attitude' whose cultivated aggressiveness was less effective. The girls' PE teacher, for example, barked at her classes with great self-assurance and authority, yet the girls clearly saw her as a soft touch. Some wore wellingtons on the games field. A third-former brought a lesson to a standstill by pretending to panic at the top of a rope, proclaiming loudly from the gym ceiling that she was stuck and didn't know how to get down. The teacher stood anxiously below issuing advice and instructions, coaxing, and getting nowhere. Like most teachers who can't control their pupils, this lady seemed not to see what was going on around her. Three girls inexplicably disappeared one day in the gym and the lesson was half way through before telltale sounds emerging from inside the vaulting horse solved the mystery.

There were other teachers who seemed to get just what they wanted from their classes without any discernible technique or show of strength: no glares, snarls or raised voices. Gladys Ross was a tall, rather elegant lady who looked precisely what she was: a retired captain of the Ladies' Team at an exclusive tennis club. She was always well-groomed and had a wicked twinkle and seductive actressy laugh. Gladys was kind and generous and a real softy with individual children, but a firm and well-organised classroom manager. When asked how she did it, she referred to her baptism of fire as a young teacher of a class of 63. Miss Ford was more difficult to fathom. She was a small rosy dumpling of a woman, the image of everyone's favourite grandmother. Her soft voice, gentle eyes and complete lack of presence defied the normal criteria for survival in the blackboard jungle.

There were some very enthusiastic and lively young men on the staff at High View. Wally Wragg ('Woolly Rug'), whom I helped with boys' games, ended each day as cheerfully and energetically as he began it. However, Harry Horlock-Stringer ('Forelock Springer') outstripped him for stamina, still exuding enthusiasm at 9 pm when his evening art class ended. I still have a passable pot, testimony to his ability to get results with the least artistic of students. Harry lived up to his surname by having a distinctly 'upper' voice and sporting a very natty hand-tied bow-tie, another set of characteristics that ought to have made for difficulties in the classroom, but did not appear to do so. All the young men on the staff paid court to a saucy and successful English teacher who was just sufficiently their senior to be interesting. Harry was the most outrageous in his advances and extolled this colleague's charms in amorous lines that he transposed into the hymns we sang in morning assembly – much to the embarrassed delight of the lady concerned.

The successful teachers brought different talents and skills to their work in the classroom but had certain key qualities in common – they were enthusiasts for their subject, they thoroughly enjoyed teaching, they liked children. And, perhaps most important of all, children liked them. The teacher's vantage point in assessing a school is of course very different from that of a pupil, but it seemed to me that the children at High View were better taught than I had been at school. Unlike grammar school teachers of the day, the staff were, of course, all professionally trained and, whatever the standard of that training, they had given some thought to what teaching entailed. Added to this, they had to be reasonably good at what they did in order to survive. Incompetents tended not to last long. Passing the room of a recent arrival, I noticed that the members of her class were all sitting on their desks and responding to each pedagogical statement with the kind of uninhibited bursts of cheering and applause normally associated with goal-scoring moments in football matches. The teacher had departed by the end of the week.

A temporary maths teacher who taught briefly in the room next to mine lasted a little longer, but gave early indications of her desire to escape by frequently abandoning her classes to post a letter or go to the shops. George Paul, the headteacher, made valiant attempts to forestall her, but she was usually too quick for him. One day a boy arrived in my room to say that he had been sent by this colleague to say that she needed my help. It proved to be a reasonable request as I found the teacher with her back to the wall and a knife held by one of her pupils a few inches from her face. If this were typical of the relationship she had with her classes, it was understandable that the occasional shopping expedition appeared an attractive proposition.

Violent conflicts between teachers and pupils were infrequent occurrences, but they did happen. One day I entered the room of another English teacher to find the furniture pushed back from the centre of the room and the attention of the class hypnotically focused on two writhing figures locked in unarmed combat on the floor. Addressing the smaller of the two adversaries, I asked, 'Are you all right, Mr Turner?' to which I received the strangulated reply, 'Yes...I think...I've... got 'im.' I withdrew, quietly closing the classroom door.

One of the most difficult pupils I had to deal with was a young lady called Priscilla whom I first encountered in the third year and then taught as a fourth-former. Loud, abusive and at times virtually uncontrollable, Priscilla was a strapping wench with a washerwoman's build and range of invective. As our routes to and from school partly coincided, I occasionally ran the gauntlet of her ribald comments as I passed her on my exercise-book-laden bicycle. I wasn't unduly surprised to learn one day that Priscilla had caused another cyclist on the staff to fall off his bike. The initial version of events was that she had felled the teacher with a single blow that had lifted him bodily out of the saddle. She would certainly have been capable of such an assault, in terms of both strength and intent, but subsequent reports implied that she had been harassing the teacher while he was trying to mount his cycle at the kerb and had then blundered into him, knocking bike and rider over. Priscilla was said to receive frequent beltings from her father and this might have explained why her bad behaviour at school was usually directed towards the male staff, whom she knew couldn't resort to physical chastisement.

As far as I knew, no male teacher at High View ever laid a hand on one of the girls, but in other respects corporal punishment was an accepted part of school life, certainly for some pupils. Formal caning was administered by the head, but all male staff carried a letter authorising their use of the slipper, if and when necessary. Some female staff applied a ruler to the bare arm or slapped pupils' outstretched palms with their own hands; one or two of the ladies had been known to bend girls over and slipper the backs of their legs above the knees.

'The slipper' usually meant one or two whacks, but there were occasional beatings of a much more severe kind. 'Bouncer' Breffit, the senior master, caught two second-formers in the playground strangling another boy by pulling on both ends of a scarf wound round his neck. The victim was in considerable distress and Breffit was incensed. He dragged the two offenders into the nearest classroom, where I was preparing for the next lesson, bent each one in turn over a desk, holding him down none too gently by the neck, and wielded his gym shoe with all the strength he could muster, continuing until he was exhausted. No-one appeared to question the principle of corporal punishment, but there was an academic debate that occasionally surfaced as to whether one should ever strike a child in anger. 'Bouncer' Breffit had no qualms on that score.

It took a lot to anger George Paul, the headteacher, who was a calm and kindly man much liked by staff and pupils. However, he completely lost his cool on one occasion. He came to my room to show a second-year form a publisher's sample of an attractively bound poetry book that was part of a new series. A bright but very cheeky boy made a disparaging remark about poetry. Over-reacting to the implication that I had failed to inculcate an appropriate love of this branch of literature, I referred to a recent lesson on Walter de la Mare's *The Listeners* that I thought had gone rather well and which I hoped might elicit a more positive response. Another disparaging remark. Mr Paul had had enough: he ordered the boy out to the front and hit him across the head – hard. I was as stunned as the class. Cuffing was not uncommon, but it was usually a mild flick issued to over-exuberant or over-talkative youngsters, more as a reminder than a punishment. Mr Paul's blow was in a different class. In today's climate it would probably have landed him in jail, where no doubt he would have had the company of most of his staff, and several of the pupils.

I had an unhappy experience with cuffing. A lively spark in one of my classes was capering all over the corridor instead of lining up quietly outside the classroom with the rest of the form. Coming up behind him I attempted to administer a corrective cuff. Aware at the last moment of my presence, the culprit swayed away from my hand, which consequently made the slightest of contact but sufficient, in combination with the impetus of his own evasive action, to land him with quite a crack against the unplastered brick wall. By the time the class was seated he had a spectacular discoloured egg emerging from his forehead with a trickle of blood oozing from a small star-shaped central hole. I was appropriately horrified and chastened and my contrition was intensified by the graciousness with which he accepted my apology: 'It's all right, sir. It was my fault.'

It is an indication of just how much attitudes have changed in 50 years that there never seemed to be any complaints from parents concerning the assaults on their offspring. Probably the pupils didn't tell them, in case they received an additional clout at home for good measure. In the same way, the occasional attacks on teachers were five-minute wonders: nothing much came of them and there were no court cases during my five years at High View. Physical abuse seemed to be regarded as a natural part of life and no big deal. Oddly it didn't appear to affect the generally good relationships between staff and pupils or most children's obvious enjoyment of school. That didn't of course make it any less reprehensible and, in looking back from a different age, it is painful to recall how readily we then all accepted the concept of corporal punishment. Perhaps some stirrings of disquiet did disturb my equanimity at the time for it became my custom to offer offenders a choice of the slipper or lines. They invariably chose the slipper.

9

# Learning by Teaching

Certification provides teachers and children with a goal, motivating them and raising their expectations and levels of performance. At the same time it can distort the curriculum, restrict syllabuses and inhibit both teaching and learning. The need to prepare children for exams often leads to premature specialisation at the expense of general education and an over-concentration on what is most easily categorised and measured. Priorities in an examined curriculum tend to be dictated by the needs of one group of children – the most academic.

Free of the demands and restrictions of certificate courses, High View pupils in the mid-fiftees enjoyed a broad curriculum consisting of academic, creative and practical subjects, thus avoiding the choices that selective school pupils had to make between different areas of human knowledge. However, the school failed to exploit a precious opportunity to define its own educational priorities and create a learning experience directly relevant to a specific group of youngsters. There was no attempt to break away from the traditional fragmented curriculum by linking or integrating subjects or to re-think either the content of courses or the way in which they were taught. In fact, there was little educational thinking at all – no policy or direction; no discussion of aims, objectives or methods; no syllabuses or course documentation; no guidance on what to teach or how to teach it. There was nothing unusual about this: schools in the fifties didn't define or direct the educational process or have management structures like faculties, departments and curricular teams. Thus at High View it was left to individual teachers to decide what and how to teach, a procedure that led to much duplicated effort and inconsistency.

Resources, as well as syllabuses, define the classroom experience and at that time were almost as scarce. Some of the textbooks must have had an antiquity value. The wonders of the spirit duplicator had not yet impinged on school staff rooms and there was no other way of producing one's own materials. I therefore wrote begging letters to numerous firms and organisations requesting multiple copies of their current publications – newspapers, magazines, brochures, advertisements, posters, correspondence, in-house documentation, anything that could be used, or adapted for use, in the classroom. For some reason, tube train advertisers were particularly generous in their response and I became quite an authority on the artistic and literary skills of those who seek to attract and retain the attention of some of the world's most switched-off commuting consumers – the zombies who ride the London underground. It is now possible to buy anthologies of 'poetry from the underground', but 50 years ago I had to do my own scavenging for accessible verse.

My hunt for appropriate materials produced many examples of the different ways in which facts and opinions can be presented and the various uses to which people put language according to their integrity, profession, purpose and audience. Several of my classes undertook an extended study of newspapers, their content, language and editorial policy. I learnt a lot from such projects and hoped that the children did too. Another happy consequence of my steadily growing resource bank was that it provided generous display material for the classroom. In my first year at High View I was peripatetic, having to use other people's rooms for my teaching. Laden as a shopping centre baglady, I manoeuvred my way along the crowded corridors with bulging tins of pens, pencils and rulers balanced precariously on top of the books required for each lesson. As soon as I graduated to a room of my own it became a priority to maintain a regularly up-dated display of illustrative material and children's work.

The completion of an extension to one wing of the school building prompted plans for a new initiative, an evening exhibition for parents. Pupils were preoccupied with preparing their work for display and I involved everyone in this process trying, by varying the length of contributions, to reconcile the conflicting desires to show off the best work and to give all children the satisfaction of exhibiting something that they had produced. All four walls of the classroom were covered with neat copies of children's creative writing. Posters outlined the teaching and learning methods. Examples of class books and materials were laid out on the desks with explanations of how they were used. When the evening arrived, I took up my post early hoping that the flow of interested parents would be sufficiently regular for me to have the opportunity to respond to everyone's queries and comments. This concern proved needless as it was three-quarters of an hour before anyone entered the room. A solitary father then put in an appearance, stood for a moment looking round and asked: 'Why do so many children nowadays write with a backward slope?' I took this to be a rhetorical question for, having made his point, the gentleman turned on his heel and left without waiting for an answer. I didn't see anyone else.

If the open evening confirmed impressions that there was

a low level of parental interest in the work of the school, the appreciation that pupils and ex-pupils often showed for our efforts to educate them was a source of much pleasure. It was my custom, whenever I could see a way of presenting an idea visually, to draw on the blackboard with coloured chalks. Years later I met ex-pupils, often serving behind shop counters, who enthusiastically recalled the pinmen and cartoon characters who had peopled their classroom. It would have been churlish to have inquired whether they also remembered the linguistic and literary points that these drawings were intended to drive home.

The less able the children, the more grateful they seemed for help given them. Similarly, those who had been the least successful at school were often the most likely, after leaving, to return to see their ex-teachers, although this may have had something to do with their ready availability during periods of being 'between jobs'. Ex-malefactors would suddenly arrive on the doorstep unannounced and add to the challenge of classroom management by interrupting one's lesson for a prolonged chat. Invariably they were young men and women with a poorly developed sense of when they were overstaying their welcome.

Two young men who regularly returned to see me were Messrs Hatcher and Sullivan from 4C, my first bottom stream form, their visits an embarrassing reminder of my early attempts to master the art of managing difficult fourth-formers. There was a lot of Hatcher and Sullivan: large, loud and oafish, their disruptiveness often set the tone for the rest of the class. At one stage, I succumbed to the temptation of temporarily foregoing their contribution to lessons. In my efforts to encourage a more positive attitude in these young men, I had enlisted their help one day in returning some texts to the walk-in English store cupboard and whilst there they had, under my supervision, re-arranged some of the piles of books for me. As often happens with badly-behaved pupils, they had enjoyed being useful and asked if there were further jobs that needed doing. The book cupboard had no catalogue system so I devised one and set them to work re-arranging and labelling the sets of books. The work progressed slowly during a number of lunch hours and my two budding librarians – who weren't lacking street wisdom – volunteered generously to carry on unsupervised in an English lesson, and then later, as the pace of progress slowed even further, to sacrifice additional lessons to the cataloguing cause.

This was a high-risk project with suspect motives. However, I overcame my misgivings by convincing myself that the two boys were benefiting from what was for them a rare experience of being gainfully employed – and in a task that was more likely to be relevant to their future employment, if any, than much of what they would be doing in class. Nevertheless, I was relieved when their ingenuity could string the task out no further and it came to an end, having been completed with no greater mishap than some damage to a shelf – and a minor head wound to one of my helpers.

As time passed, I discovered ways of transferring the principles of gainful employment and job satisfaction from the book cupboard to the classroom. The key to 4C's application to study and enjoyment of lessons was to set achievable goals, to help pupils to attain them, and then to be generous in one's recognition of their success. These principles are, of course, applicable to all learners, from nursery school to university, but they are particularly important in building up confidence in children with learning difficulties who have experienced years of failure and frustration with schoolwork. I was very pedantic over the way classes presented their written work, laying down unequivocal rules over headings, underlining, spacing, procedures for correcting mistakes and so on. The A forms took these idiosyncrasies on board reasonably effortlessly, but for the bottom streams it was a real challenge to remember all the rules of the game. Pupils sat back and admired each correct step they made in the presentation procedure. Mistakes produced consternation. A perfectly executed layout was a cause for great celebration.

At times, when they became absorbed in some routine task, 4C belied their reputation as the most difficult class in the school, but there were too many eccentrics and potentially disruptive elements for one ever to relax. One of the most unpredictable pupils was a gangly unco-ordinated youth called Evans. All arms and legs at the best of times, he had sudden convulsive spasms during which his limbs threshed about wildly before he ended up sprawled across his desk like a battered spider crab on the seashore. These frantic episodes lasted only a few seconds and he recovered immediately, straightening his glasses and appearing none the worse for his brief journeys into the unknown. It was generally accepted that he suffered from some kind of epilepsy, but I had my suspicions of Master Evans. Some of his 'silly' questions and remarks in class were a little too clever to be entirely innocent and the timing of his 'involuntary' contortions raised doubts in my mind.

On the 'teacher's eye' principle I kept a close watch on young Evans and had his desk jammed up against my own. There was a large misshapen girl in 4C who from time to time became disconcertingly absorbed in her own body, discreetly smelling her armpits or handling even more private parts that most of us try to avoid inspecting in public. One day, when 4C were having one of their preoccupied spells, I must have been surreptitiously watching one of these distasteful yet compelling performances, for I suddenly became aware of Evans' maniacal face six inches away from my own. 'Keep watching, sir,' he whispered. 'She'll do it again in a minute.'

A generally accepted compensation for teaching 4C was

that on Tuesdays, when the local courts sat, the group was pleasantly small and manageable. One week, when the form was more than usually depleted, curiosity overcame my normal tact in not inquiring about reasons for Tuesday absence and on the Wednesday morning I buttonholed Staple Causton, one of the previous day's absentees. Staple was a cheerful, likeable lad but not one of the world's fastest thinkers. It transpired that, some weeks earlier, he had been posted as a lookout in a mass break-in at the local chocolate factory. However, while other members of 4C were packing their pockets full of Payne's poppets, Staple was failing to conceal himself from the local bobby on his beat. It wasn't difficult to envisage the ensuing exchange:

Bobby: 'Ullo, 'ullo, 'ullo, what might you be doing, young man?
Staple: Waiting for me mates.
Bobby: And where might they be, sonny Jim?
Staple (indicating broken window): In there.

Staple's real name was Stanley, but in his early efforts to get this down on paper the 'n' had acquired a tail and the 'y' had gone walkabout. 'Staple' had stuck and become the normal written version of his name. Jeffey Ashey had also experienced difficulties with the 'ley' syllable; however, he had omitted the first and not the last letter, thereby acquiring the surname 'Ashey' instead of Ashley. Like Staple, he had found writing his forename a tiring process and reduced Jeffrey to 'Jeffey'. No appropriate workbooks existed for such pupils so I had to produce my own, writing on one side of an exercise book and leaving the other side blank for Staple's and Jeffey's response. This wasn't quite as time-consuming as it sounds, as the pupils concerned worked so slowly. And it was very satisfying, particularly when Friday arrived with 'Stanley' and 'Jeffery' painstakingly but legibly inscribed in their owners' home-produced workbooks. On Monday, however, euphoria gave way to despair: after the weekend break the shorter versions reasserted themselves. Even in the 1950s it is unlikely that pupils like Staple and Jeffey would have remained in mainstream education had they not been very docile and amenable characters.

Most of the members of 4C with severe learning difficulties were hardworking and conscientious. We did a lot of work on spelling and one of those who never failed to obtain full marks in tests was a girl whose answers appeared in a different order to everyone else's: she learnt how to spell the words but couldn't match their visual and spoken forms. It was a salutary reminder that the process of rote learning can result in 100% accuracy and 0% comprehension.

I was keen that all classes should become proficient at spelling and devised various ways of clarifying the English language's complex orthography. Thus spelling lists always illustrated particular rules, sounds, syllables or letter combinations, and avoided popular, but ineffective, strategies such as pairing easily-confused words or dealing with examples of a rule and the exceptions at the same time. Similar principles and strategies were applied to vocabulary work and, indeed, all routine learning tasks. We would look at the derivation of words, how they could be broken down into their component parts, any simple associations and groupings that would aid the memory. In this way some of the barriers to memorising were removed and the prospect of success opened up.

I instituted a principle of 100% accuracy for spelling tests. Those who fell short of perfection repeated the test in class and then, if necessary, once again in their own time. Every few weeks there were re-tests of previously-learnt spellings. The same principle was employed: full marks or repeat the test. The 100% rule applied also to routine vocabulary work

111

– masculines and feminines, singulars and plurals, parents and young, synonyms, antonyms, diminutives and homonyms. Every week lists of such pairings were committed to memory and then tested. The concept of 100% accuracy was, of course, a novelty and it took a while to bring about a sea change in expectations. Once the principle was established, however, few fell short of the spelling and vocabulary targets each week. The aim was not to set easy tasks, but to show children how to make seemingly difficult tasks easy – or, at least, straight-forward. Gradually pupils found that regular exercising of their memories improved their efficiency. The 100% principle gave pupils immense satisfaction and did much for the self-confidence and self-esteem of those who were unused to regular success. It also gave pupils a welcome break from competing with each other, as everyone was deemed capable of reaching the targets set.

We pay insufficient attention to the concept of 100% accuracy in education. We are too concerned to place children in order and achieve a neat curve of distribution in the marks and grades we award them. Our educational system is constantly classifying people and assigning them to different categories of success or failure. We design examinations specifically for that purpose. Every time that the nation's annual A-level or GCSE results show an improvement on the previous year's there is an outcry that too many candidates are succeeding, the implication being, not that standards are improving, but that the exams are getting too easy. Particular concern is expressed at any increase in the number of candidates obtaining the top grades. New levels of super-achievement are then introduced in order to distinguish the élite from the rest, an obsession imposed by academia and its desire to groom potential scholars for post-graduate research. The pass rates for separate levels of achievement are readjusted to limit the number of higher grades awarded.

One of the consequences of this syndrome is that the level of exam achievement for most children is artificially restricted. The pass mark for School Certificate when I was at school was 33%; in some current GCSE exams a C grade can be awarded for less than 20%. Where, outside the academic community, would that level of competence be acceptable? Would we employ an interior decorator to hang our wallpaper, knowing he would only be 20% efficient? Or contemplate going under the knife when the surgeon was reputed to possess 20% of the knowledge required to carry out the operation? Or buy a car assembled by workers known to be only 20% accurate in their conveyor belt adjustments? We want these people's work to be perfect.

In the 1950s teachers were left to work out their own strategies and to set their own standards, blissfully unaware of the systems of quality assurance, self-assessment, target setting, performance reviews and individual education planning lying in wait for their 21st century successors. Basic responsibilities at High View, such as lesson preparation and marking, were assumed, but not prescribed. Management and administration were left to the head and his two deputies and didn't seem to cause much loss of sleep on their part. George Paul was very laid back and returned from the summer holiday having done no planning for the new academic year: we worked to a makeshift timetable based on the previous year's arrangements while George retired to his study with pencil, paper and rubber to produce something more appropriate.

The one additional responsibility that staff undertook was form teaching, or 'tutoring', as we now call it. Everyone was a form teacher, except the art mistress, who made such a hash of keeping the register that George had to relieve her of the rôle. The special relationship that built up between form teacher and class was very rewarding and, with the energy and enthusiasm of youth, I sought to extend the time that I spent with members

113

of my own form. There were trips to the cinema, for example to see *The Great Adventure*, a charming sub-titled Swedish film about a boy and his otter, and to the West End theatre, most notably for the original production of *West Side Story*, with its exhilarating dancing and exciting Leonard Bernstein score. One Saturday, 2A took over the top deck of a Croydon bus and travelled into Kent for a scavenge hunt and picnic. The sedate and eminently respectable inhabitants of the small town of Hayes were taken aback but rallied to the cause, helping or hindering the young scavengers according to their different capabilities and personalities.

Children's lives were less varied and eventful 50 years ago and breaks in school routine were therefore more memorable. Similarly, the professional lives of teachers proceeded without the stimulus (and frustration) of today's constant changes and innovations. Partway through my time at High View, however, there was a mild flurry of excitement caused by a decision of the Burnham Committee, the body that determined teachers' salaries. Traditionally, variations in remuneration, apart from those arising from differences in length of service, had occurred only in the grammar schools, where some staff received additional payments in return for the burdensome task of teaching small groups of able and responsive pupils in the sixth form. Then, in 1956, a small number of 'responsibility allowances' and 'graded posts' were made available to other secondary schools. High View received three, two A allowances worth £125 per annum each, and one scale 1 graded post valued at £75. George had the pleasant task of deciding which members of staff should receive these windfalls. Chippie Chapman, the woodwork teacher, was awarded one of the A allowances in formal recognition of his being the senior of three members of staff who taught at an annexe situated half a mile from the school. I received the other for a newly-created but undefined rôle as 'Head of English'. George was puzzled

114

as to how he might use the smaller graded post allowance, but eventually decided that it should go to the National Union of Teachers' rep for keeping the staff room notice board tidy. Anyone who was unhappy with the way the handouts had been distributed was invited to see George. He was apparently taken aback that one person, a possible candidate for a 'Head of Science' position, actually did express his disappointment.

Life returned to its uneventful norm after the excitement of the new appointments, but one day George aroused mild interest by declaring that he was going to do some teaching. George was very involved in promoting national savings in schools and spent half the week pursuing this interest up and down the country. He was therefore unable to undertake a regular teaching commitment, but he posted prominently in his study a ghost timetable of classes that he would take over from English staff from time to time, if he were available. The prospect of some additional marking time was attractive to the recently-designated department, but, before George could implement his good intentions, he informed us of a major distraction: the school was to receive a full-scale inspection. Shortly after the inspectors' visit George's timetable disappeared and we heard no more of his desire to help out in the classroom.

Staff reaction to George's little subterfuge was tolerant: he was a good bloke and we were all guilty of similar inspection games, beavering away to devise hitherto non-existent syllabuses and schemes of work and thinking up other strategies to mislead the HMIs. How far these people see beneath the surface is a trade secret but we thought that several of our inspectorial visitors were quite sharp and astute. The English specialist persistently questioned one of my classes about their newspaper project. What was the point of the work? Where was it leading? What were the aims, objectives and likely outcomes? The pupils did their best to answer these questions and actually demonstrated good understanding of the purpose of the particular lesson that was being observed. However, not having had it properly explained to them, they had little idea how it fitted into the general scheme of things. The point was taken.

The HMIs' report was typically bland but made a number of interesting observations, one of which was that the teachers worked harder than the pupils. This could have been interpreted in various ways but, taken at its face value, it was a fair comment. Most of the staff were committed and industrious but, as a school we had not found an alternative to certification as a means of motivating pupils to make the most of their talents.

# 10

## Some Way to Go

Two years into my teaching career I resurrected the idea of studying for an English degree. There was still the small matter of a Latin qualification, which I addressed with the help of a genteel and elderly headmistress who rounded off her educational week by teaching an earnest but undistinguished O-level Latin class for three hours at Norwood Evening Institute. A year later, in 1957, I registered for a four-year, four-nights-a-week BA honours degree course at Birkbeck College, formerly the London Mechanics Institute. Birkbeck enabled men and women in full-time employment to register as internal students of London University and to sit the same exams as internal students – a significant detail because of the prejudice that existed in some quarters against external degrees. I have frequently taken my metaphorical cap off to George Birkbeck who, 200 years ago, gave free evening lectures to working men and founded the unique institution that now bears his name.

The Birkbeck English department turned my understanding of the educational process upside down. For the first time in my life I learnt how to learn. The opening lecture of the course was delivered by the Professor, Geoffrey Tillotson, an authority on 18th century poetry in general and Alexander Pope, the malign satirist, in particular. A few minutes into his presentation, Tillotson paused melodramatically and looked down from his rostrum with a pained expression on his face. 'There are people writing,' he said, with studied incredulity. 'Please don't write while I'm speaking. My lectures are an experience and you can't experience them if you're busy scribbling.' This completely flummoxed me. My only understanding of the student's rôle in the lecturing process was that assumed by RGS sixth formers and Borough Road students – writing non-stop to get down as much as one could of what was said. To sit and simply listen was a novel experience and strangely disconcerting. It was difficult to know what to do, particularly with one's hands. And how was one to retain the pearls of wisdom so that one could hand them back four years later in the examination hall?

Worse was to come. It had been established that we were allowed to ask questions and express opinions in lectures and one of the older students called Levy, who had made an early bid for recognition as a scholarly contributor, stood up during one of Tillotson's lectures and referred to a view expounded by the Cambridge professor, F R Leavis, the most influential and well-known literary critic of the day. Tillotson's by now familiar pained expression spread across his face. 'F R Leavis?' he repeated, very slowly and thoughtfully, as if searching way back in his mind for some clue that would enable him to place the person named. 'Is his opinion relevant? Is it more significant than your own, Mr Levy? Why, your name is almost the same as his.'

We were forbidden to read the critics and had to rely on our own judgement of the literature that we studied. This was a significant culture shock. Although in the past I had obviously formed opinions on the books I'd read, I'd never assumed that these were of much use as academic criticism. My literature essays had consisted of a clumsy fusion of what we were told in class and the views of arbitrarily-chosen commentators. Occasionally I acknowledged a source: most of the time I plagiarised unashamedly, stringing together extracts from different critics' works with no attempt to put them into my own words. The only excuse for such a lamentable practice was that no-one ever complained about it and at Borough Road, where it was perfected, I obtained consistently good marks.

At Birkbeck we had personally to analyse, criticise and evaluate the works that we read. In seminars we sat at a large table, a sub-group of about seven or eight students. Tillotson would distribute a sheet of paper containing a short poem that we spent a few minutes reading. 'Would you like to comment, please?' he'd say, indicating someone by name. 'We'll then go round clockwise. Anything you notice. The number of stanzas or lines. The rhyme scheme.' A round of introductory and not very erudite observations would be followed by a second turn, when we obviously had to work much harder to say something worthwhile. All contributions were received with courtesy. If a statement lacked substance or validity, someone was invited to develop or qualify it. We progressed from describing simply what we saw on the printed page to an analysis of the poet's intentions and methods, and an appreciation of the poem's meaning and effectiveness. This was Tillotson's method: to start with the obvious and peripheral and work towards a definitive statement on the poet's purpose and achievement.

I adjusted eventually to Tillotson's injunction to listen to lectures, and found them much more interesting as a result. He was of course right: you can't fully appreciate what someone is saying if you are occupied doing something else. Neither was his assertion concerning the quality of his own lectures an idle boast. He wasn't a charismatic or dynamic speaker and spent much time just reading poetry in a rather dry voice. But he read with a wonderful sense of a poem's meaning, its nuances, rhythms and changes of pace. As in a Pinter play, every emphasis, pause and variation was given a precise weight.

It took considerably longer to learn to trust my own judgement of literature. It was a process that had to start almost at the beginning, as with the technical school art classes when, as 16-year-olds, we were shown how to hold a pencil. Everything was a revelation. The study of plays, for example. At school and teachers' training college, they were read much in the same way as a novel, with the focus on character and plot. Birkbeck's Dr Harold Brookes, however, was steeped in the theatre and saw every play in relation to its production. His specialism was restoration comedy and he made us keenly aware of the ways in which the elegant repartee of the plays was matched and enhanced by their choreographic qualities, the visual impact of the protagonists' movements, stances and adversarial pairings.

We never missed an opportunity to see a production of a play that we studied, whether professional or amateur. Harold often came with us. He was a small, wizened old man who bubbled with enthusiasm and restless energy. Full of eccentric mannerisms – he lectured with a forefinger stuck firmly in one ear – he was something of a liability in the theatre. I sat next to him for a RADA production of Sir George Etherege's *The Man of Mode*. He was totally involved in everything that was happening on the stage, willing the actors on with muttered encouragement, squirming with delight at subtleties of interpretation of which he approved and shaking his head sadly at any aspect of the direction that he thought misguided. At one point he was unable to contain his disappointment at one of a number of deletions that the director had made from the original text and cried out, 'No! No! The unkindest cut of all!' (Julius Caesar, III, 2, line 188).

Dr Brookes took us for all our studies of Shakespeare, but fortunately wasn't present on the evening that we tracked down a unique production of *Macbeth*, part of an amateur drama festival held in a cramped church hall in Peckham. The stage was minute and the actors inconveniently large. Banquo, played by a front row forward in a huge Viking helmet and mangy bearskin, created havoc whenever he elbowed his way centre-stage. The challenge of finding a space from which to speak their lines seemed to preoccupy the actors and their delivery became increasingly self-conscious and inaudible. There was a brief moment of expectation in Act II when the porter began his big speech in fine declamatory style, only to subside into embarrassed confusion when he reached the bawdy lines describing the practical problems encountered by a drunken lecher. Notwithstanding its limitations, the production was very well received by the audience – presumably predominantly friends and relations of the cast – and we gained the impression that it was a serious contender for the cup to be presented at the end of the week for the winning festival entry. The previous night's *Two Gentlemen of Verona* had apparently been something of a disaster: the scenery had collapsed on top of the actors and Crab, the dog, had peed on his master's hose.

Shakespearian disasters were not confined to the Peckham church hall. My first attempt at unaided critical appreciation for Dr Brookes was an essay on the structure of *A Midsummer Night's Dream* in which I described the play's constantly changing groupings of characters – the scenelets within the designated scenes. It was wholly original, but, as I realised afterwards, unspeakably pedestrian and devoid of any penetrating insights into structural purpose and effect. Dr Brookes, the kindest and mildest of men, gave it C double-minus. His comment when he handed back the heavily-annotated piece of work was: 'Well, ahem, you've, um, some way to, um, go.' It was the harshest thing I ever heard him say and I was mortified.

In theory, our lecturers used a 20-point marking scale, A++ to D--. However, not all grades were attainable: we were reliably informed that A++ was reserved for the deity and that A+ was what the professor would get if he had studied the set authors and works. The D categories were also unused. However, Harold Brookes considerably extended the range of grades by using a question mark to designate that an essay was tantalisingly poised between two possible classifications, for example, B+?+, or even B++?A- -. Thus, allowing for the unattainability of A++ and A+ and the non-use of D grades, my *Midsummer Night's Dream* essay was assessed, in numerical terms, as meriting a score of 1 out of 26, which was probably about right.

Although we were very fond of Harold, we were in love with the blonde and provocatively bejumpered Mrs Hardy – or at least the male half of the class were. Barbara Hardy held all the aces as a lecturer: not only was she young, highly attractive and sexually desirable, but she had the pleasantest of assignments – to encourage and guide us in our appreciation of prose fiction. The special buzz of enjoyment that I receive from a good novelist's stylistic skill owes much to my attentiveness to Mrs Hardy – and, of course, to her lively analysis of carefully-chosen passages from Jane Austen, George Eliot and Charles Dickens.

The staff naturally varied in the quality of their scholarship and teaching, but they were almost all enthusiasts for their subject and anxious to transfer their love of literature to their students. Immersed in the academic way of life, they automatically assumed that we shared their devotion and single-mindedness. There were no concessions made for our part-time status. The programme of written assignments and preparation tasks was relentless and little patience was shown over missed deadlines. At the end of one term a cross-section of the 40 or so students in the year were hauled in front of a staff panel, chaired by the professor, and interrogated on their level of attainment. They included conscientious and successful students who, nevertheless, were thought to be under-achieving. They were visibly shaken and at least one perfectly respectable performer withdrew from the course following his interview. It seemed to us that the academics were oblivious of our other lives as full-time workers in the real world and students never dared to admit that their motivation for study was mainly in order to further their career. Nevertheless, whether by accident or design, several of the learning processes developed by the department were particularly appropriate to our situation as part-timers. The embargo on reading the critics was, for a start, a blessed time-saver.

Most of the literature courses were taught by means of a 'burst' system: a series of lectures and seminars on a particular author would be concentrated into a three-week period, at the end of which we would have an essay to complete under exam conditions. Getting to grips with Dickens' novels or the complete works of D H Lawrence in three weeks was tough going, but it concentrated the mind wonderfully and forced our studies up the scale of priorities in our busy lives. The three-weekly timed essay routine was a speedy and economical way of getting us to reach conclusions on the authors we studied and an excellent preparation for Finals. A few authors were taught in a more conventional way by means of a series of weekly lectures lasting a whole term. I have no recollection now who these writers were or what was said about them, but the authors who were 'burst' upon us became part of an ongoing literary experience.

Observing the way in which children can become absorbed in projects, fieldwork and other situations that require sustained effort, one cannot help feeling that there must be a better way

123

of timetabling the secondary school curriculum than shunting children from room to room throughout the school day and requiring them to jump from one uncompleted job to another. The rationale behind such a system is presumably that children cannot concentrate on one subject for any length of time, but that implies that teachers are incapable of providing a range of work tasks and learning situations to ensure a varied and stimulating classroom experience. Daily contact time is probably right for acquiring linguistic and mathematical skills, but most other subjects would benefit from the 'burst' approach, an allocation of significant blocks of time in which a major topic, set book or practical task could be seen through from beginning to end.

From time to time Birkbeck lecturers descended from their ivory towers to run eminently useful practical sessions. There were some quizzical looks among the students when a dictionary workshop was timetabled, but few of us, until then, had been aware of the detail and variety of information available in the 20 enormous volumes of the Oxford English Dictionary. The great man himself, Professor Tillotson, wasn't averse to rolling his sleeves up and dirtying his hands with such mundane matters as examination technique. He was full of essay-writing tips, presented in his inimitably laconic and unequivocal way:

The process: 'Don't use the title as a starting point from which to move off in ever-widening circles. Work inwards to the heart of the question to reach a conclusion.'
On keeping to the question: 'Use the words of the title in every paragraph.'
On timing: 'When your time's up on a question, stop writing, even if you're in the middle of a sentence. The first marks on the next question will be easier to obtain than adding to your total on the essay you're finishing.'

Like most university studies, the Birkbeck English course was historical: it was concerned with the language and literature of a bygone age. The further one went back in time, the more important the work was considered: both Anglo Saxon and Middle English (c. 1150 – 1500) were compulsory elements of the course. Students then chose a further seven components from a small range of options. There was considerable scepticism about the value of studying ancient poetry written in what was, to all intents and purposes, a foreign language, and most students confined their language work to the two obligatory units. I decided, however, that I would take two further language options – Old Icelandic and the Development of the Language. My remaining units were Shakespeare and four literature options based on different historical periods.

My thinking in committing myself to substantial language work was that the linguistic skills that I would have to develop to cope with the Anglo-Saxon and Middle English might as well be applied as fully as possible. Also much of the translation work was precisely defined, a part of the course with clear goals and predictable exams that consisted mainly of prepared translations of prescribed texts. This would be a welcome change from the more usual game of chance in which one has to guess what aspects of the course will feature on the exam paper.

The class routine was much the same for each language component of the course. We worked painstakingly through the set texts preparing a specified number of pages for each session. My strategy was to be in a position to give an oral line-by-line translation in class but also to have a polished written version, which, if necessary, I then corrected in the light of the lecturer's comments and student discussion. By the time Finals arrived I possessed an accurate translation of all the set texts, most of which I could recall when confronted with the originals. In Old Icelandic the texts were mainly prose and not unduly complex: in the exam I was able to write the translations straight out, which gave me significant extra time for other parts of the paper – an unseen translation and essay. When I got home I checked the accuracy of my translations and was disappointed to realise that I had inexplicably translated the common adjective 'svartr' (our word 'swarthy') as 'white' instead of 'black'. It was, however, my only mistake.

University Finals are a selection procedure for academia. The papers are designed by academics for potential academics – those high fliers who, it is hoped, will proceed to research and devote the rest of their lives to perpetuating the system. Students of this ilk are reputedly distinguished by their ability to produce erudite and scholarly answers to academic questions, without needing to employ anything as demeaning as a strategy to achieve success. The writer, playwright and actor, Alan Bennett, likes to recall how he obtained a 'First' at Oxford 'by cheating'. Deciding that he wasn't 'bright enough' to achieve the highest academic honours without a game plan, he prepared for his exams by reducing everything he knew to an examination kit – a pack of postcards on which he wrote key points, useful quotations and skeleton answers to questions. He carried these cards with him at all times, learning their contents on buses, in queues and at odd moments throughout the day. Bennett has, of course, cultivated a self-deprecatory persona throughout his life but, even so, the fact that he regarded his expediences for preparing for exams as a form of cheating indicates just how élitist the system was, and how remote the academic community can be from the real world. What Alan Bennett doesn't recognise is that generations of students have employed similar practical, but entirely legitimate, methods to beat the academics at the examination game – and good luck to them.

Not everything went according to plan in my Finals,

the formidable Will Shakespeare again threatening to be my undoing. The examination paper covered the whole of Shakespeare's considerable output, but there was a compulsory section on six selected plays that we had had to subject to the close textual study that is the hallmark of academic practice in the university study of English. This work was tested in two ways – firstly, by means of a translation or paraphrase of a complex speech from one of the set texts and, secondly, with a 'gobbet', an appropriately unpleasantly-named procedure in which one supplied detailed linguistic comment on an extract full of disputed interpretations, manuscript uncertainties, obscure references and pedantic technical points. Dr Brookes' enthusiasm was such that he spent too long on each set play, with the consequence that he was a long way from completing the syllabus: we did no work on either *The Winter's Tale* or *Coriolanus*. I had hoped not to employ the banker system of preparation for Finals – revising selected parts of the syllabus that one hoped would appear on the paper. However, I came under increasing pressure in my final year, a change of job having precluded an application for a sabbatical, which most of my fellow students were able to obtain for the fourth year of the course. The Shakespeare paper was one for which I was unable to cover all the ground: I prepared *The Winter's Tale* but *Coriolanus* remained unstudied, and indeed unread.

The inevitable happened. The Shakespeare paper was the first of the nine Finals exams and at 9 am on the Monday of the week for which we had been preparing for four years a pamphlet of questions on the great dramatist was duly placed on my desk. There on the very front was the obligatory paraphrase question – a passage from *Coriolanus*. I felt physically sick and had every sympathy for the candidate who, a few moments later, rose and walked purposefully out of the room. Any thoughts of following suit, however, were forestalled by a glance at the second compulsory question

127

– a passage from *Macbeth* on which Dr Brookes had at some time supplied us with a detailed commentary, as a means of demonstrating the mysteries of the gobbet procedure. I knew his model answer more or less by heart. Thus what must have been an O-level standard paraphrase was followed by a gobbet answer that neither God nor Professor Tillotson could have bettered – a splendid illustration of the 'hit and miss' aspect of examinations. I couldn't help wondering what the marker would make of the juxtaposition, but afterwards noticed that the initials of the three examiners who had set the paper included the letters 'HB'. Perhaps this feature of my script would, after all, cause little surprise.

Following the acquisition of my degree, Professor Tillotson wrote to me on two separate occasions to draw my attention to assistant lectureships in Anglo-Saxon that were becoming available at London colleges. Of course I was flattered, but the prospect of spending the rest of my life coaxing translations of *Beowulf* out of unresponsive undergraduates appealed even less than the £16-a-week salary. Tillotson was a bit miffed at my lack of enthusiasm: he wrote wishing me well for my choice of 'a straight downhill run to the grave', although I think my subsequent career proved to be more challenging, and certainly more rewarding, than a lifetime in academia would have been.

Dr Brookes suggested that I might like to consider embarking on a PhD as a part-time student and I showed more interest in this idea, becoming quite excited by the thought of producing a first annotated edition of Congreve's *Way of the World* for students – with introduction, study notes, and background information on the Restoration period and its drama. We had felt the lack of such an edition when we studied the play. I quickly found, however, that my unscholarly tendency to favour topics that might have some current application was once again a problem. It was the human geography/social history/modern English usage syndrome all over again. Editing a play was (just about) acceptable as a PhD qualifying task, but it would have to be carried out according to time-honoured procedures. The requirement was for the textual minutiae to be subjected to a degree of anal scrutiny that would be of interest to no-one other than members of the academic community researching in the same area. As my subversive aspirations to provide an accessible text for undergraduates became clear, the alarm bells began to ring for Dr Brookes. He was too kind to tell me outright that I had got it all wrong, but his gentle attempts to keep me on the straight and narrow spoke eloquently of the problems my approach would encounter with the examiners. In the meantime, my evenings in the British Museum were rapidly confirming my suspicions that I wasn't suited to the academic lifestyle in its purest form. Demanding as part-time undergraduate studies had been, the nightly contact with lecturers and other students had motivated me to keep going. Sitting for hours in lonely isolation at the end of a tiring day, with the marking and lesson preparation awaiting my return home, was a different kind of challenge and not one to which I found myself warming. My academic life went on hold – for about 20 years.

# 11

## Sports Academy

After several years of cycling 20 miles a day to and from school, I acquired a chauffeur, a primary school head who travelled a similar daily route by car and offered me a lift. It was she who drew my attention to a basic scale post being advertised by Sutton Boys' Grammar School, to which some of her pupils transferred at 11. The last thing I needed in the run-up to my Finals at Birkbeck was a fresh teaching challenge, and the drop in salary was not a big incentive either. Nevertheless, the advertised post offered A-level work and thus the prospect of putting my graduate studies to fuller use. I was tempted, put in a speculative application and moved schools in January, 1960.

Sutton's idiosyncratic action in appointing an undergraduate to its otherwise graduate Common Room created a serious problem: I had no gown to wear. A solution was, however, to hand: I resurrected a forgotten right that London University students had to wear an undergraduate gown. It wasn't an altogether satisfactory arrangement. Being an indication of inferior academic status, the undergraduate gown was conspicuously shorter than its graduate counterpart and, because of my size, my garment looked rather like a badly-made black shirt worn outside my trousers. I just hoped that people would think it had shrunk in the wash. There was also a practical disadvantage in that, unlike my colleagues, I had great difficulty in using the tail to clean the blackboard.

In reverting to the status of new boy and basic scale teacher, I once again became peripatetic, wandering at each lesson bell from one to another of Sutton's bare and dingy classrooms. My least congenial teaching room during my itinerant year at High View had been Hazel Abrenowitz's chaotic art studio; here it was Hutchins' hallowed biology lab. It was all serried rank teaching at Sutton so the daily adjustments from parallel rows of desks to laboratory benching wasn't much of a problem. What I couldn't get used to, though, was trying to hold a class's attention while bloody old Hutchins was prowling around checking that no-one was unscrewing the bench fittings. One bonus in my new school was that I didn't have to hump all the pupils' equipment from room to room: 11+ success guaranteed that proud parents and doting aunts happily stumped up for all the necessary instruments and aids to study that Johnnie required – and quite a few that he didn't.

My translation from secondary modern to grammar school brought a return to the all-consuming routine of marks, grades and form positions of my own schooldays. The fortnightly positions and reports were given added significance at Sutton by being presented to each form by the headmaster in person. Unfavourable comments were given a public airing. To provide the data for the fortnightly reports, every piece of written work was awarded a mark and every learning homework tested. The able and conscientious received constant pleasure and encouragement from their good marks and grades. They couldn't wait to get their marked exercise books back. The challenge for the teacher was to maintain the interest and effort

131

of those boys who showed no desire to open their returned books, knowing that they would contain another slap in the face.

During the Burt IQ controversy in the sixties and seventies, there was a more general debate, conducted with similar acrimony, on the nature and purposes of assessment. At the time I was at Sutton the issue had not yet reached our country from America and I knew nothing of the experts' views on norm-, criterion- and self-referencing. What I did know, however, was that the relentless publicising of pupils' performance measured against that of their classmates made it very difficult for teachers to maintain widespread enthusiasm for schoolwork. I responded to this situation, as many teachers have done, by using the marking process to encourage and coach pupils individually. I spent many hours writing in boys' books, commenting on each piece of work, saying what I liked about it and suggesting ways in which pupils could build on what was successful and eliminate obvious weaknesses. I emphasised that the comments on their work were more important than the marks or grades awarded. The system, of course, sent out a different message and one was under no illusions as to which was the more powerful.

The mark routine does for classroom activities what the examination system does for education as a whole – forces teachers, and therefore pupils, to focus on what can be most readily assessed. Other equally-important educational processes then get devalued, either omitted altogether or not taken seriously by pupils because they are not awarded a mark. I was particularly keen to elevate the status of oral work and to allow substantial time for developing boys' speaking and reading skills. In order to do this within the prevailing culture I decided I would simply have to mark all forms of oral contribution – drama and prose readings, prepared talks, impromptu contributions to discussion.

I regularly played the 100% card at Sutton and found it particularly effective with grammar work. The O-level examination was the customary combination of essay, précis and comprehension, with a fourth question offering candidates a choice between a grammar and vocabulary exercise. The grammar question never varied: it was always a mechanical clause analysis task in which a sentence had to be broken down into its component parts. It looked formidable to the uninitiated, and weaker pupils steered clear of it. However, for the stronger candidates, particularly those studying Latin, this question was about as difficult as the ten times table to a competent mathematician. With training, they not only achieved full marks but did so at a speed that, in an exam, gave them precisely the same advantage that I had in my Old Icelandic Finals paper – valuable extra time for the other questions.

Despite sharing the same mark culture, Sutton County Grammar School and High Wycombe Royal Grammar School were surprisingly dissimilar. The RGS was a caricature of a very traditional grammar school. Sutton deviated from the norm in significant ways and had its own distinctive character. Atypically, Sutton's headmasters had all been scientists or mathematicians. Dr Walch, who became headmaster in 1956, was a physicist, as was his deputy. Not surprisingly, the school had a strong science and mathematics tradition, a feature that has been maintained into the 21st century by an unbroken line of science and maths heads dating back to the school's foundation in 1899.

There was little of the ivory tower about Sutton, few aspirations to emulate the rarefied atmosphere of those prestigious public schools that measured success in terms of the number of Oxbridge scholarships that their pupils achieved. Academic honours were, of course, important and able boys did win awards, sometimes to Oxford and Cambridge, but also to London, Nottingham and elsewhere. Others won direct entry to the Civil Service Executive and to commissions in the armed forces. Most boys saw education less as an end in itself than as a means to a successful career. This might entail going to university or entering employment straight from school; the latter route didn't seem to carry a stigma. There was inevitably pressure on staff and boys to obtain good examination results, but the place wasn't an archetypal academic hothouse.

Dr Walch was a product of the grammar school system and a graduate of London University, whereas the usual route to the post he held would have been public school and Oxford or Cambridge. The Oxbridge hold on grammar school headships was particularly strong: some education authorities, as I was to discover several years later, would never risk tainting the reputation of one of their selective schools by appointing a headmaster who was not an Oxbridge man.

Another odd thing about Dr Walch was that he had a teaching diploma and was very interested in the craft of teaching. This undoubtedly affected staff attitudes. There was a refreshing, if occasional, common room discussion of methods and current trends in education. When the Nuffield Science schemes were launched, the Sutton science departments were well placed to respond. There was a tradition of teaching through the scientific method of observing, hypothesising and predicting in order to prompt further experimentation. The science staff were sympathetic to the Nuffield philosophy with its emphasis on recent developments, experiential learning and a more questioning approach. In May 1962 the Nuffield physics programme was inaugurated and the school became part of the national pilot scheme. The biology and chemistry departments adopted the Nuffield schemes two years later. The mathematics department was also responsive to similar approaches that were being introduced in that subject.

The headmaster either led or supported these moves to

keep up-to-date. He was very much part of the real world, a vigorous, no-nonsense, short-back-and-sides professional. Well-groomed and always smartly turned out in a city suit, he looked the part of a Chief Executive, long before the job of headteacher acquired overtones of that rôle. He would have relished the financial control that 21$^{st}$ century heads exert over their schools. There was a sense of purpose and commitment about Dr Walch that was reflected in his staff and, indeed, in the school as a whole. The sixth form wore smart black blazers that matched his dark suits.

Dr Walch had a natural authority without being authoritarian. Although firm and direct, he was sensitive to circumstances when dealing with transgressors. He liked young people and was ahead of his time in being opposed to any form of corporal punishment. Freddie Walch was a compassionate man and regularly visited one of my form who was hospitalised with leukaemia. He enjoyed his headmastering and was noted for his ready smile and the way in which his gravelly voice often broke into a guttural chuckle.

Freddie was very supportive of staff, particularly young men learning their trade. There was an occasion when I committed a cardinal form-mastering sin in not taking action over a pupil's absence, a truancy that, because of my omission, entered a second week and culminated in the boy's getting into trouble with the police. The headmaster would have been fully justified in coming down on me from a great height. He was obviously concerned but actually said very little, leaving me to assess the situation and my own unfortunate part in it for myself. This was strangely disconcerting and I made very sure that I never again gave him cause to be disappointed in me.

Among my biggest challenges at Sutton were those members of the science sixth who were struggling to pass English language O-level after two or three previous failures. They were a bunch of earnest and anxious young men, united by their linguistic incompetence and failure to understand where they were going wrong in their regular tussles with the English examiners. Their work usually held out some hope of a narrow pass, but on the day of their retake they were just as likely to fail again, possibly with a lower grade than before. This was depressingly familiar territory to me: the lottery of the school exam system and the puzzling elusiveness of a basic qualification in English language. I had never been able to predict or understand my own results during my time as a grammar school pupil. For example, in my first year I came top of the form in history for the year's work and spectacularly bottom in the end-of-year exams. In my second attempt at School Certificate I turned a fail in geography into a distinction, whilst registering a drop in grade in several other subjects. Perhaps this is why I've never seen the point of a game like snakes and ladders with its constant ups and downs determined by a throw of the dice.

English language and mathematics differ from most other school subjects in that no amount of hard work will bring success if you haven't understood the mechanical processes that you are handling: without the requisite skills, you spend your time just shuffling the words or figures around, hoping that they'll come out in the right order. My sixth form O-level English language class toiled manfully to comprehend the incomprehensible, but they exacerbated their problems by trying to write above themselves, in emulation of the inflated prose passages that they encountered on the exam papers. Exams are like interviews: you have to be yourself, not act a part you cannot sustain. My main task, in the limited periods of time between the repeated O-level attempts, was to get the candidates to stop striving for effects that were beyond them and to express themselves in words that they themselves could understand.

It was the creative part of the English language paper, the

essay question, that most cruelly exposed the deep-seated inadequacies of the re-take group. The sad reality was that, asked to be imaginative, they had little to say, and no effective means of saying it. A topic such as *My School Desk* was likely to produce a dictionary definition and some carefully worked out dimensions. There would be little subjective response, no reflection, for example, on the parts of the world whence the materials had come, the craftsmanship of the prototype and the technical advances demonstrated by the mass-produced article, the generations of studious, idle and refractory schoolboys who had sat at the same desk, or the boredom, fantasies and aspirations of those who'd scratched and carved its surface. The re-take group had experienced 11 or 12 years of schooling without apparently developing a personal response to the world around them, without exercising their imagination, senses or feelings, without marvelling at life's wonders, mysteries, contradictions – without even experiencing these things vicariously through the observations of a charismatic teacher or creative writer. Needless to say, none of them ever read for pleasure.

One of the essay questions in the first exam for which I prepared my sixth-formers was *A Railway Station*. It may have been prompted by a short art documentary called *Terminus*, commissioned by British Rail and directed by John Schlesinger, before he became famous as a director of full-length feature films. As a Londoner, Schlesinger was no doubt very familiar with his subject, but, before he began filming *Terminus*, he spent a fortnight on Waterloo Station just observing, listening, and breathing its atmosphere. He viewed the scene throughout its variations and his own shifting moods, constantly changing his vantage points, angles and perspectives. In the finished work there was a wonderful sequence in which one saw the station concourse from knee height through the bewildered eyes of a lost and frightened toddler. In contrast to Schlesinger's approach, O-level candidates were expected to produce their imaginative work in one hour without forewarning or any kind of preparation. This would have been a formidable task even for pupils with some of the perceptions and sensitivities of a creative writer, but for the Sutton retake group it constituted a challenge comparable to climbing Everest without any of the right equipment.

Today's schools have become places of perpetual motion where children are subjected, from an increasingly early age, to the pressures of competitive striving for supremacy over their peers, a microcosm of an adult world obsessed with the ruthless pursuit of status and greater spending power. We have brought about W H Davies' nightmare of a world so careworn that it allows no time for one to stand and stare. If we want to develop children's imaginative and creative talents we need to give them more space to be themselves, to grow in awareness, to think and reflect, to see things through the contemplative eyes of the poet and artist, to produce individual portfolios of work in which they can express themselves freely without worrying whether, according to a limited set of measurable criteria, the results are 'better' or 'worse' than their neighbour's. The secondary school day requires restructuring to avoid the scenario in which pupils scurry from one compartmentalised chunk of knowledge to another, leaving a trail of unfinished tasks behind them. Children need more time out of the classroom and out of school, more opportunities to observe and record, to keep a journal of their ideas and experiences, to follow up their own interests.

Schools divide their time between fostering competition and devising ways of mitigating its worst effects. Sutton had an interesting policy of treating academic success not as the prerogative of a privileged few but as something that could be shared by many pupils. It was very generous in its public recognition of good work and progress and a large number of boys received prizes each year; it was not uncommon for as many as two dozen of the upper sixth to be presented with a form prize and there were also awards in every subject. A slight disadvantage of this beneficence was that the annual prize-giving ceremony held at the Cheam Swimming Baths was a very protracted affair. Staff interest in the occasion, however, was maintained by a sweepstake, which entailed betting on the time that the eminent visiting speaker would take to deliver his address. Waller of the maths department took his annual duties as timekeeper very seriously, using a stopwatch to measure the carefully-observed bum-rise to bum-set.

There were many alternatives to academic success. House and individual competitions were held in rhetoric, drama and music for separate age groups. Annual prizes were awarded for achievements ranging from leadership and service to prowess in gymnastics, rifle shooting and reading the lesson in Morning Prayers. Sutton was a relatively small school – only three-form entry – and yet it offered a wide choice of games activity with both football and rugby among the numerous winter options. One of the merits of school games is often said to be that they offer an alternative form of human endeavour in which non-academic pupils have an opportunity to shine and succeed. True, but one does have to recognise that, perversely, many of those who achieve sporting honours are the same people who are good at their studies. What was impressive at Sutton was that any boy with four intact limbs, or even three, could find some sporting activity in which he could aspire to represent the school within his age group. Even if he didn't become a star, he could enjoy contributing to a team's achievements and benefit from the social experience of belonging to a group working together with a shared objective.

Considering the inclusive nature of the school teams, the standard was exceptionally high. The PE department concentrated on getting the boys fit through timetabled gym periods and circuit training sessions. The Common Room, with some outside help, provided the managers and trainers of the various teams. Dr Walch was alert to opportunities to involve Old Boys, parents and other members of the local community in the school's activities and he had persuaded a highly-successful coach from the Cheam Swimming Club to train the school swimming and water-polo teams, with the result that they were the best in Southern England. Basketball was another strength, most of the team gaining county caps.

Freddie Walch was himself a passionate sportsman who had represented his school and college at football, boxing and cricket (and was still, according to Mr Doon, the groundsman, 'a very pretty bat'). He believed that 'a fit body produces a lively mind' and was in favour of full participation in physical activity. The annual house cross-country run on Banstead Downs involved every member of the school – the boys as participants, the staff as stewards posted the length of the course to ensure that no-one took short cuts or sneaky bus rides. He also introduced mandatory ballroom dancing lessons for the sixth form as a *quid pro quo* for releasing them from the obligation to wear caps. This trade-off received a mixed reception: initial horror, but then growing enthusiasm as increased expertise brought the initiates into ever closer contact with the sixth form girls from the Sutton High School.

Freddie was a strong supporter of the school's extra-curricular activities and a regular spectator at Saturday matches. At the time I was appointed, I was blissfully unaware of the level of staff and pupil extra-curricular involvement at Sutton. Shortly after my interview and acceptance of the post, Dr Walch wrote to me saying that he had read in my curriculum vitae that I had obtained college colours in athletics and cross-country and he wondered if I would like to take charge of these activities as my contribution to the extra-curricular life of the school. Assuming from my High View games teaching experiences that this would probably entail a bit of training supervision, prior to taking selected boys on the bus to an annual district sports meeting, I readily accepted.

On a subsequent visit to the school, ostensibly to discuss my English teaching, I spent much of the day with the master who was relinquishing the athletics and cross-country responsibility. He was extremely helpful and talked me through the twice-weekly training routines and the summer and winter fixtures. The junior and intermediate cross-country teams only had weekly fixtures, but the senior side often raced on Saturdays as well as mid-week. The weekend races, some of which were relays and steeplechases, were major events organised by various athletics clubs and prestigious schools for teams from across the south of England. We discussed the transport arrangements and other aspects of administration for these occasions.

In the summer there were three-cornered athletics meetings involving all the standard field and track events. When Sutton hosted these meetings the Common Room had to be mobilised to produce the necessary stewards, judges, starters, timekeepers and other officials that an athletics meeting requires to make sure everything runs smoothly. I was advised on the safety precautions one had to take on these occasions and the need to plan well ahead when hiring an athletics track with field-event facilities. We also discussed the insurance procedures and catering arrangements. Both the winter and summer fixture lists were carefully programmed to ensure that the school teams peaked at the right time for the county and national championships, in which many of the boys would be participating. Particular emphasis was placed on the procedure for briefing the headmaster on the presentation of the medals and cups in morning assembly following the teams' successes. The outgoing manager of athletics and cross-country ran a non-profit-making equipment and clothing business which ensured that the boys were impeccably turned out and possessed the most appropriate running shoes for different race and field-event conditions. There was a slight problem which I would need to sort out over storing all this kit: an early version of a premiership football team's megastore appeared to be the sort of premises that he had in mind. It was a most interesting and illuminating day.

On the way home I stopped at a public telephone booth and made a sheepish call to Dr Walch. Much as I would like to take on the athletics and cross-country team management, I felt that, all things considered, I was not, by and large, quite ready, at that moment in time, to take on the responsibilities that had been outlined to me earlier in the day. Dr Walch was very understanding – it was one of his qualities – and said he would ask someone else. Perhaps I would be willing to give that person some assistance? Of course, Dr Walch. No problem.

Thus I arrived at Sutton with my confidence a little dented. I had no qualms over the teaching side of the job, but felt that I had made an unpropitious start to my wider contribution to the school. In the early weeks, however, I saw that, given the demands of my studies, I had made the right decision. I noted just how hectic life was for the staff who ran time-consuming extra-curricular activities. The No 1 cautionary figure was Major Wall, who was in charge of all the rugby XVs and also Commanding Officer of the CCF. He lived life on the run, not least from Dr Walch, who kept a watchful eye on the number of times in a day that he left his classes to make urgent telephone calls concerning pitches and parades, fixtures and firing ranges, visiting teams and VIP army officers.

A feature of teaching and other caring professions is that only part of the job is defined: there are areas of discretion and choice, opportunities for a personal contribution, a chance to make a difference to the organisation in which one works and the quality of the service it provides. Taking on a major extra-curricular or managerial responsibility in a school adds considerably to the defined core of one's job. The same is true of the large number of bureaucratic tasks that have been imposed on teachers in the accountability age – and some would question whether these are as worthwhile as the voluntary activities that they have replaced. As the core of one's job expands, so the space available for developing one's own initiatives recedes. Of course, the enthusiastic teacher quickly fills that space, however big or small it is, and ends up frustrated that there always seems to be so much more that could be done if only there were time. Young teachers, in particular, often become aware too late of the catch 22 nature of this dilemma, pursuing their early enthusiasms and saying yes to additional responsibilities, without always adequately ordering their priorities or ensuring that they are making informed decisions. There are teachers who move jobs for no other reason than a need to empty their undefined space and start again, a little more circumspectly.

The master who took on the management of the Sutton athletics and cross-country teams was a young chemist, Alan Robinson, who was only in his second year of teaching. My conscience over his workload wasn't eased by the knowledge that he too was studying in the evenings – for a higher degree. Some sort of justice was achieved, however, for after I had obtained my BA I assumed responsibility for the teams during the final year of Alan's study. I inherited a very smooth operation. Alan's management left nothing to chance and he was meticulous in ensuring that boys knew precisely what was expected of them on training and match days, particularly with respect to the correct procedures for obtaining early release from lessons, whenever this was required for away matches. Alan studied form and at the big cross-country races and athletics meetings knew who would provide the main opposition to our teams and the times and distances that our boys would have to beat.

We had some outstanding athletes who belonged to the Mitcham Athletics Club. Malcolm Burton, our cross-country captain in the year that I assumed responsibility for the teams, was a mature and self-contained young man with a Michael Johnson running style – upright, controlled and economical. He often won the big races looking almost as fresh as he started, a feat that never failed to mystify me. Jim Colwell, the vice-captain, was a much lighter and looser runner who seemed to skim the ground, an impression created partly by his always doing his cross-country running barefoot. Jim chose the All England Championships to finish ahead of Malcolm for the first time and was leading the whole field at the start of the final straight, only to be overtaken and beaten into second place a few yards from home. He admitted afterwards that he'd been so elated at how well he'd done he hadn't focused on what was happening around him on the final run in and thus had completely failed to respond to the challenge from the eventual winner.

Outstanding individuals are obviously a great asset to a team, but it was our strength in depth that made us really formidable opponents and ensured a steady supply of pots for Freddie Walch to present in morning assembly on Monday mornings. He must have enjoyed these frequent reminders of his pupils' fitness. Freddie's fit-body-equals-lively-mind equation reminded me of a unique period at Borough Road when, for the first time in my life, I prepared seriously for a sporting event. The daily training runs ceased to be hard work and became enjoyable, even exhilarating. The feeling of general physical well-being affected my whole outlook. I think that some of the Sutton boys were fit in that very special sense.

Although the level of my involvement in the boys'

training sessions was never sufficient for me to regain my peak Borough Road fitness, it was a useful form of exercise in a mainly sedentary profession. Participation in school games can be as rewarding for teachers as for pupils. The team-training and management rôle brings one into a closer and more informal relationship with pupils than most other teaching situations and the understanding that develops is mutually beneficial. The breaks from the classroom are mentally refreshing and matches against other teams provide opportunities to meet people from different backgrounds. Some school sides compete not only against other schools but club sides and teams from universities, colleges and the services. At Sutton we travelled all over the southern counties to different establishments and venues. The team-building process is very satisfying and one shares in the excitement and adrenaline rush that the competitive matches give participants. I rarely lost sleep over my work in the classroom, but prior to big athletics meetings I spent some exhausting nights working out tactics and running races in my mind.

Another very valuable experience that the teacher gains from managing school teams is in organising people and events. In the 1960s, genuine management responsibilities in schools were very limited and both Alan Robinson and I had reason to be grateful for the opportunities we had as young teachers at Sutton to develop a few of the skills that we would subsequently require as headteachers. Headship didn't enter my thoughts at this stage of my career, but the acquisition of what the teachers' salary regulations described as a 'good degree' opened up promotion prospects and in 1962 I took up a post in Kent as head of English at Maidstone Grammar School.

# 12

## Maidstonenses Gaudeamus

Maidstone Grammar School was one of the country's best
known state schools and its headmaster, William Arthur
Claydon (WAC) CBE, MA, had established a formidable
personal reputation for his championing of the day grammar
schools as providers of an academic education for 'able and
industrious boys from all social backgrounds'. Schools like
Maidstone ensured, in words often quoted by its headmaster,
that 'there may never be wanting a supply of fit persons to serve
God in Church and State'. Claydon believed in the principle
that aptitude and ability should be the sole considerations in
determining educational opportunity. Nowadays such a view
would only be voiced by right-wing politicians (in private).
However, in 1953, when the headmaster of Maidstone
Grammar School had expressed these sentiments at a speech
day, the normal assumption was that educational opportunity
was the prerogative of those who could pay for it. Claydon's
crusade to extend the boundaries earned him notoriety as an
egalitarian.

Claydon regarded the detection and nurturing of

scholastic potential as the most important of a headmaster's responsibilities. He believed that academic distinction was the highest form of human achievement and that the greatest honour a pupil could bring upon himself and his school was an award conferred by Oxford or Cambridge. School reports of star performers in the third year informed parents of their son's destiny in the headmaster's portentous words: 'a potential Oxbridge scholar'. From that heart-stopping moment pupils were marked men, the outcome of their studies determined for them. It never occurred to Claydon that ability and industry, far from prematurely narrowing a boy's career path, opened up a whole range of options, many of which would not be best served by attending Oxford or Cambridge. Clever and hard-working boys might, for example, wish to study a university subject not available at either of these two universities or to follow a course that had a better reputation than its Oxbridge equivalent. They might – say it quietly – want to pursue an artistic rather than academic career and gain admission to a college of art, music or drama.

Claydon was a scholar through and through. Watching him from inside the Big Hall as he made his begowned and dignified way through the cloisters to lead Morning Prayers, one felt instinctively that he should have stayed in Oxford, become a don and eventually Master of Balliol, where he had been a student. This surely was his true milieu. Probably that is what he would have wished, but his degree result let him down – a second, not a first. His class of degree was a source of great regret to Claydon and it left him with an exaggerated sense of admiration for anyone who had achieved the ultimate academic accolade.

At least that is how I tried to explain to myself how I came to be appointed head of English at Maidstone. The interview could hardly have been a factor. The first question put to me was, in retrospect, entirely predictable: what did I know about the place in which I was apparently keen to spend the next stage of my career? Unfortunately, the honest answer would have been 'precious little': I had been too busy to do much preparation for the interview and my main concern over the preceding few days had been whether the process would end in time for me to get back to Sutton for an evening athletics meeting for which I was responsible. My ignorance was too palpable to conceal and Claydon was visibly shaken. Another puzzling aspect of my appointment was that it broke a distinct mould. The English department was staffed entirely by Oxbridge graduates and eight of those during my time as head of department were scholars or exhibitioners, an élite within an élite. Most were experienced teachers and included both the Second Master and the Master of the Lower School. Their reputation was second to none in achieving success in the school's terms – excellent exam results and a steady flow of Oxbridge awards and places. With my evening class London degree and two-and-a-half years' GCE teaching experience I was a conspicuous oddity in this environment.

By the time that I took up my appointment I had done my homework on the school and was duly impressed. Claydon's distinguished career was nearing an end and by 1966, when he was due to retire, he would have completed 30 years of headship, 25 of them at Maidstone. Long service had been a tradition of the school's headmasters, although not all had distinguished themselves as positively as Claydon had done. One John Law, for example, had been admonished in 1668 for frequenting alehouses and taverns and then, some years later, indicted for murder. The circumstances were unclear but the victim appears to have been neither pupil nor parent, but a drinking companion with whom the headmaster had had a disagreement. Notwithstanding his unacceptable social habits and the trouble they brought upon him, Law was not lacking in commitment to his headmasterly responsibilities: having been convicted of manslaughter, he escaped from prison – taking his jailer with him – and returned to his school, where he apparently held out for some considerable time before disappearing altogether.

Long service was not confined to the school's headmasters. Two legendary members of staff had retired in 1960, but lived on in people's memories and conversations. G B Phillips, the senior master, had served the school for 46 years; Sarge (Bennet), the ex-army caretaker, a mere 40. In 1962, when I joined the school, there were several masters approaching retirement after lifelong service, but none was looking likely to mount a serious challenge to Phillips' record. Not surprisingly, given the continuity provided by such staff, the school had a very strong commitment to tradition and traditional values. Its motto was *olim meminisse juvabit* – 'one day we shall like to have remembered', from Virgil's *Aeneid*. More demandingly, the school song, *Maidstonenses Gaudeamus*, was also in Latin. It ran to 20 verses but, as a concession to the pace of modern life, we only ever sang three. Prefects were 'praefects' (from Latin *praefectus*) and each year's leavers were listed in the school magazine in a *Valete*.

Latin was an extremely important language in the day grammar schools as a GCE O-level pass in the subject was still a requirement for Oxbridge entry and for BA courses at the so-called 'lesser' universities. Thus, within a year of their admission, pupils' destination at 18 had to be estimated – to ensure that those who would require a Latin qualification started the appropriate course. Latin and German streams were formed in the second year and the L stream prepared for early GCE entry in four subjects. The other two forms remained unstreamed for a further year when the least successful boys were demoted to a bottom stream (form B). Thus, by the age of 12 or 13, boys were pigeonholed according to the school's assessment of their potential level of examination

149

success. Inevitably they tended to live up, or down, to those expectations.

The boys who joined Maidstone Grammar School each year were used to academic success. This was, of course, true of all grammar school entrants, but Maidstone's intake was extra special. Whereas Sutton, for example, served just its immediate urban neighbourhood and lost some potential high-fliers to outer London public schools, Maidstone drew from a wide area, cherry-picking the very ablest boys from primary and junior schools throughout mid-Kent and, because of its consequent reputation, attracting pupils whose parents would, in another part of the country, have felt the need to pay for private education.

As soon as the new intake had arrived, all the familiar paraphernalia of tests, exams and grades swung into action to produce a regular form order. An added refinement at Maidstone was the recording and reporting of a grade for effort. There were four categories of industry, which were explained in a key; for example, A – 'deserves praise for really hard work'; D –'little or no effort, really lazy'. By October, many of September's 11+ successes were having to adjust to very different perceptions of themselves, perceptions that would condition their response to school for many years.

Any comparison between Maidstone and High View ought to have been ludicrous: their worlds were as far apart as the lifestyles of the Royal Family and Calcutta street dwellers. And yet I was constantly fascinated by the similarities between the attitudes of the top streams in the two schools and also, to some extent, between those of the bottom streams. In both the secondary modern and the grammar school the most successful pupils tended to be keen, hardworking and confident, whereas the least successful were often bored, unresponsive and lacking in self-esteem. In a highly competitive system these differences are noticeable not only between streams but between pupils within a form. Some of the saddest grammar school pupils are those who have languished for several years at the bottom of the top stream. Picked out as the brightest of the bright, these pupils have to live, day in and day out, with their failure to come up to expectations. There were boys in the Latin stream at Maidstone who left school after O-level not because they weren't capable of sixth form work and a university place, but because after years of conditioning to a lowly position in their form they were not persuaded, even by respectable O-level results, that they had the potential to go any further with their studies.

All teaching is mixed ability teaching. No matter how hard a school tries to create homogeneous groups of able and weak pupils the success/failure syndrome will work on the different personalities, temperaments, aptitudes, types of intelligence within the group and produce a wide range of responses. Teaching entails sensitivity to the differences that emerge, constant adjustment of the pace and level of the work and a sympathetic response to individual needs. My first A-level lesson at Maidstone was a forcible reminder that there is no stage in the educational system where one can expect uniformity of response. We started reading *David Copperfield* and, during discussion, one member of the class launched a scathing attack on Dickens, as a person and an author, backed up by detailed references to his life and works. I was taken aback by the vehemence with which he dismissed man and writer as a petty-minded, nasty little you-in-your-corner-and-me-in-mine Victorian. At the end of the lesson another member of the class lingered nervously behind and asked me earnestly if I would tell him the meaning of several words in the passage we had read.

My early sixth form lessons at Maidstone demonstrated the power that a teacher has to build or destroy pupils' confidence. Impressed by the academic standards and reputation of the school, and keen to rise to the challenge of the work, I badly overestimated a group of third-year-sixth Oxbridge candidates whom I was timetabled to prepare for their general essay paper. The stratospheric demands I made of them quickly destroyed their self-assurance and produced a state of drivelling incompetence.

Maidstone was not oblivious to the pressures it put boys under by its emphasis on academic success and this was reflected particularly in attitudes towards the bottom stream. Class size worked in favour of the least able, not – as often happened elsewhere – the highfliers. Members of the B Form were encouraged to think in terms of passing five or six O-levels, but to take six years to do so instead of five. I never heard the bottom streams reviled at Maidstone, whereas there was a stage at High Wycombe RGS when the weaker forms were referred to as the 'snake pits' or just 'the pits'. I once had the misfortune to be paired in an extended exam-marking exercise with a young master from Manchester Grammar School whose main topic of conversation for three days was the lamentable ignorance and ineptitude of one of the lower streams it was his misfortune to teach in that most selective of schools.

Keen as Claydon was to instil academic ambition in boys, he was, paradoxically, responsible during his headmastering career for a number of measures to ease workloads. Two of his initial reforms in his first headship, at Borden Grammar School in North Kent, had been to increase the proportion of the timetable devoted to PE and games and reduce the amount of homework that junior and middle school boys were expected to complete each night. In the sixth form at Maidstone no-one took more than three A-levels and nearly all the arts sixth were limited to two. This was a significant statement on the importance of providing time for senior pupils to read round their subjects and to do other things that were important: there was no sixth form general studies programme, but all sixth-formers, other than those studying A-level English, followed a two-year, three-period-a-week course in English. The two-A-level policy for arts sixth-formers was a particularly courageous innovation and, but for the school's reputation, might well have jeopardised boys' university prospects. The references supplied for university applicants explained the policy and the thinking behind it. Bucking the system as blatantly as this wasn't a process normally associated with traditional grammar schools and Maidstone's individuality in this matter said much for Claydon's self-confidence and authority.

The headmaster's national standing undoubtedly benefited the school, as a situation over examination grades showed. Like many teachers, we were frequently puzzled by our pupils' GCE results and found those in O-level English language particularly inexplicable. Early in 1964 I responded to an advertisement for O-level examiners and marked papers in the summer of that year for the first time. Although the exam board was not the same as that used by the school, I hoped that I would gain insights into the mysteries of the system that would be helpful to the English department. The experience was certainly illuminating, but not quite in the way I had anticipated. Not only were the instructions that I received extremely brief, but there was no meeting of examiners and no additional guidance for someone like myself new to examining. The main method of support was by an arrangement whereby I sent six marked scripts to the chief examiner for his comments. In the meantime, I continued marking in accordance with instructions. The return of my annotated scripts was delayed by a postal strike and they arrived too late to influence my marking.

When our 1964 Maidstone results came through, we received a set of O-level English grades that contained fail or low pass grades for some of the ablest and most conscientious boys and high grades for some of those whose classwork and homework had not suggested that they would do particularly well. This was long before the age of litigation and automatic protest and appeals, but Claydon wrote a personal letter to the secretary of the examining board expressing our concern and asking for several scripts to be re-marked. To our considerable surprise, the secretary ordered a re-mark of all our English language scripts, numbering over 100. When this exercise had been completed, we were informed that 22 candidates had been upgraded, more than half of them by over three classifications on the nine-point scale in use at the time (1-6 were pass grades; 7-9 failures). One candidate moved up five grades. The board mentioned that some of our other candidates had initially been awarded higher grades than their scripts merited, but these were to remain unaltered.

The secretary's explanation of what had happened was that the examiner who had marked the essay question on our candidates' English language papers had concentrated too much on linguistic accuracy and given insufficient credit for imaginative and innovative content; the rest of the paper had been correctly marked by another examiner. Whilst we were impressed by the board's magnanimity and courage in admitting a basic error of judgement, we could not but feel that the explanation given was disingenuous. The essay carried 40% of the total marks for the exam. For its re-marking to affect a candidate's overall result by as many as four grades, an essay must have been undervalued initially to the extent of some 25 marks; in other words, a piece of work that merited a distinction had been awarded a mere handful of marks, say five out of a possible 40. The candidate whose result was adjusted five grades must have received nought for an essay of distinction standard. Either the original essay examiner was certifiable or there was some more sinister or embarrassing explanation that the board felt it could not reveal.

We ought, of course, to have taken the matter further. But our gratitude to the board for admitting an error and re-marking the papers, our pleasure at achieving justice for our candidates and our habitual inclination as teachers not to cause any trouble meant that we simply returned to our classrooms and did nothing. However, another school that had tired of its unpredictable exam results tried an interesting experiment the following year: it entered its candidates for O-level English language with two different boards, and then published the parallel sets of results in the national press. There were, of course, very significant differences between the two. One candidate was awarded grade 1 by one board and grade 9 by the other. From that point onwards the various exam boards made sure that their O-level English language exams were always held on the same day. One wished that, as well as taking this evasive action, the boards might have got their examiners together to see if they could agree on measures to ensure more equitable treatment of candidates. What would be really refreshing, though, would be for those who control the education system to admit that exams are a lottery, particularly in subjects where examiners are expected to make an objective assessment of something as personal and subjective as an imaginative essay.

The concept of management in education was virtually non-existent in the 1960s. Although grammar schools had for some years employed a nominal departmental system it had made very little impact. At Maidstone there was no head of department job description and little attempt by those fulfilling the rôle to formulate one for themselves. On the science side some oversight of laboratories, equipment and safety was necessary, but in arts subjects the head of department's responsibilities were usually confined to two tasks of preparation for the start of a new academic year: ordering any new books that were required and agreeing each

155

master's teaching timetable. No-one appeared to question whether these duties were sufficiently onerous to merit the extra cash that went with the job. Responsibility allowances tended to be regarded as rewards for experience and long service. Again my appointment didn't fit the norm.

As a teacher you defined for yourself how you taught and then got on with it. Provided your classes didn't create a degree of mayhem that made other people's working conditions intolerable, you knew you would receive neither direction nor interference. This system was not merely tolerated but highly regarded. In schools like Maidstone, where class control wasn't a problem, masters greatly valued and jealously guarded their independence from any form of management. In return, the headmaster was left to make major decisions over the organisation and administration of the school; Claydon sometimes went through the motions of consultation, but normally made his own mind up after sounding out one or two senior colleagues.

Given the prevailing culture of individual autonomy I trod warily at first, suggesting just a few fairly obvious ways in which the English staff might function as a team rather than a collection of gifted individuals. The freedom-to-do-as-you-like rule meant that staff chose whatever books from the store cupboard that they thought they would like to read with their classes. Thus a master might look to titillate the literary taste buds of a class of 13-year-olds with the delights of Sheridan's *School for Scandal* only to be greeted, when he distributed copies of the play, with a chorus of groans and cries of 'We read this last year, sir!' An early initiative was, therefore, to seek agreement on which prose, drama and poetry books were appropriate for different age groups and ability streams, and then to ask members of the department to adhere to that allocation. Not unreasonable. There were similar co-ordinating tasks over aspects of language teaching, internal examination papers and – more tricky this one – marking policies.

There was an immediate need to do something about the language course books, particularly those used in the middle school. The existing books, and indeed most of the available alternatives, were simply sets of graded exercises for use as test questions. These were the boys' only aids to study: they had no handbook to provide support or guidance in their efforts to master the complexities of the English language, no manual of instruction to which they could refer to check basic rules of grammar, syntax, spelling and punctuation, nothing that would help them to speak articulately, to write fluently, to read with comprehension. It was a situation that spoke eloquently of the priorities of English education with its unequivocal preference for testing over helping people to learn.

What struck me most forcibly about most of the Maidstone teach-by-testing books was that they appeared to be written in a foreign language: the passages selected for the précis, comprehension and other routine exam exercises were all drawn from obscure and idiosyncratic historical sources. The final test in each chapter always consisted of a convoluted dialogue which had the punctuation and paragraphing omitted. Pupils were instructed to write the passage out, supplying all the missing features. The confusion that results from trying to teach rules of spelling, punctuation and grammar by presenting pupils with incorrect forms was then compounded by a bizarre choice of passages involving 19th century rustics, Dickensian grotesques and First World War infantrymen exchanging witticisms in the trenches. Try your orthographic skills out on this one:

they didnt shout more at the news of the battle of waterloo now this is our speciality this absence of extreme centralisation it must be encouraged local jealousies local rivalries local triumphs these are the strength of the kingdom if you mean to say that crickets a the old squire speaking squire uploft of fallow field remembered the saving presences and coughed good thing im one with ye sir george encouraged egad they dont want much of that here give some of your lean London straws a strip o clean grass and a bit of liberty and youll do em a service what a beautiful hit exclaimed one of the ladies languidly watching the ascent of the ball beautiful dye call it muttered the squire the ball indeed was dropping straight into the hands of long off instantly a thunder rolled

What teenager is likely to know whether the obsolete aristocratic oath 'egad' takes an apostrophe or not? And does it matter? One wonders at the mentality of someone who thought that such exercises were relevant components of a teenager's education. But they were, of course, only old-fashioned examples of an all-too-familiar exam strategy: that of introducing gratuitous difficulties in order to separate the sheep from the goats and to ensure that too many candidates do not gain high marks. It is a nasty little trick designed to keep the less intelligent candidates in their place, regardless of how conscientiously they may have worked.

Potentially the most contentious policy issue on which I sought agreement was concerned with making space on the GCE courses for general reading. The grammar school curriculum was designed to meet the perceived needs of the universities. In the senior school the content and teaching of each subject mirrored its university counterpart, thereby giving pupils a foretaste of what it would be like to study that particular specialism at honours degree level and actually preparing them for doing so. Thus, in English, instead of reading as widely as possible and exploring a range of literature appropriate to their age and interests, pupils had to spend their time scrutinising a few classics in great detail, for the supposed benefit of the small number who would actually go on to read the subject at university and therefore be engaged in that kind of esoteric activity. No-one appeared to question whether the set text approach was the most effective way of developing a potential English scholar's understanding of authors, genres and periods of literature. What certainly wasn't in doubt was that the majority of pupils found the detailed and repetitive analysis of a small number of texts an excruciatingly tedious procedure. What should have been the beginning of a lifetime's enjoyment of reading and theatre-going proved a negative experience that risked deterring pupils from any future engagement with serious literature.

In an attempt to introduce some sanity into this system I delayed the study of A-level texts with my teaching groups to provide time for wider reading. However, in deference to the exam syllabus, this reading was always pertinent to the set works. Thus, if the A-level syllabus required the study of *King Lear*, sixth-formers read and discussed some of the other great dramatic tragedies so that, when they came to study *Lear* in detail, they did so, not in a vacuum, but with some understanding of the nature of tragedy in the theatre. The suggestion that the department should adopt this approach was accepted with surprisingly little opposition: some did feel, however, that the proposed 50/50 split between background reading and prescribed texts was a tad too risky, so we settled for two terms' preparatory reading and discussion, followed by three for the set works (the final term of the two-year course being taken up with revision and the A-level exam itself).

At O-level we introduced a newly-devised alternative syllabus for the top stream, which involved the reading of a wider range of literature. This course provided a better educational experience than its conventional counterpart, but was appreciably more demanding – which deterred us from offering it to any but the top stream. This is a familiar situation with new syllabuses that adopt a more general approach to study: aware that purists will attack such reforms as 'dumming down', examination boards contort themselves to ensure that the new course is in fact more difficult than the traditional alternative, thereby excluding many of those who would stand to gain most from a less narrowly-specialised syllabus.

Running the Maidstone English department was about as demanding as managing a football side that could be relied upon to win all its matches. It was a very strong team full of star players. Several of the masters had a passion for literature and a facility for quoting their favourite poets that I could only admire, not emulate. I think I differed from the rest of the department in being just as interested in the language work as the literature. The discussion documents that I circulated reflected this and I gained a reputation for my efforts to raise the standard of boys' creative work. Another difference of emphasis was that, because of my High View experience, I had developed a particularly keen interest in the learning and teaching processes and a heightened awareness of what worked and didn't work in the classroom. I was an enthusiast for teaching who enjoyed his subject. My colleagues were subject enthusiasts who enjoyed their teaching.

# 13

## WAC

If academic success was the first aim of Maidstone Grammar
School, the second was that boys should not lag behind the
public schools in gentlemanly behaviour. Claydon, who had
a fondness for quotations, liked to use a phrase from a 1953
inspectors' report that described the school as 'a civilised and
virile community'. As an all-male establishment, Maidstone
obviously had high virility potential, but the boys' intellectual
precociousness was perhaps more noticeable than any
special manliness or robust masculinity. Sporting prowess
was encouraged and respected, but the general level of
participation and achievement wasn't exceptional – certainly
not in the Sutton league. 'Civilised', on the other hand, was
fair comment: the boys were mostly very well-behaved and
orderly; they didn't rush along corridors shoving and shouting;
they were respectful to masters and, if they did misbehave,
they apologised when chastised and accepted their punishment.
It was the only school in which I have worked where pupils
automatically opened doors for staff.

The general orderliness of the school owed much to the

efficient day-to-day organisation and administration. Bob Rylands, the Second Master, had been a major in the King's Shropshire Light Infantry during the war and his standing orders were drawn up with military precision. Duty masters, for example, admitted boys to corridors after morning break at 11.02, not 11.00 or 11.05. The way a school starts a new academic year reveals a great deal about its organisational and administrative strength: Maidstone's 'first day of the year' was planned in minute detail and masters were carefully briefed at an evening staff meeting held on the final day of the holiday.

The boys' behaviour at Maidstone reflected that of the staff. The Common Room contained some delightfully urbane and cultured gentlemen and there was a general attentiveness to courtesy and good manners that inevitably impacted on the boys. Most masters treated their pupils decently and humanely. From early times, the school appeared to have had a progressive tendency with regard to human relationships: another inspectors' report, this time from 1869, noted that corporal punishment was rarely used and then only 'by the headmaster in private'. A century later the school had regressed slightly in that both the Second Master and Master of the Lower School caned, in addition to the headmaster. Such punishment was, however, occasional and still discreetly administered. I looked back with embarrassment at the readiness with which we employed corporal punishment at High View and made sure that I never had cause at Maidstone to send a boy to be beaten.

The physical environment played an important rôle in Maidstone's civilised lifestyle: there was a spaciousness and sense of style that I had not previously experienced in a school building. High View and Sutton occupied cramped sites with their main buildings almost abutting the street pavement. The entrance to High View had been a narrow, badly-lit corridor through which one squeezed one's way past a pile of staff bicycles. The Sutton staff room resembled a furniture salesroom before an auction: staff were allocated two-foot square spaces at back-to-back carrels so close that gaining access to the inner berths involved clambering over the occupants of those on the outside.

Maidstone Grammar School stood well back from its gatehouse and archway entrance. The main building was built in the style of a public school and modelled on an Oxbridge college, with a quad, cloisters and sacrosanct lawn. The staff accommodation was on two levels – a lower common room and a long upper workroom large enough to accommodate meetings of all 50 masters. There was a very attractive foyer with highly-polished floor and professional-looking floral display. On one side swing doors opened into the Big Hall and on the other a corridor led past the school office to the headmaster's study. Those summoned or courageous enough to venture into this inner sanctum found themselves in a light and spacious room adjacent to Claydon's private residence and garden, the latter maintained by pacifists who opted out of the CCF. The vicinity of the Study was out-of-bounds to pupils, a superfluous restriction since boys instinctively gave it a wide berth.

Claydon was an awesome figure – tall, gaunt and austere. Slow and deliberate in his movements, he wore a grey suit, knitted cardigan and habitually pained expression. He gave the impression of great age. There were two alternative theories on this matter: (i) that he had been born middle-aged and so naturally, by his mid-fifties, looked like Methuselah, and (ii) that, having been appointed to his first headship when only 29, he had sought to give himself a touch of gravitas by adopting an elderly manner, which had then become habitual. Common sense favoured the latter explanation, but there was anecdotal evidence to support the first hypothesis: apparently right from the outset at Borden Grammar School boys had referred to their phenomenally young headmaster as 'Old Claydon'.

On the infrequent occasions that Claydon emerged from his study, the corridors emptied instantly. Even staff suddenly recalled an important reason for heading off in the opposite direction. One day I failed to spot him approaching and, more unfortunately, so did Pope, a quiet and singularly harmless young man in one of the fifth-form classes that I taught. 'Come here, boy!' ordered Claydon. Pope took six paces forward, raised an arm and asked desperately, 'Please, sir, may I be excused?' In the two seconds between command and response, Pope's bowels had started to emit unmistakable signals.

Perhaps because he encountered pupils infrequently, Claydon seemed somewhat puzzled when they did enter his line of vision. Having scrutinised the object in front of him, he was often affronted by what he saw. On one occasion my form of 16-year-olds were only just in time for Morning Prayers – my fault, not theirs – and the final stragglers were still entering the rear of the Big Hall as Claydon emerged from his study corridor to make his measured way through the cloisters. He stopped irascibly at the unwonted sight of feckless youth before him and then, spotting some minor discrepancy of dress that I'd obviously failed to correct, he issued his customary command, 'Come here, boy!' and then, indignantly, 'You look like something out of a circus!'

Boys didn't deviate in any significant way from the uniform requirements, but Claydon fretted at the small variations they occasionally introduced. At a staff meeting prior to the start of a new term, one of the Common Room elders gave an impassioned plea for us to be watchful of certain fashion trends that he feared might become features of boys' dress in the coming weeks. Thanking this gentleman for his timely observations, Claydon expressed his personal aversion to some current styles of footwear, particularly suedes, or 'cads' shoes', as he called them. I stirred uneasily, checking surreptitiously that my feet were well out of view.

Notwithstanding the boys' generally good behaviour, Claydon was always alive to the possibility of insurrection and had a batten-down-the-hatches approach to the end of a term. He opened one December staff meeting with the alarming words, 'Gentlemen, we are sitting on a powder keg!' (His metaphors were invariably antiquated.) Hints of rebellion were, in fact, few and far between and hardly any masters had discipline problems. One exception, though, was an elderly classicist who contributed a small amount of teaching to the English department. The extent of his ineffectualness was brought home to me when I apprehended a youngster from one of his classes on his way down the corridor during lesson time. I was never as punctilious as High View's Miss Clarke in automatically asking anyone I passed in such circumstances what he was doing, but this boy was conspicuous because he had his desk with him. The Maidstone desks had a bench-seat attached to them and were made of solid wood set into an iron frame. Despite their considerable weight, it was possible for boys to move them around while appearing to remain seated. It was an acquired skill, necessitating lifting with the arms and shuffling with the feet in the way that a young child moves a toy car before he has learnt to control the pedals. This particular boy was clearly an experienced practitioner, having taken the opportunity, while the master was writing on the board, to manoeuvre his desk up to the classroom door, out of the room and down the corridor. I'm not sure where he thought he was going.

Established staff recalled one or two earlier incidents that were said to have contributed to Claydon's insecurity concerning boys' behaviour. Apparently everyone had arrived at school one morning to find a china chamber pot ensconced on a pinnacle above the Big Hall. Sarge had shot down the

165

intruding Jerry with a .22 rifle. Then there had been the unforeseen outcome of a decision to release fifth-formers from the obligation to wear caps. On the day of this pronouncement a significant number of Year 5 had assembled after school on Maidstone Bridge for a *valete* ceremony in which the now obsolete items of headgear were cast with a flourish into the Medway, accompanied by wild cheering. Claydon had apparently been particularly distressed at this public display of disrespect for the school uniform. It had obviously not occurred to him, when making this uniform concession, that the boys might not wish to keep their caps as a memento of a school tradition.

All heads tend to be watchful of their school's image and Claydon was hypersensitive to anything that might sully Maidstone's considerable reputation. One of my upper sixth A-level candidates discovered this to his cost. He was a seriously intellectual young man, a prefect and school chorister who had never been guilty of the smallest misdemeanour. However, he hit the jackpot one momentous evening during an SCM sixth form social at the Maidstone Girls' Grammar School, when he did a turn as a stand-up comic, using some unsuitably blue material. The headmistress, who was one of the staff chaperoning the girls at this event, registered her disapproval by walking out. Next morning she rang Claydon. The skies darkened and the school held its collective breath.

No-one at that time had dreamt up the exhaustive and exhausting procedures that heads currently have to follow when excluding pupils. The sixth-former was suspended immediately and indefinitely. The timing was unfortunate as the offender's A-level exams were a few weeks away, but no-one dared enquire whether he would be allowed back to take his papers. I never received a definitive account of the SCM entertainment but the sixth-formers who were present were adamant that he had not intended to be offensive, a view that certainly accorded with his character and school record. The prefects went to see Claydon *en bloc*, an unheard-of event. The incident – or rather the handling of it – divided the staff: the more elderly masters believed that Claydon's action had been entirely justified; the younger members of the Common Room, among whom I included myself, thought that he had over-reacted. The debate dragged on, corroding relationships, until the young man was eventually reinstated in time to take his examinations.

I found myself wondering how Dr Walch would have dealt with this schoolboy misdemeanour and concluded that his response would have been more considered and diplomatic, a bit more centred on the transgressor and less on his own anger. The sixth-former had clearly offended, but almost certainly hadn't intended to do so. Intelligent and scholarly, he had strayed into an area where he lacked nous and sensitivity. Like my RGS Polish classmate with his football match essay, he had made an error of judgement. He needed to understand precisely what this was, why his behaviour had caused offence. Dr Walch would have worked on him to the point where the young man genuinely recognised that he owed the headmistress of the Girls' School an apology. Freddie would then have allowed himself one of his gruff little chuckles at the thought of the ensuing interview.

Arthur Claydon belonged to a bye-gone age and was easily bewildered by deviations from the norm and the need for change. As the master in charge of the team of sixth-formers who edited the school magazine, I wanted to replace the traditional journal-style booklet with a larger, landscape magazine that would give more scope for photographs and original artwork. This kind of initiative required the headmaster's approval and I sought a meeting to state my case. Perplexity furrowed Claydon's craggy brow, but he heard me out. But then, turning towards his bookcase, he indicated with an expansive wave of the hand the generations of identically-sized *Maidstonians* erect in their serried ranks: 'But Macfarlane, it wouldn't fit on the shelf.' There was no answer to that. However, a compromise was reached: photographs and artwork, yes, but no change of size or shape.

There was a warmer, more human side to Claydon that belied his austere manner and aura of uncompromising authority. He and his wife, Ruth, were a conscientious host and hostess to senior masters and their wives, whom they invited to the Lodge for dinner – one couple at a time, not in groups. On the way to our first visit my wife ran through a few of the basic table manners for my benefit. Soup looked like being the first challenge, but Ruth had barely finished serving before the great man began attacking his bowl with great gusto, slurping noisily. I kept my head down, frantically fighting off the alarming spasms that threatened to overcome me. The fearsome Arthur was human after all – and indeed quite relaxed in his own home. One brave master and his wife who plucked up courage to reciprocate the Claydons' dinner invitation reported that he was even more at ease as a guest, and touchingly appreciative of the hospitality shown him.

Genuine appreciation was a hallmark of the man and he never missed an opportunity to thank masters for their work. No summer holiday passed without my receiving a letter from him – expressing his pleasure at the latest edition of the *Maidstonian* (read after term ended); sending congratulations on a set of examination results; thanking me for some particular task undertaken. He once wrote to me in the West Country in response to some edited material I'd sent him from my holiday address. These weren't conventional notes, but personalised letters of some substance. They were always handwritten.

Claydon's handwriting was distinctive: very neat, regular and unadorned, but cramped and painstaking, as if the effort of composition had been hard work. It may indeed have been so, for as a writer Claydon was an inveterate polisher. He once told me that it took him a day to write a staff reference: he wanted to be quite sure that he said everything that needed saying, but on a single side of A4. His speech day addresses, always models of linguistic and structural clarity, were meticulously planned and timed. Whatever they cost him in effort, Claydon's letters bore little sign of artifice or formality. They were surprisingly natural and relaxed, free of clichés and popular colloquialisms, but lively in their asides, emphases, exclamations and personal expressions of feeling. They were warm, enthusiastic and quite intimate. I kept everything he wrote to me, including his handwritten invitation to interview containing train and bus times and precise directions for finding the school.

Nearly 70 years after Claydon took up his first headship, at Borden Grammar School, I met John Spice, an Old Boy of that school who vividly recalled the new headmaster's arrival and the impact that he made. John, too, had a collection of his letters, written to him when he was a sixth-former – to congratulate him on his Higher Certificate results; to wish him well in his Oxford entrance exam; to thank him for a set of gramophone records presented by the prefects when he left to take up his Maidstone headship. The latter contained a request for the names of everyone who had contributed to his leaving present, as he would 'of course like to write to each of them individually'.

John Spice was one of the first to experience the warmth of Claydon's patronage. I was one of the last. Just as Claydon guided selected academic pupils towards Oxbridge, so he groomed certain members of his staff for headship. He was proud of the number of men who went on from Maidstone to run their own day grammar schools and ensure 'the spreading of the gospel (good works and practices) elsewhere'. Whenever I had an audience with him, and sometimes in his letters to me, he would pass on gratuitous pieces of advice on the nature of a job that he found extremely demanding but very rewarding. One of his comments shed fresh light on how I came to be appointed to Maidstone Grammar School: 'When you become a headmaster, Macfarlane (he always said 'when', never 'if') take care not to fill the common room with replicas of yourself.' His golden rule for headmastering was 'patience and proportion', wise words but not ones that would have sprung readily to the minds of some of the pupils with whom he had dealings in the final years of his career. But then other people's perceptions can be very different from one's own.

There was an aloofness about Claydon that kept people at arm's length and no-one on the staff knew him well, not even Bob Rylands who spent time with him daily. He had qualities that would have made him a sensitive and compassionate friend, but his rôle – or his interpretation of it – prevented his forming any close relationship. One assumed that he shared his problems and anxieties with Ruth, but he must, nevertheless, have experienced considerable loneliness. I often wondered how he coped privately with the crises and traumas of headship and particularly those that a head sometimes brings upon himself and his staff. His aspirations, standards and reputation put pressure on both staff and pupils to succeed and, long before stress became a recognised occupational hazard for teachers, a number of masters suffered intense anxiety over their work. Claydon endured three staff suicides during his Maidstone reign, one near the beginning, one in the middle and another near the end. No-one openly linked these tragedies with the work situation, but they must have preyed on Claydon's mind, for he was not unaware of the demands that he and the school made of staff. Certainly the suicide that occurred during my time in the school affected me: when I became a head I was very conscious of the heavy responsibility I had for the welfare of the staff and students in my charge.

Claydon retired in the spring of 1966 shortly after his

sixtieth birthday. On the day of the interviews for his successor an incident occurred – of the sort that he always knew could happen at any time but very rarely did. A night intruder – or probably several – scaled the outer walls of the Big Hall, not to deposit a chamber pot but to paint on the roof in immaculate six-foot-high lettering a cryptic slogan – PEACE AT LAST. We arrived in the morning to find a workforce of builders attempting to remove the paint but succeeding only in smearing it over a much wider area, without obliterating the outline of the message. The disturbance to our normal calm routine seemed to unsettle everyone and the Common Room was restless. When at break we discovered a WAC-initialled notice on the board requesting us to line up at lunchtime in the quad wearing our gowns and ready to be introduced to the day's candidates, there were mutterings of rebellion. Whether anyone would actually have gone so far as to boycott the parade we never knew for one of our number, scrutinising the notice more closely than the rest of us, observed that the C in 'WAC' was in fact a G.

The successful candidate was a Mr Bernard Moody. Having doubtlessly taken note of the rooftop activities on the day of his interview, Mr Moody appeared to conclude that the school was out of control and requiring an early version of 'special measures'. He put his not inconsiderable weight behind a clean-up exercise – not so much a new broom as a vigorous dusting of the pants of any boy failing to adhere punctiliously to the school rules. Boys were beaten in droves for offences normally corrected by means of a quiet word from a prefect. Moody showed no respect for the tradition of 'discreet application of corporal punishment' noted by the 1869 inspectors: he published a daily list of beatings stating the offence and the number of strokes awarded. Crowds gathered to get a sight of each day's posting and a popular early morning greeting among the boys was 'Been beaten today?' It was not long before another slogan appeared – 'Come back, WAC. All is forgiven.'

Claydon retired with Ruth to Gloucester, but kept in touch with his ex-colleagues. I left Maidstone a term later to become headmaster of Letchworth Grammar School in Hertfordshire. Claydon wrote with typical warmth when I informed him of my new appointment and again a day or two before the start of my first term to wish me well. There was a pressing invitation to come down to Gloucester to tell him all about my early experiences of headship. I never got round to going and not long afterwards Claydon died.

# 14

## Lighting up Letchworth

I prepared for headship by attending a weekend course and reading a two-page article on *Pomposity in Headmasters*. Teachers of my generation made the transition from classroom to head's study without training, and usually without any significant management experience. Deputy heads tended to be long-serving members of staff who saw their time out in the same school: few applied for headships. Senior management positions, such as faculty or year head, were still in their infancy. Thus the normal launching pad for a headship was a head of department post, itself largely undeveloped as a management rôle. The prevailing view appeared to be that managing a school was just an extension of teaching a class, which was presumably why, in the past, many heads were inclined to adopt much the same manner to their staff as they did to their pupils.

It was a steep learning curve. In my first weeks at Letchworth I reviewed the day's action each evening and tried to assess the effectiveness of my responses: if pluses outnumbered minuses, it had been a good day. Staff were, of course, watching every move as closely as a class observes a new teacher. First contacts were significant, particularly those initiated by the staff themselves – the supplicants wishing to establish an early case for recognition, to ride a hobbyhorse or air a long-standing grievance, to offer gratuitous advice.

Among the first of my visitors were a number of senior staff bearing gifts in the form of files and documents which they sought to deposit on my desk. My predecessor had had a prolonged illness and, during his 12-month absence, the counselling, organisational and administrative tasks of the school, which he had monopolised, were shared around. It was assumed that, with my arrival, the careers work and higher education guidance, the timetabling, the organisation of exams and collating of results and numerous other jobs of this kind would return to the centre. Not everyone was disappointed to find that this was not so. Responsibility usually increases job satisfaction and, just as I was pleasantly surprised to discover that the Hertfordshire Education Authority gave its heads a cheque book and a degree of financial control uncustomary at that time in the state sector, so the LGS staff responded positively to the realisation that they were to retain a rôle in running the school.

It hadn't been my intention to arrive in Letchworth firing from the hip. The modest aim was to observe and listen before deciding what needed doing. Like many good intentions, however, this strategy rather assumed a situation in which one could control events and choose when to make a move. The reality was that the daily surgery of troubles, complaints and requests for direction or advice required a response. There was also an ominously large stack of papers in my in-tray relating to matters deferred during the previous year's interregnum. Thus without setting out, Moody-like, to make an immediate impact on the school, I found myself quickly acquiring credentials as a bit of an action man – 'Batman' was the pupils' name for me, although this probably arose less from my problem-solving and trouble-shooting exploits than for the way that my gown – now full-length – billowed out behind me like a black slipstream when I strode purposefully along the corridors.

There could have been few cosier places in which to pursue an educational career in the 1960s than a coeducational grammar school with a largely middle class catchment area. LGS was an extremely congenial resting place. Its gentle pace of life obviously agreed with the staff, most of whom appeared to be comfortably ensconced there for life. The eccentricities and frailties of the elderly – of whom there were a fair number – were good-humouredly indulged: the head of department who shuffled off to the common room to put his feet up for a while in the middle of a lesson; the senior member of staff who always took a day off during Wimbledon fortnight. Notwithstanding their suspicions that certain aspects of their lifestyle were about to change, the Old Brigade were warm in their welcome. Several of the elderly spinsters appeared to relish having a young head that they could take under their wing, and their venerable male colleagues also proved very supportive, once they had worked out how to address a boss who was the age of their sons and daughters.

As a teacher I had been pedantic over classroom procedures. Lessons were tightly structured and the work always had a clear framework. Pupils knew exactly what was expected of them. Within the security of that situation I had been able to innovate and extend the normal range of learning experiences. As a head, I wanted an orderly, disciplined and well-organised school in which it would be possible to pursue a dynamic and radical educational agenda. Fortunately, I realised that, although these teaching and headteaching aims and objectives were similar, the approaches and methods for attaining them would need to be different. With both pupils and staff you have to earn respect, but it's a quicker process in the classroom, where you start with so many advantages – not merely status and position, but height (usually), age, experience, knowledge

175

of the world, greater articulacy, and so on. Whilst both children and adults deserve explanations for why you want things done in a particular way, you can specify requirements more directly and unequivocally with pupils than with teachers. Haranguing the Common Room over routines, standards and deadlines is nearly always counterproductive. I concentrated on briefing the pupils, hoping that the staff would get the message and appreciate the implications.

Policy statements to parents were another indirect way of reminding staff of their responsibilities. An unfortunate father who wrote to request time off for his daughter to end term early was quickly disabused of his assumption that pupils' attendance became less important as the holidays approached. My written response – copied to the Common Room – described an impressive scenario of industrious teachers building systematically to the climax of their term's courses, summarising key topics, organising crucial concluding activities to units of work, setting homework assignments designed to consolidate the term's studies. The parental request was hastily and apologetically withdrawn: parent power had yet to be invented and parents of grammar school children readily bowed to headmasterly high-handedness in their anxiety not to give the impression that they undervalued their son's or daughter's selective school place. Whether or not staff recognised my vision of an end-of-term classroom was beside the point: the aim was not to turn everyone into a star performer overnight – attractive as that prospect would have been – but simply to establish unequivocally that classes were expected to continue working effectively until term ended.

Whilst none of my previous schools had exactly fallen apart at the end of term, stress levels had been raised by a premature holiday mood and deteriorating pupil behaviour – not unconnected with the fact that a proportion of the staff appeared to take a sudden aversion to teaching in favour of doing their own thing, while their classes occupied themselves playing hangman, battleships and other tedious time-filling pencil-and-paper games. Any hopes that LGS might have succeeded in rising above this depressing syndrome were quickly dispelled soon after my arrival when I learnt that end-of-term pupil pranks had become something of a tradition in recent years, a practice that had started with an early morning greasing of classroom doorknobs and progressed to more imaginative but irksome projects such as a middle-of-the-night removal of every book and shelf from the school's extensive library. I felt I'd earned a brownie point when my first term concluded without incident.

I arrived in Letchworth with no master plan of action, but, nevertheless, with strong views on both the curriculum and ways of delivering it. These inevitably affected the way in which the school developed over the next five years. LGS was refreshingly free of the more extreme forms of academic paranoia: there was no streaming and little setting, and the staff were quite receptive to suggestions for broadening pupils' educational experience. A proposal not to hold any internal examinations until the end of the fourth year went through on the nod. There were, however, some raised eyebrows when I publicly floated the idea of dispensing with O-level and delaying the examination-orientated curriculum until the sixth form. Of course, to have realised that dream all pupils would have had to commit themselves to continuing at school until they were 18 and Letchworth, like most grammar schools, was well short of that target. Once we'd dispensed with internal exams for those under 15, it became a natural step to discontinue providing termly marks and positions for the same age group. Reports to parents concentrated on written comments on pupils' response to school and study. However, the human obsession with status and comparative levels of performance was appeased by the use of subject grades that enabled parents to measure their child's combined achievement and effort on a nine-point scale.

The premature introduction of the examination system in schools not only exposes children to unnecessary pressure and anxiety, but distorts the classroom experience by obliging teachers to concentrate on those processes and forms of knowledge that can be readily tested in a written examination. The reforms undertaken at LGS enabled us to take a fresh look at the kind of education we were providing for the lower and middle school pupils. The starting point was to consider how best to use the teaching and learning time gained by dispensing with exams and all their attendant baggage of question-setting, revision, marking, classifying results and analysing performance. The opportunity was there to introduce a wider range of group activities, projects and fieldwork, to raise the status and standard of coursework and pupils' oral contributions, and generally to shift the emphasis from teaching to learning by encouraging more active pupil-participation.

That was the challenge. Meeting it required staff conviction, energy and skill. The management of pupils' learning makes much more complex demands on teachers than their traditional rôle of imparting knowledge and setting standardised written exercises and tests. Helpfully, there were a number of young, recently-trained teachers at Letchworth who brought new classroom approaches into the school. Our debate was also well informed by ideas and materials emanating from the Nuffield Projects, the General Studies Association and, most particularly, the recently-formed Schools Council, an organisation that provided a unique opportunity for able and imaginative teachers to influence the curriculum and the way in which it was delivered. The sixties were a good time to be in teaching, particularly for those who questioned the whole basis of traditional classroom practice. There was a prospect of a sea change: the task was to get a conservative profession to do more than merely dip its toes in the water. At Letchworth, heads of department undertook an annual evaluation of the initiatives taken by their team in response to the opportunities for change. Their reports and outline plans for the forthcoming year were revealing. In Dr Brookes' memorable words, there was some way to go.

Having eschewed the administrative tasks that had occupied so much of my predecessor's time, I was free to make a contribution to what interested me most – the quality of education that the school provided. While the staff were, I hoped, beavering away at extending the range of pupils' learning experiences in their specialist subjects, I was exploring ways of achieving the same objective with respect to their general education. An early move was to use the Morning Assembly as a forum for stimulating discussion on all kinds of human issues – personal relationships, topical debating points, different beliefs and philosophies of life. Themes were presented through readings, recordings, live music, staff talks, panels and visiting speakers. Although the spiritual aspects of life remained a recurring topic, with the RE department making a major input, Morning Assembly moved further and further away from the legally required 'act of Christian worship'. No-one seemed unduly concerned by this, least of all those with a religious faith – neither the Christians, who had found the generally apathetic response to the conventional ritual of hymn, bible reading and prayer an impossible context for genuine worship, nor those of other religions, whose participation in Assembly had hitherto been limited to a hang-dog appearance at the end of the proceedings in order to hear the notices and sports results.

Visitors became a familiar feature of school life, bringing specialist knowledge and expertise to various courses. Outside speakers were a particularly useful dimension to sixth form work when the general studies topics crossed the disciplines and specialisms of the staff. As a contributor to a course ambitiously designed to deepen the upper sixth's understanding of *The Nature of Man*, I spent a considerable time matching speakers to topics. There was an occasion when I felt especially pleased at the outcome of my efforts in procuring the German economist and visionary, E F Schumacher, to speak on a very precise subject, *Technology and the Underdeveloped World*. Schumacher was founder of the Intermediate Technology Group, which developed tools and ideas appropriate to the culture and traditions of the people using them. He was a leading authority on the Third World and later expressed his concerns in an influential book, *Small is Beautiful*.

Pursuing my normal policy of telephoning speakers a day or two before their visit – ostensibly as a courtesy to ensure that they were happy with arrangements, but more especially to allay my anxieties that they might have forgotten the engagement – I reminded Schumacher of the agreed title for his talk, *Technology and the Underdeveloped World*. 'Yes, fine,' he said, 'but perhaps we could make it *Technology and Life*.' Not having much option, I concealed my disappointment at suddenly losing half my carefully-chosen subject. The day of the talk arrived and we walked together down to the library where the upper sixth were waiting. As I opened the library door, I checked again: '*Technology and Life*.' 'Well,' said Schumacher, 'let's just call it *Life*.' It was a good topic and he spoke very well on it. The speaker is often more important than the subject.

Famous and much sought after speakers had, of course, to be booked well ahead and there was always a risk that some unforeseen commitment might arise to prevent their visit. There was a longstanding arrangement for Edward Heath to speak in Morning Assembly. However, in a particularly ironic operation of Sod's Law, the agreed date turned out to be that chosen for the opening of Parliament after the 1970 election, in which the electorate returned a Conservative Government led by Mr Heath. The Prime Minister elect wrote a charming letter saying how much he regretted having to disappoint us. On the morning for which his visit had been planned I arrived at school to find a national newspaper photographer waiting on the doorstep. I was incredulous that he appeared to be unaware of the Prime Minister's changed programme for that day. It transpired, however, that he knew all about the State Opening of Parliament, but he'd assumed that Mr Heath would be popping along to Letchworth Grammar School first: apparently he never missed a commitment of this kind. Ted Heath was said to lack the common touch of the pipe-smoking and beer-imbibing Harold Wilson, but my informant painted a very different picture of the two men in which Heath was much the readier to devote time to ordinary people.

Another politician with a reputation for honouring all commitments was Shirley Williams, at that time MP for the Hitchin and Letchworth constituency. Shirley was a good friend of the school and a frequent visitor. One evening she came straight from Westminster to speak to parents and afterwards returned to the House of Commons for an important vote after midnight. A few hours later she was heading for Heathrow and an early morning flight to the United States. That particular schedule persuaded me that I had no right to continue exploiting her generosity.

In inviting people from all walks of life to visit the school, I sought speakers whose talks could be followed up in class. Some visitors came for a day to run mini-conferences involving group discussion and workshops. John Laing and Company, the construction firm, ran three different all-day projects for the school. At one that I attended students worked in teams on a critical path analysis exercise that introduced them to the processes involved in planning and constructing a substantial cricket pavilion within a fixed budget and set timescale. The exercise significantly overran the school day but students showed no awareness of the time. No-one observing the intensity of effort and sense of achievement that activities of this kind generated could have any doubts about the merits of student-centred learning. Yet it was precisely this kind of departure from didactic teaching that eventually led to widespread condemnation of the 'progressive' educational methods of the sixties.

Another initiative that became a regular feature of the sixth form general studies programme was a 'personal encounter' exercise designed to develop students' powers of self-analysis and self-expression. A team of appropriately-briefed visitors held one-to-one conversations with students, encouraging them to talk openly about their interests and aspirations and to reflect on the issues that were important to them and the principles by which they wished to lead their lives. The aim was to go beyond the standard mock interview agenda and encourage students to analyse and articulate their thoughts more frankly than they had perhaps had an opportunity to do before.

Parents gave generously of their time to support activities of this kind, thereby increasing the opportunities that pupils had for meeting and talking to adults other than teachers and family. They ran evening hobby clubs, initiated a prize to encourage individual projects and responded enthusiastically to new initiatives for combined pupil and parent activities. A parents' team just managed to defeat their middle school opponents in a quiz chaired by the producer of BBC Television's *Top of the Form*, but another panel surprisingly and ignominiously lost to a sixth form team in a contest designed to discover which generation was the more proficient in dealing with problems and dilemmas of everyday living – accidents in the home, tricky personal relationships, embarrassing social situations, legal disputes. The students on this occasion not only amazed the audience by their knowledge and understanding, but delighted everyone with their ingenuity in inventing solutions to problems for which they didn't have a ready answer.

In the computer age we have to recognise, as adults, that children's technological understanding often exceeds our own, but the young age at which this supremacy manifests itself is a constant surprise. The remote control to my recently-purchased car has an unnecessarily complicated array of buttons which have to be clicked or double-clicked to open and close doors singly or in different combinations. My uncertainty over precisely how to access the boot independently, without embarrassingly setting off the car alarm, persisted until my four-year-old grandson sorted it out for me. But it's not just their knowledge that's impressive but their street wisdom, resourcefulness and common sense. I recently had a conversation with a nine-year-old young lady whose perceptive comments on the problems of playground bullying left me marvelling at the maturity of some young children.

We ought constantly to be tapping into children's perceptions of the world: the freshness and relevance of their observations can add to our own understanding and greatly enhance the pupil/teacher relationship. Every act of respectful listening by a teacher is a boost to the pupil's confidence and self-esteem. The classroom manager needs constantly to be looking for opportunities to draw upon children's special interests, talents and first-hand experiences, and thinking of ways of encouraging the ungifted to develop some pursuit, body of knowledge or area of comparative expertise upon which they can eventually speak with a degree of assurance. The Gradgrind School of Didactic Pedagogy is, of course, totally dismissive of such procedures – and the quality of education in our schools has long suffered as a result.

'Learning from each other' was, I suppose, one of the unstated themes of my LGS headship, as I strove for an integrated community in which people worked together and came to appreciate each other's different contributions. A coeducational school is an excellent context for furthering such an ideal for the two sexes bring different qualities to the learning process. Letchworth appeared to have taken some time coming to terms with its coeducational status and opportunities. Senior pupils could recall the days when the opposite sex were a species that inhabited the other side of the playground, classroom and assembly hall. A number of anomalies survived from this time: boys and girls used different entrances to the school, were segregated for all physical education and studied different practical subjects. Most bizarrely, only the girls attended the annual house music competition, the boys being taken off to the games field, where presumably it was thought there was no risk of their masculinity being threatened by the sounds emanating from the school hall. Miss Falkner had allowed me to listen to music-making but not to participate; in this instance, boys could take part as performers but not listen as members of the audience. Given the context, however, performing in the house music competition was about as appealing to the male half of the community as having to play one's party piece at a family gathering while one's contemporaries were enjoying ice-creams on the lawn.

The integration of different age groups was more fully developed and senior pupils were very occupied running all-age clubs and societies and organising various events for the younger years. A familial model was used for organising school lunch with a prefect serving a mixed-age group of pupils at each table. Encouraged by the easy relationships between the different years, I indulged myself by teaching my two favourite age groups simultaneously in a curricular drama course for sixth and first formers.

To extend the responsibilities undertaken by senior pupils certain headteacher tasks were delegated to members of the sixth form – chairing panels, reporting on the school year to parents and guests at the annual prize giving, announcing sports results and giving out notices in Morning Assembly. The policy of increasing contacts with the outside world created additional pupil responsibilities – for entertaining visitors, thanking speakers, representing the school at various community events. Although confident of pupils' abilities to rise to such occasions, I was nevertheless frequently surprised at the assurance with which they carried out even the more difficult of these assignments. Their growing confidence and articulacy received recognition when a school team won the first prize in a competition organised by the Council of Europe for the best discussion by a group of European secondary school pupils on ways of improving relations between the peoples of Europe.

The level of staff guidance and support given to pupils who assume management and organisational responsibilities is always a fine judgement. The sixth form sometimes got into difficulty in the management of its social events. On one occasion they hired a public hall for a dance and didn't master the security problems. Towards mid-night, gatecrashers began to make a nuisance of themselves and a hastily-assembled posse from the local rugby club had to be mobilised to lend a hand. If you encourage young people to assume responsibility, there will inevitably be times when they make mistakes or take initiatives of which you disapprove. The caretaker took me to view a den that had been lovingly created in a spacious loft above the woodwork room. The facilities were impressive and included lighting, a very respectable carpet and a handsome television set, an acquisition to which my family had not at that time aspired. There were no sleeping quarters, but I viewed the number of couches with some suspicion. The woodwork' teacher had some explaining to do.

The most alarming moment I experienced with regard to over-ambitious projects was, however, in connection with a Christmas drama production. Shortly before the play opened the normal hazards attendant upon such events were increased by a series of strikes by power workers. Each evening a quarter of Letchworth was blacked out, but no-one knew beforehand which sector of the town would be without power on a given day. Twenty-four hours before the first performance, the member of staff directing the play mentioned that his stage manager had a contingency plan to cope with the power workers' action, should it threaten to disrupt any of the performances. He thought perhaps I ought to know about it. I was fairly well acquainted with the sixth-former who was stage-managing the production and had in fact had a brush with him a few days previously. For some time the stage-management team appeared to have been in semi-permanent residence in the school hall and one lunch-hour the building had begun to heave with the throb of over-amplified pop music. I had ventured down the corridor to enquire politely of the SM what he thought he was doing. 'Just providing some light entertainment for the inmates, sir,' was the prompt reply. He was a highly confident young man with a ready answer for every occasion, the sort of person likely to end up either in government or being detained at Her Majesty's pleasure – or possibly both.

It transpired that the SM had friends in high places and that he was on particularly good terms with the head technician at the Letchworth College of Technology, which occupied an extensive site next to the school. The power strikes that had already taken place had established that the school and college, although adjacent, were in different quarters of the town with respect to power supply and would not therefore be blacked out on the same evening. The SM and head technician had deduced that, if the power supplies of the two sectors of the town containing the school and the college respectively could be connected up, there would be a means of bringing the electricity back on, should we unfortunately be blacked out on one of the nights of the drama production.

I smiled indulgently when the producer mentioned this ingenious fantasy – only to be informed that everything was actually in place to implement the plan should it prove necessary. Batman took off and winged his way down to the school hall. Ascending the stage steps, I could see through the hall windows a set of heavy cables suspended on teetering wooden props stretching from the college across the school car park to the hall. A public footpath ran between the school and the college sites and the loose roll of cables crossed this at an inviting height for any budding Tarzan to demonstrate his prowess on his way home from the pub of an evening. On the stage the SM proudly outlined the procedure for returning power to our quarter of the town should it be blacked out during a performance. It was breathtakingly simple: a heavy metal bar like an old-fashioned railway signalman's lever had been crudely bolted to the floor and, with one wobbling 180° degree heave, would release a mighty surge of power into the building and the surrounding neighbourhood.

The College of Technology's autocratic principal was a notoriously inaccessible supremo, but the urgency in my voice must have been palpable for his PA put me through immediately. He listened to the account of what I had just witnessed without comment, but the silence was electrically charged, so to speak. Within half an hour the cables, posts and stage fitting had all disappeared, just four small holes in the floor remaining to verify that it had all actually happened. I received no subsequent communication from the principal, but did notice a fortnight later that the college was advertising for a senior technician. The last I saw of our resourceful stage manager was towards the end of my headship, in fact on the day that the school governors were appointing my successor. One of the candidates had detached himself from the organised tour of the school in order to nobble a passing pupil, presumably to get the low-down on the place. Of the 630 youngsters that he might have accosted he'd chosen the smoothest talker in the school. The SM was in full flow and I had no doubt that the candidate would be receiving a glowing account of the school's achievements, together with full details of the part played in its success by his informant.

15

## To a Student from His Students

The latter half of the swinging sixties with its strongly defined youth culture and mood of protest against authority was an interesting time to take over the management of an 11-18 school. The first half of the decade had produced the mini-skirt and the contraceptive pill, Carnaby Street and a distinctive pop lifestyle, irreverent pirate radio stations and the scurrilous *Private Eye*. Nineteen sixty-seven was the year of flower power and hippy festivals, fuelled by LSD and serenaded by rock music. March 1968 saw the violent Grosvenor Square clash between police and anti-Vietnam-War demonstrators. Student protests and sit-ins were spreading throughout higher education institutions, and the National Union of Students – noted hitherto mainly for its organisation of cheap touring holidays – was, by 1968, a potent political force co-ordinating demands for student involvement in the running of their institutions. University students, whose excesses had previously been at the level of ritual pantie raids on girls' dorms and some over-exuberance during rag weeks, suddenly started behaving like anarchists and revolutionaries. Only a small minority were involved, of course, but the media conveyed the impression that youth protest was an all-pervasive force sweeping the country. Certainly the generation gap had significantly widened.

The most obvious way in which the sixties' youth culture impinged on Letchworth Grammar School was in the hirsute appearance of the older males. Boys' team photographs looked like pictures of Jesus and his disciples in a biblical play. This never became a contentious issue, as I simply couldn't get worked up about hair length. My ultra-short back-and-sides days in the Military Police had left me with a distinct predilection for longish hair, which remained with me for most of my life. At High View I answered to the name of Ted because of my Teddy Boy sideboards (although I always maintained that my carefully-nurtured whiskers were Dickensian rather than Edwardian).

The deep aversion that some young men had in the late sixties to having their hair cut was far more than a mere fashion statement: their hair was part of themselves and its removal as unacceptable as having their ears lopped off. Parents found this attitude difficult to tolerate, let alone understand. The father of one of our fourth-formers completely lost the plot one evening, wrestling his 15-year-old son to the floor and forcibly shearing his offending locks. The boy walked out and, as far as we knew, was never heard of again. His sudden departure reduced the school's number of what Claydon would have termed 'potential Oxbridge scholars'.

The other big manifestation of teenage rebellion was, of course, the way in which the young wanted to dress. Letchworth, the first garden city and home of many avant-garde thinkers, boasted one of the country's best-known 'progressive' schools and the St Christopher's youngsters responded extravagantly to the hippies' do-your-own-thing clarion call. They roamed the town in every conceivable form of fancy dress – Napoleonic army and navy uniforms,

190

flowing eastern robes, scanty leather-thonged garments. Their appearance aroused predictable adult prejudices and encouraged allegations of irresponsibility, promiscuity and lawlessness. A well-circulated, but no doubt apocryphal, story was that all police investigations of criminal activity in the town began with enquiries at St Christopher School. The progressive schools, like the new 1960s' universities, became victims of their own too keenly-publicised liberal philosophy, which attracted individualists and misfits of all persuasions and stimulated their natural inclination towards extremes of behaviour. It was no accident that Essex University led the way in student outrageousness, its Vice-Chancellor having trumpeted the institution's progressive approach and built up student expectations that couldn't be met.

A well-established school uniform enabled us to avoid most of the problems that can arise in schools over teenage fashions in dress. The only significant debate on clothing focused on the sixth form, whose members asked if they might be released from the requirement to wear uniform. This seemed an eminently reasonable request. We were conferring increasing adult responsibility on the 16-18 age group in numerous other ways, seeking their views on structures and routines, encouraging more initiative and decision-making, allowing them to revise at home in the weeks leading up to the O- and A-level exams. We took the sixth form transition from uniform to 'appropriate dress' quite slowly, discussing the pros and cons with the students and then instituting a six-month trial period before making the change permanent. It was a good opportunity for people to air their views on freedom and responsibility, the individual and the community, the relationship between sixth-formers and staff, and between senior pupils and the rest of the school. As a staff we tried to listen as well as pontificate. The transition, when it eventually came, was relatively painless: one non-conformist stubbornly retained his uniform for the

191

remainder of his sixth form days and inevitably there were a few who, after a while, sought to put the new boundaries to the test. There was little reaction from the younger pupils. No doubt the changed appearance of the sixth increased the desire of some of the middle school for a premature emergence from childhood and we had a few battles with girls over skirt length, but it was pretty innocuous stuff. They were co-operative and non-confrontational youngsters.

Not all parents, however, would have agreed with that assessment. There was no doubt that the prevailing youth culture intensified normal parent-teenager tensions and there were some spectacular family bust-ups when spirited rebelliousness clashed with expectations of unquestioning conformity to traditional standards of behaviour. Sometimes communication broke down completely. One 14-year-old was confined to her bedroom by her parents for a prolonged period, meals being placed outside her door. Her birthday came and went without any concessions or attempt at reconciliation. Elsewhere, families were learning the difficult art of compromise, talking through problems as they arose and seeking to resolve conflict through dialogue. Our own developing belief in this approach as a school prompted us to bring current manifestations of the generation gap out into the open. A team of staff devised a course for the sixth form on the subject of *The Family*, based on materials produced by the University of York General Studies Project.

There was no shortage of theories on the sixties' teenage phenomenon and when the local Rotarians produced a report on *Current Attitudes of Young People* they were invited to the school to meet senior pupils socially and to discuss the report's conclusions. Several evening meetings were held for parents and sixth-formers. The lower sixth hosted an event attended by 80 parents and 40 students at which some of the parents' association and members of staff chaired mixed adult and teenage groups in a discussion on *Trends in Adolescent Behaviour*. A more light-hearted evening produced a lively debate between two teams, one of parents and one of teenagers, to ascertain the extent to which the two generations understood how each other's minds worked. Adults played the rôle of teenagers whilst the students adopted the views of parents. There was a particularly spirited defence of the long-haired male by two fathers and an equally convincing performance by two female members of the students' team who, as mothers, stoutly resisted their daughters' arguments for attending an Isle of Wight pop festival. It was a great evening and excellently attended, but of course, as so often happens with parents' meetings, those who probably had most to learn from such an occasion were not present.

Parents felt the stigma of their children's bad behaviour more keenly in the sixties. One of our fifth-formers got into trouble with the police, having been a member of a group that went joy riding in a stolen car. The parents were devastated and within a few weeks had sold up their business in the High Street and left the area. Many years later I was watching a football match at the recreation ground in the Hampshire village in which I was then living and found myself standing near to three people whom I recognised immediately as Mr and Mrs Standen and their son, whose trouble with the police had long ago led to their hasty departure from Letchworth. I went up to them: 'Hello, John. Hello, Mr and Mrs Standen.' The look of complete incredulity and dismay that appeared on all three faces told me instantly that I should never have revealed myself. After a few mumbled exchanges they slunk away, presumably to pack and take renewed flight from the past.

Dropping out of the grammar school was a stigma that families wished to avoid at all costs and it was a rare occurrence at LGS before the O-level stage. Demotions to one of the secondary modern schools were virtually unknown and transfers the other way equally uncommon – the secondary modern schools were naturally loath to part with their ablest pupils, no matter how much they might justify a belated grammar school place. Thus, despite the rhetoric about opportunities for re-assessment, the classification of children at 11 as 'academic' or 'non-academic' was almost always final. This was nothing new: High View had had numerous pupils who clearly should have been in a grammar school, and there had been boys at both Sutton and Maidstone who would have been happier and more successful following a practical or technical course elsewhere.

One of our least successful and most troublesome fifth-formers had Saturday employment in the butcher's that my family patronised. I was fascinated by his consummate skills in the workplace, cutting bacon, trussing chickens, dealing with customers – all in marked contrast to his poor response to study. The school leaving age was still 15 in the sixties and occasionally we parted company with fifth-formers before they sat any external exams. I attended an open day with other Hertfordshire headteachers at a large aerospace factory in Stevenage. We were shown round by a very articulate, knowledgeable and personable young man, no doubt someone with manager potential who had been hand-picked to impress visitors. He was vaguely familiar, but it was quite some time before I recognised him as an ex-pupil whom I had expelled from the fifth form 18 months previously. People who malfunction in one context don't necessarily do so in another and formal schooling isn't the only route to success in life. Gainsborough played hookey and forged his father's signature on sick notes. Winston Churchill was no great shakes as a scholar and had three attempts at the entrance exam to Sandhurst.

We had a number of outstanding sportsmen and women at Letchworth who sought, with varying degrees of success, to

194

balance their academic and sporting commitments. Parents and teachers were inclined to be ambivalent in these situations, hoping that both scholarly and sporting aspirations could be realised. The situation varied with the individual, but when students had the ability and desire to compete at the highest level I inclined to the unpedagogical view that they should go all out to achieve their sporting ambitions. The chance to gain the highest honours in sport, if missed when young, is unlikely to recur, and this might become a lifelong regret. One can always return to study later in life. Better to get the sport thing out of one's system. No doubt my views on this subject have something to do with the admiration I have always felt for those with the dedication and determination to perfect a practical or technical skill, whether it be trussing a chicken or hitting an immaculate drive down the fairway.

There was an A-level student at LGS who had entered the sixth form at 16 from a secondary modern school and was, like the members of the 1940s' Shell form at the Royal Grammar School in High Wycombe, extremely keen to make the most of his belated academic opportunities. He was also a nationally-recognised athlete who thrilled us with his diving exhibitions at the school's annual swimming gala. He was a natural joker and there was an occasion when he held a high-board handstand, preparatory to plunging to the distant pool below, while he very slowly and deliberately bent one leg to scratch the other calf with his big toe. What need for A-levels when you have the bottle to do that? Chris made the right choice and took time out from his studies to ensure his place in the British team for the 1974 Olympics. He subsequently obtained a degree and PGCE and, when I looked round the secondary school that he now runs, I felt the same admiration for his headteaching accomplishments as I had done many years ago for his athletic prowess.

The relationship that teachers establish with many of

those whom they teach extends well beyond the school day and the years of school attendance. Schools take an interest and pride in the achievements of their pupils and ex-pupils that is second only to that of parents and close relatives. This was particularly so in Letchworth, where so many of the staff were long-established members of the local community. The heavy parental involvement in the school was also a factor: we were in regular contact with many families and got to know them really well. An increasing number of parents looked to the school for support and advice when they were having difficulties with their children at home.

Such requests for help were unpredictable and I was accustomed to receiving parental telephone calls at some fairly inconvenient times. Even so, I was somewhat taken aback one day in the summer holidays to have a father ring me up at 5.00 in the morning concerning an absent daughter. Normally this was well before the time of day when I was in a fit state for coherent conversation, but, by an odd co-incidence, I was already up and about on the morning in question: Jill had just informed me that her contractions were coming with increased frequency and we needed to set off to hospital without delay for the delivery of our third child. When the phone rang I was busy organising the other two sproggets, who were to accompany us on this early morning jaunt. I sensed, as I listened to my caller's tale of woe, that Jill's normal patience over the time I devoted to school affairs was quickly likely to wear thin on this occasion and that some ordering of priorities in favour of parental responsibilities would be appreciated.

As a head one suffers from being a minor local celebrity and, if one lives in the catchment area, privacy is virtually impossible. Our next-door neighbour in Letchworth was a house-and-garden maintenance fanatic. He was the only person I have ever known who painted the *inside* of his overflow pipes. Every morning at the crack of dawn he lit a neat little bonfire to dispose of any stray leaves and twigs that had encroached upon the immaculate lawns and dust free concrete paths during the night. A family of smartly turned out gnomes inhabited his front garden, grouped round an enormous concrete toadstool which was regularly re-painted, red with cream spots. Unfortunately, our houses were situated in a road that led to a local hostelry that was regularly frequented by members of the LGS sixth form and, if I rose at a sufficiently early hour in the morning and took the trouble to look out of the bedroom window, I was on occasions rewarded with the sight of my punctilious neighbour embracing his giant toadstool in a valiant attempt to remove it from the middle of our front lawn.

Some heads become very active in their local community, joining a host of committees and organisations. Others make an impact nationally; George Paul, for example, had received an MBE for absenting himself two or three days a week from High View in order to promote a national savings campaign. I never went down this route. The work in school was totally absorbing and I resented commitments that took me away from it: certainly I had no desire to be constantly gallivanting off to receptions, ceremonies, dignitaries' luncheons, union meetings and so on. There were, though, some responsibilities that unavoidably took me out of school. We had a close relationship with our junior and primary schools, which was partly a consequence of the LEA's 11+ strategy. Selection for the grammar schools in Hertfordshire was based on the recommendations of the children's teachers and headteachers. The grammar school heads acted as moderators for their own intake, visiting partner schools to discuss borderline candidates in an attempt to ensure a consistent standard of selection across the catchment area. No procedure can conceal the absurdity of classifying and segregating children at 11 into educational types, but the Hertfordshire system was at least less crude and manifestly flawed than the customary method of relying on a single day's written tests, without any reference to teachers' assessments or the children's day-to-day work in the classroom. I was impressed by the conscientiousness and objectivity with which schools carried out a potentially very tricky exercise.

There were, of course, difficulties. Whereas one-off written tests favour the bright, alert, confident children, and particularly those unphased by examination pressures, selection by recommendation gives more weight to qualities of conscientiousness, perseverance and consistency of application. A specific problem for a visitor trying to differentiate between borderline candidates on the basis of a brief assessment of written work was that the girls' exercise books were generally neater and more attractively presented than the boys'. Despite my efforts not to be over-impressed by appearances, girls nearly always outnumbered boys in the annual LGS intake of 11-year-olds.

The biggest challenge that I'd accepted with my Letchworth appointment was to oversee the transition of LGS to a comprehensive school. Hertfordshire was one of the first large LEAs to dispute the validity of the 11+ selection/rejection system and had already drawn up plans to reorganise its secondary schools along comprehensive lines before the Labour Government's 1965 circular required all LEAs to submit proposals to that end. The Hertfordshire scheme sought to provide a uniform countywide comprehensive system based on existing schools and to achieve this without the need for closures and staff redeployment. The timing of the transition was to vary according to circumstances in different parts of the county. The implementation of the LEA's plans in Letchworth was dependent upon new accommodation being provided for the grammar school staff and pupils on a larger site than the restricted space that the existing buildings occupied in the town square. Time slipped by without the necessary

198

funds being released and the secondary modern schools, all with enhanced facilities in readiness for their changed status, became increasingly restless at the delay. This situation was doubly frustrating for me: not only was I unable to undertake the key task for which I'd been appointed but, as head of the institution that was the stumbling block to progress, I felt cast in the unwelcome rôle of reactionary.

I no doubt exacerbated this situation by making it clear what I thought of a series of ill-conceived proposals, put forward by my headteacher colleagues, for reorganising before the conditions stipulated by the Authority had been satisfied. One suggestion was that the grammar school might go comprehensive on its restricted site – and without the additional practical accommodation that it would require – by admitting no pupils in alternate years and taking a full comprehensive intake every other year. There was no chance of the Authority's accepting such a hare-brained scheme and the wise reaction on my part would have been to say nothing and let such ideas die a natural death. But the public disclosure of such suggestions unsettled staff and undermined their faith in the LEA's efforts to ensure a smooth and efficient reorganisation process. I made it well known that I would not agree to a botched job. My first duty was to the school's current staff and pupils.

The comprehensive reorganisation having stalled in Letchworth, I began to scan the *Times Educational Supplement* for other possibilities. There was a new comprehensive school opening on the outskirts of Leicester, to be run on similar innovative lines as the infamous Countesthorpe, another institution that had courted trouble by too vigorously advertising its liberal and progressive intentions. The Leicestershire Authority had a good reputation, with a legendary CEO in charge who was renowned for his eccentric interviewing of applicants for headships. Waiting for our turn to lay claim to the Upper Wreake Valley post, the candidates shared suggestions for countering such alleged opening gambits as 'What is truth?' and 'There are fairies at the bottom of my garden.' In the event, I received only a mild googly: what original paintings did I have in my home? With three young children, we hadn't got round to amassing our collection of old masters; thus I had to register a nil return. The post went to the county's audio-visual aids and technology adviser — fair enough, as the school was to be a showcase in that area. Or – cynical thought – perhaps it had been set up and advertised in that way to accommodate the internal candidate. A lot of time can be spent at interviews just going through the motions for the sake of form.

My worst experience of that kind was some months later at Bishop Otter College of Education in Chichester. I had views on how teachers should be trained and when the principalship of Bishop Otter became available I was tempted and short-listed. The selection process was spread over a weekend: a tour of the site and separate meetings with the retiring principal, groups of staff and governors, members of the students' union. We were cosseted and cocktailed and on the Saturday night dined at High Table, a slightly unnerving experience against a background of student hubbub that contained a distinct element of insurrection. The formal interviews were held on the Sunday, culminating in a lengthy session with a committee of 12 governors, all of whom had questions to ask each candidate. Then at the end of an exhausting two days we were informed, for the first time, that the procedure we had been through was merely the first round; four of us, from the original eight, were invited back in a fortnight's time for another two-day exercise which would include an interview with the whole governing body. And this time we were to bring our spouses. Outcry. One of the four final-round candidates was moving house on the weekend in question. Another declared emphatically that she would never get her husband along. Baby-sitting was our particular problem: Jill had considerable difficulty persuading her elderly parents that they'd enjoy a weekend looking after their three lively young grandchildren. Despite their difficulties, the four candidates duly presented themselves, complete with spouses, for another two days of meetings, wining and dining, and interviews. At lunch on the final day we were joined by a professor of education, conspicuously spouseless, who had flown in that morning from Cape Town. A few hours later he was declared the new principal of Bishop Otter College.

I had no further interest in job seeking for about a year after the Bishop Otter experience. By then, however, I was becoming attracted to the sixth form college concept, and particularly the Hampshire LEA open-access model, designed to encourage all 16-year-olds to continue with their education beyond the statutory school leaving age. The county seemed genuine in its desire to break new ground and, when the principalship of Queen Mary's Basingstoke was advertised, the LEA sought applicants from all walks of life and included the captain of a ship on its short list. I would have been intrigued to see how the latter's maritime skills transferred to education had I not myself obtained the post. I took up the principalship of Queen Mary's in 1971.

The evening before my final day at Letchworth I was preparing for bed when it suddenly occurred to me that some of the pupils might decide to mark the end of my reign in some youthful way. Not wishing to bequeath to the school a resurrection of the old tradition of end-of-term pranks, I decided on a late-night recce of the premises. Having assured my wife of my sanity, I set off for the centre of the town, parked my car a few streets away from the school and climbed over the rear gate into the playground. A quick inspection of doors and windows revealed nothing untoward so I found a quiet corner where I could conceal myself whilst observing the rear of the building. It was a balmy summer's night full of the promise of the holiday ahead, but tinged with the sadness of my imminent departure. Musing upon such things, I found the time passing pleasantly enough and it was well after midnight before I conceded that I was wasting my time. I was just setting off across the playground when I detected the sound of subdued voices on the night air. Scuttling back to my vantage point, I resumed my vigil and, moments later, a file of shadowy figures rounded the end of the main school building carrying on their shoulders what looked like a giant cherry-picking ladder. After some whispered discussion, this was placed carefully against the rear of the building, tested for firmness and then ascended gingerly by the four figures, one of them carrying a large white bundle.

Letchworth Grammar School was an imposing two-storey building with a very high roof. It was some time before the young stevedores had reached the summit, attached their homemade banner to the town square side of the roof and begun their slow descent to the foot of the ladder where I was waiting. I felt a bit of a heel as I watched them repeat their perilous ascent to retrieve their elongated sheet, and even more so when I read the inscription on it – *We Luv Eric*.

The next morning in Assembly the pupils said their farewells. Appropriately, the spokesman was the leader of the previous night's gang of four. As he came forward to the edge of the stage, he was groping in the breast pocket of his jacket. 'I had a sheet here somewhere,' he said, apparently trying to locate his notes. A loud voice spoke up from the back of the hall, none other than Chris of the high diving board, 'I think you left it on the roof last night, Nick!' Judging from the school's reaction there was no-one who hadn't heard of the previous night's escapade. The silver tray with which I was presented was inscribed with the words *Discipulo Discipuli Sui* – 'To a Student from His Students'. It was a moment on which I have always looked back with intense pleasure.

# 16

## Bear Garden or Academic Factory?

The Hampshire reorganisation scheme completely changed the face of the county's secondary school provision in the space of a few years. With just one or two local variations, Hampshire decided on a system of 11-16 co-educational, comprehensive schools with sixth form education concentrated in open-access junior colleges. The greater autonomy enjoyed by today's schools would now preclude such a co-ordinated reorganisation of secondary education. Even in 1970 the Hampshire LEA encountered considerable opposition and the Basingstoke plans, in particular, were fiercely contested. There was major concern, not so much over the principle of comprehensive education, but with regard to the way in which it was being implemented locally and the upheaval that would be entailed. A highly-regarded girls' secondary school was to be phased out to provide accommodation for the junior college and each of the two grammar schools would lose its sixth form and absorb a neighbouring secondary modern. The demise of the Queen Mary's Boys' Grammar School was a particular cause for regret: the school had a proud tradition dating back to the mid-16$^{th}$ century, when Mary Tudor renewed the charter of a local religious guild and directed that a priest be appointed to instruct the boys of the town.

The strongest opposition to the Basingstoke scheme, however, came not from the oldest school in the town but the newest, a recently-formed bilateral whose governors and staff were greatly disappointed at the prospect of losing a sixth form that was non-existent but eagerly awaited. The head of this school was said to have had some experience of journalism and there was certainly a whiff of Fleet Street about some of the tactics employed by the protesters. The LEA officers were given a rough ride at a succession of local meetings and every one of their arguments and statements was taped and scrutinised for flaws and inconsistencies. The first intimation that I had of all this was the warmth of the officers' welcome when I arrived to relieve them of their public relations responsibilities.

There were a few other matters that required my attention. For example, advising on major additions and improvements to the accommodation inherited from the girls' secondary modern school, appointing the college staff, planning the curriculum and ordering equipment. Ideally these tasks would have been undertaken before I attempted to answer too many questions about the nature of Queen Mary's College, but that proved impossible. The LEA had stalled over giving details of the college's provision until the principal took up his appointment. With my arrival in the town, the expectation was that all would be revealed. The questions ranged from the basic to the bizarre. Querulous technology teacher: How many power points were envisaged for the classroom being converted into a design and technology workshop? Earnest parent: Would the extra-curricular activities include rifle shooting? I spoke at separate meetings to the governors, the staff, the parents and the senior pupils of each of the six schools due to become the college's partner comprehensives. Other groups requested an audience – subject panels, councillors, representatives of outlying rural schools. Bright-eyed and bushy-tailed, I pontificated about the sixth form college concept and devised policies on the hoof for the Basingstoke version.

In addition to the specific anxieties of individuals and groups at the sharp end of the reorganisation, two major but conflicting concerns surfaced at the meetings that I addressed. Traditionalists were troubled by the re-designation of schoolchildren as 'college students', a loaded term that suggested to them the relaxation of appropriate controls and restraints. The 'open-access' label was another red alert, implying the admission of all sorts of undesirables and an inevitable weakening of the single-minded grammar school focus on the needs of the most academically gifted. These two features of the sixth form college conjured up visions of a bear garden of permissiveness – drunken drop-outs prostrate in the rose beds, condom dispensers in the foyer and dope readily available in the student common room. On the other hand, some strong supporters of comprehensive education were very sceptical of the 'open-access' claim, fearing that the college would simply be an enlarged community of academic high-fliers, admission to which would be even more daunting for ex-11+ failures than it had been to the two grammar school sixth forms. There were serious doubts whether the college would have the will or expertise to meet the needs of a truly comprehensive intake. In refuting the extremes of unbridled licence and élitism and explaining how I saw the new system working, I began to shape the character of the college long before it opened.

The Hampshire LEA's decision to use the premises of a secondary modern school for the Basingstoke college proved fortuitous, even inspirational. It was assumed nationally that sixth form colleges would develop on the site of grammar schools, usually boys' schools with their impeccable academic traditions and time-honoured procedures. We had none of this baggage: the site for Queen Mary's College had no sixth form accommodation, courses or structures. Most significantly, with no sitting-tenants in the staff common room, I had the freedom to appoint staff who were excited by a new vision of post-16 provision. It was a unique opportunity to found a college on a set of principles that challenged conventional thinking about sixth form education – the curriculum, the learning experience, the relationship between teachers and learners, the organisational systems.

Arthur Claydon had been personally responsible for all staff appointments to Maidstone Grammar School and, when I became a head, I had simply assumed that this was the normal procedure. It was not until some time after I had taken up my post at Letchworth that I became aware of a few grumbles that neither education officers nor governors were ever involved in the staff interviewing procedure. When I moved to Basingstoke, I expected to continue my sole responsibility for staffing and no-one challenged this assumption. The LEA officers appeared to have had sufficient contact with the town to last them for quite a while and I didn't raise the matter with the governing body. The appointment of staff is the most important of a head's responsibilities and I guarded it jealously throughout my time at Queen Mary's College. I readily shared the task with professional colleagues and gave heads of department a big say in junior appointments; but, except for deputy principal posts, there were no interviewing panels of politicians, freemasons and local candlestick-makers.

Before reorganisation the LEA invited all Basingstoke secondary teachers to declare if they wished to be considered for a post in a particular institution within the new system. There were 81 applicants for a place in the college, nearly all of them from the three schools most affected by re-organisation –

the two grammar schools and the secondary modern designated for closure. I interviewed each of them and recommended 21 appointments to the Authority. Two features were a surprise to observers: the equal distribution of men and women and the appointment of six secondary modern teachers to head of department posts. It had been assumed that the bulk of the QMC staff would come from the boys' grammar school which, after all, was bequeathing its name, if not its premises, to the new college. A further 26 appointments were made following national advertisements.

Sixth form colleges interpreted the comprehensive principle in different ways – and they still do. In the early seventies the traditional image of the sixth form as an élite and privileged group of scholars led some educationists to regard even a slight relaxation of its exclusiveness as a sufficiently radical reform to merit the 'open-access' label. There were, therefore, 'comprehensive' colleges that merely extended their GCE A-level curriculum to give school leavers who had achieved only modest GCE O-level results a chance to improve their school qualifications, and perhaps make a late start on A-level courses. Others sought, in addition, to develop a range of pre-vocational courses for students unsuited to the GCE route to qualifications.

Queen Mary's took the term 'open-access' at its face value and offered a place to all who wished to continue their education beyond the age of 16. From the outset, students came from very different backgrounds, including remedial departments and special schools. For some – school refusers, the behaviourally difficult, those who had fallen well below their potential at school – the college provided an opportunity for a fresh start. There was a big intake from the independent sector, mostly youngsters who were kicking against archaic practices at second-rate private schools and causing parents to question the return they were getting for their considerable financial outlay.

The social mix was refreshing and the college looked to exploit its educational opportunities. We employed a familial model for the care system in which all students belonged to a tutor group with about 15 members, mixed in ability, age, sex and background. Initially four, and eventually six, senior tutors co-ordinated the pastoral care work of teams of 12 or more tutors. Tutor groups met twice a day and were, for many students, an important reference point and source of support and companionship. Groups went picnicking, ice-skating and tenpin bowling, visited the theatre and the coast, and occasionally spent a weekend together at the college's residential centre. They participated in inter-group sports tournaments and fund-raising initiatives for charity. The competition for the most ingenious tutor group entry in the annual fancy dress fun run was always keenly contested.

Before the college opened, I walked the miles of London-overspill council estates that were enveloping the small market town of Basingstoke and concluded that, for many of the teenagers who would be coming to QMC, this would be the final stage of their formal education and their only collegiate experience. I felt that it would be pleasant if the college could give them just a taste of the lifestyle that they would miss by not going to a university. This thought influenced several features of QMC, not least the freedom that students were given to choose how they spent part of their day – working in the library or one of the supervised or unsupervised study rooms, or socialising with their friends. One of my happiest memories of the college is of summer days when the grounds took on the appearance of a university campus with groups of students dotted across the lawns.

Tutor group lunch was another collegiate-style experience. Each day a different group lunched in the college's conference room with its personal tutor, senior tutor and either the principal or deputy principal. The meal was at a long, highly-polished boardroom table once used for Basingstoke town council meetings. Coffee was served in a lounge recess. It was a little bit of 'high table' style and formality that I hoped might stand students in good stead.

I enjoyed tutor group lunch and never tired of the occasion. It enabled me to meet all members of the college socially and to learn something of their interests and programmes of study. It was a good opportunity to speak to individuals about specific situations – to have a word with someone going through a bad patch; to comment on a recent musical or dramatic performance, a sporting achievement or academic success; or to get back on terms with a student whose only previous contact with me had not been of the congratulatory kind. There were frequent guests at tutor group lunch and it was one of several ways in which students could take a share in entertaining the college's many visitors. As at Letchworth, students were given every opportunity to represent the college to the outside world.

Tutor group lunch wasn't intended to be a threatening occasion, but it was no doubt a bit daunting first time round. Old hands enjoyed building up its aura and warning initiates of the rituals and pitfalls. A cardinal sin was to take the last banana from the fruit bowl if the principal hadn't already helped himself to his favourite fruit. Chocolate nutcake with custard was a legendary menu hazard: undue spoon pressure would discharge fragments across the table with devastating consequences for visitors in their best suits. Turnout was always at its smartest for tutor group lunch and sometimes students really dressed up for the occasion. One fine spring day all the young ladies came in delightful Easter bonnets. Occasionally a group prepared an entertainment or brought the lunchtime equivalent of after-eights to accompany the coffee. Attendance was high: cutting the occasion was regarded as very bad form, a breach of loyalty to the group and, more particularly, to one's tutor. There was a strong bond between most groups and their tutor.

Visitors to the college commented on the maturity of the students and the close relationship they had with both tutors and teachers. The college saw a major shift from didactic teaching to a participatory style of learning. Many of the courses, particularly those devised by the college itself, involved fieldwork and other off-site activities in which staff worked alongside students in a way that removed traditional barriers. A plethora of extra-curricular activities provided opportunities for students to take on management and administrative rôles. Staff joined the college choir and orchestra and participated in many of the sports activities, often partnering students in tennis, badminton, squash and table-tennis tournaments.

These features of the college all contributed to the more adult relationship between staff and students that is a natural consequence of separating the 16-19 age group from a school. Not everyone found this situation easy to handle at first. For most of us it entailed some adjustment to the way in which we related and spoke to those whom we taught. For some this was a slow process; others, young and inexperienced, went too fast, trying to establish rapport by invitation ('Call me Pete'), instead of allowing it to develop naturally out of mutual trust and respect. Students invariably react badly to that sort of thing.

First names gradually became the norm between staff and students. It took me a while to accept this situation and my instinctive reaction when students talked to me of Val or Gareth was to arch an eyebrow and say, 'Do you mean Mrs Tierney?' or 'Are you referring to Mr Thomas?' But I came to regard this feature of the college as a natural and attractive outcome of the good relationship that existed between students and staff. I was aware that, in conversation among themselves and with staff, students usually referred to me as Eric – or Big Eric.

One day I was in the college street, a wide thoroughfare that doubled as an exhibition area, when a student came bounding up to me and asked: 'Eric, will you sponsor me for the Basingstoke half-marathon?' I felt a glow of pleasure, a sudden sense of arrival: I was a *bona fide* member of the college, no longer just an authority figure. The remainder of the day was punctuated by a recurring image of an imaginary member of the Maidstone sixth form cheerfully hailing Claydon – 'Morning, Arthur.'

The kind of instinctive door-opening deference that Maidstonians showed their teachers didn't seem appropriate in a sixth form college. Nevertheless, I was determined that, in seizing new opportunities, we didn't automatically discard all the civilised and orderly qualities of a 'good school' like Maidstone. I talked a lot about 'community' and the courtesies and considerations that enabled people to work together towards a common purpose. The 16-19 age group, poised between childhood and adulthood, needed to exercise independence and responsibility, but within a supportive and structured environment where there were clear parameters and ground rules. Relationships, style, methods were all changing, but the rôle of staff continued to include the well-established schoolteacher's responsibility for providing sensitive pastoral care, exercising social control and communicating an agreed set of values.

Some applicants for sixth form college posts failed to understand that these dimensions to the job still applied. I made a mistake in appointing one young refugee from the school environment who was intellectually very impressive at interview but soon revealed that he had no interest in fitting into a community himself, let alone helping teenagers to do so. Arriving late and unkempt on his first day, he immediately fell foul of the caretaker who, spotting him mooching along the corridor with his backpack of personal effects, mistook him for a vagrant and ordered him off the premises. Later in the week, in the first 'college hour' of the new academic year, he created another diversion. College hour was a weekly gathering of the whole college which I normally chaired. It was customary for everyone to stand when I entered the assembly hall, but our new recruit to the staff common room remained ostentatiously in his seat. I asked to see him afterwards and, when he entered my room, I rose pointedly from my desk. I explained this idiosyncratic gesture to my new friend – the courtesy of showing those entering my room, staff or students, that I was stopping what I was doing and demonstrating that I was ready to give them my undivided attention. Nothing further was said and the young man managed to get painfully to his feet at subsequent college hours. It was not long, however, before he moved on to look for a less demanding environment.

The most problematic of the non-curricular demands made of QMC students were the dress regulations. Students had to be smart in their appearance, a requirement that ran counter to the trend in the burgeoning 16-19 colleges to give up the struggle against the jeans and sloppy t-shirt teenage culture. There were regular grumbles about the dress code, not least from staff who had, of course, to enforce it and – perhaps more significantly – by implication, to observe it themselves. Surprisingly, the students rarely challenged the principle of a dress code, but there were inevitably frequent skirmishes over interpretation. This led us down the slippery slope of subjective judgement on teenage fashion. The boys hadn't much room for manoeuvre – a collar and tie are a collar and tie – but there was an ongoing debate on what constituted smart trouserwear for girls. Jeans, ski-pants, pantaloons, leotards, shorts, pyjama and tracksuit bottoms were obvious non-starters, but that left plenty of other options for consideration. Maintaining the dress regulations was just one of the many responsibilities of the personal tutors: the trick was vigilance with a light touch – and a good store of Oxfam ties for forgetful males.

212

Some staff argued cogently that the dress regulations introduced an unhelpful ambivalence into the way we treated students – seeking opportunities for students to exercise adult responsibilities whilst laying down the law on how they dressed. There was a feeling that a college that had had the courage to challenge the Establishment's views on the curriculum and the ways in which it should be delivered ought not to be kow-towing to questionable middle-class conventions of dress. My argument, as always, was that there is no incongruity in a blend of freedom and responsibility, self-discipline and institutional control, and that the good impression our students' appearance and behaviour normally made on the general public helped to provide the goodwill and support that we needed in order to pursue our educational objectives.

It was generally assumed that my commitment to a smart turnout was all to do with public image. However, my first reason for wanting students to make an effort over their appearance was simply that a great deal of time, hard work and money had gone into providing them with an attractive and congenial environment – pleasant grounds, well-appointed teaching and social accommodation, non-institutional furnishings – and it seemed reasonable to expect them to make a contribution to the overall effect. Six months before QMC opened I visited a college in another part of the country that I understood had acquired substantial new accommodation furnished in a collegiate style. I was impressed by the provision, but not by the appearance of the place after six months' usage. Classroom partitions had been kicked in, tangled curtains trailed from broken runners, carpeting had been heavily pock-marked with black cigarette stub marks and – most depressingly – unwashed Geldorf look-alikes lolled in damaged armchairs with their bovver boots on the Ercol coffee tables. That wasn't my vision of a sixth form college.

# 17

# College Hour

College hour was a QMC initiative that became an institution, a weekly manifestation of the college as a community in which staff, students and visitors shared ideas, experiences and expertise and so furthered that most important of educational objectives – the widening of horizons. The occasion owed much to personal memories of the impact that certain one-off events had made on me when I was young.

Each term's college hour programme sought a balance between home-produced events and contributions from outside the college. Students talked about their fieldtrips, expeditions, work placements and community projects. They joined staff for panel discussions, formal debates and group presentations. The music and drama departments gave tasters of forthcoming public concerts and productions and there were numerous recitals and plays, and the occasional poetry reading. Staff reputations were made and lost in a series of Christmas pantos. Departments provided commentary on topical events and matters of general concern – environmental and political issues, natural disasters, scientific and technological developments. There were some memorable virtuoso presentations by individual members of staff who responded to the challenge of a 600-strong audience and an old-fashioned barn of a school hall with larger-than-life performances and eye-catching visual aids: a Rolf-Harris-style demonstration of painting techniques that covered a vast canvas stretching almost the width of the stage; a powerful representation of how the national economy works, employing pulleys and giant sacks; an entertaining introduction to scientific puzzles, paradoxes and party tricks, using everyday household articles.

Visiting speakers gave the college a great variety of vicarious experiences. They included a commander of a Polaris submarine and a newly-released convict, a zoo director and an ex-Japanese prisoner-of-war, a whistle-blower and a barge and roundabout decorator, the Editor of the Guinness Book of Records and the Chief Constables of London and of Northern Ireland. There were surgeons and psychiatrists; bishops and barristers; vets and environmentalists; farmers and physicians; politicians, poets and protesters; scientists, economists and therapists; TV directors, presenters, sports commentators; newspaper and magazine editors, paparazzi and war correspondents. The pattern of presentation varied: talks, panels, TV-style chats with the principal trying to out-Parkinson Parkinson, himself a visiting speaker. Some participants in college hour came in complementary or conflicting pairings, for example the founder of the London dungeon and a film censor discussed horror as entertainment, an Oxford don and a probation officer talked about privilege and deprivation. Ex-students described the transition to higher education and employment, their travels and research, their achievements and aspirations. Directors of major charities gave case studies of the work carried out by their organisations – Oxfam, Shelter, VSO, Community Service Volunteers, Amnesty International, Greenpeace, Friends of the Earth. Medical and social workers described their experiences rehabilitating prisoners, protecting battered wives, caring for the mentally ill, working with the blind and the deaf. Many health and social education issues – such as addiction to smoking, gambling, alcohol and drugs – were dealt with in this way.

There were a number of inspiring young people who made repeated visits to the college to speak with optimism and good humour of their personal disabilities. Neil Slatter, who was paralysed from the neck down as a result of a teenage motor-cycle accident, described his long battle to regain the use of his body and told of his personal campaign to raise public awareness of how much more could be done for the physically disabled. Beverly Ashton, who suffered from osteogenesis imperfecta, or brittle-bone disease, was very small physically – probably about two feet tall, had she been able to stand – but her big heart and indomitable spirit made up for her modest size. She spoke in a high piping voice and was a natural raconteur, quick to see the funny side of tribulations such as falling into the frying pan while cooking her breakfast or trying to park her specially-adapted but spectacularly-battered car. Bev's sense of humour and ready laugh added to her daily hazards as any convulsive movement of her tiny body risked fracturing her ribs.

College hour speakers opened students' eyes to lives and situations outside their own experience. People like Neil and Bev brought an added dimension, powerfully demonstrating the strength of the human spirit to overcome adversity and fulfil the potential we all possess to make something significant of our lives. Another young visitor who made a great impression on the students was Evelyn Glennie. She was just 19 when she made the first of several visits to play her marimba, glockenspiel and many other percussion instruments – and to talk about her profound deafness and the way in which she felt her music through vibrations in various parts of her body. She was a great favourite, a stunning performer and captivating speaker with her lilting Scots accent and warm personality. No-one doubted her future stardom.

Most of the musicians who performed in college hour were young – university and music college students, winners of the BBC Young Musician of the Year Competition, and our own rising stars who played for the National and European Youth Orchestras. Experienced professionals also performed, but the students responded most warmly to their contemporaries, who often brought a freshness and youthful enthusiasm to the occasion that not all their elders were able to emulate. There were also more practical considerations: even the 'small' fee of established soloists was often beyond our modest means. There were, however, some celebrated performers whose commitment to the musical education of the young meant that they required minimal payment. Gary Karr, the charismatic American double-bass player, included us in two of his European tours and Jack Brymer, principal clarinettist with the LSO for many years, made several visits. Both were big characters, full of fun and energy, who clearly enjoyed talking to young people as well as playing to them.

We exploited the college's strong representation in both the County and National Youth Orchestras to bring these talented orchestras to college hour. The National Youth Jazz Orchestra and the Royal College of Music Chamber Orchestra also gave concerts, both sponsored by local firms. Performances by the British All-Stars Jazz Band, led by the versatile Andy Dickens of the college's English and music departments, became something of a tradition. Gareth Thomas, charismatic head of drama, brought a steady stream of touring companies to the college theatre some of which performed in college hour in the afternoon before their public performance in the evening. There were also solo artists – actors, opera singers, dancers, mime artists and, on one occasion, an exponent of the art of stage fighting.

The college hall, with its high stage, wasn't the most congenial and intimate of settings for performers and speakers, and was particularly unsympathetic to panel discussions and chat sessions. Flexible and unobtrusive amplification wasn't around – or at least hadn't impinged on our consciousness – and stand-up-and-beg microphones, even if their squealing could be stifled, set their users even further apart from the audience. We experimented with different seating arrangements to close the gap between presenters and audience, using rostra to build a platform at the rear of the hall, or on the side with the chairs placed in an arc and some seating on the stage. Whatever the format, the occasion was always a challenge to those with a leading part to play. During an Any Questions discussion, Kathy Smallwood, ex-student and British athletics record holder at 100m, 200m and 400m, was asked if she felt nervous before a big race. 'Not as much as I am taking part in this college hour,' was her reply. She was in good company: the Right Honourable Lord Chief Justice Roskill admitted to 'a suspicion of panic' as he entered the hall to address the multitude.

College hour visitors were very well briefed. The letter of invitation spelt out the nature and purpose of the occasion; a subsequent phone call gave further details, and all speakers and individual performers were invited to tutor group lunch to meet students and get an impression of the college before their presentation. It was often quite difficult to dispel conventional images of the traditional sixth form and thus to dissuade speakers from coming armed with a few handouts or artefacts that they envisaged passing round a group of 30 or so young boffins gathered together in the library. It was also essential to establish the comprehensive nature of the audience. A challenge for most speakers was that, amidst the hundreds who would probably know little about their subject, there would be some able specialists in their field looking for explanations of complex problems. The students were never reticent when it came to asking questions.

Occasionally all my preparatory efforts were thwarted and then everything depended upon the skill and adaptability of the speaker. Lawrie McMenemy, legendary manager of Southampton FC, accepted an invitation to speak on *Man Management*, but proved to be wholly inaccessible in the weeks prior to his visit: his PA handled all correspondence, repeated attempts to contact him personally by phone were abortive, and he was unable to come for lunch. The big man arrived straight from the training ground and I met him in the car park where he emerged from his Jaguar with two minutes to spare before his talk. As we entered the packed hall and for the first time comprehended the nature of his assignment, he gave a classic Laurel and Hardy double take, straightened his guardsman's back, took a deep breath, and purposefully mounted the platform. No problem.

QMC students participating in college hour usually coped well. They didn't, of course, come to the situation cold: the college experience provided many opportunities for students to speak up for themselves and to develop the confidence required to meet the college hour challenge. They were also assured of a very sympathetic audience. Student speakers had a partial run through beforehand, mainly to ensure that they could be heard from all parts of the hall. Panels gave some preliminary thought to the areas for discussion, but didn't rehearse answers to specific questions: spontaneity was more important than perfect presentation. For the same reason I cajoled and bullied student speakers not to write their talks out beforehand or to use extensive notes, but to rely on a few headings as a reminder of what they wanted to say. They were apprehensive of this policy, but invariably communicated more naturally and effectively using speech forms and rhythms, rather than the written conventions and formalities that take over when one reads from a script or tries to recall a prepared speech verbatim. The occasional irregularities and stumbles that creep into an unscripted talk are a natural and acceptable part of oral presentation and a small price to pay for its greater directness and immediacy.

Visitors were more problematic than students. My aim was to confine invitations to those of whom I had personal foreknowledge or, failing that, people who were strongly recommended by a member of staff or someone else who understood the precise nature and purpose of the college hour event. Deviation from this policy was highly risky, but occasionally unavoidable. An example, etched permanently on my mind, was *Costumes through the Ages*, an illustrated talk and demonstration that resulted from a last-minute re-arrangement. In retrospect the topic had 'loser' written all over it, but I must have been seduced by the accolades quoted in the advertising literature. The event did, in fact, live up to its billing as 'a highly original and entertaining presentation', but not quite in the way one would have wished. It was a one-woman performance, an ambitious combination of lecture, slide show, fashion display and tantalising strip-tease, the presenter changing costumes on the stage to the accompaniment of recorded zither music. Initially intrigued, the college became increasingly diverted by the performer's efforts to struggle from one voluminous garment to another. The diversions and incidentals became the main focus of attention: the constant hazard of trailing leads from the amplifying and projection equipment, the phallic shadows flashed across the screen by a hand-held mike, the *double-entendres* that peppered the commentary ('Henry VIII was very fond of music and went touring the countryside looking for talent.') Each costume, once donned, was presented with a simpering curtsy and greeted with increasingly uninhibited enthusiasm by the audience. The final curtain came down to tumultuous applause for 'my impression of Her Majesty Queen Elizabeth II', presented against a background slide of the Royal corgies sniffing at the feet of a family group gathered on the lawn in front of Windsor Castle. My mounting concern throughout this remarkable entertainment was what precisely I would say to the lady afterwards when she joined me in my room for much-needed tea and biscuits. Fortunately she made it easy for me. 'They sent me up, didn't they?' she said. I could only agree and we chatted amicably enough before she went on her way, vowing no doubt to keep to townswomen's guilds and the WI in future.

None of us ever knew quite what to expect from college hour. One very warm afternoon we screened a road safety film aimed at making all road users aware of the vulnerability of motorcyclists. Compared to the hard-hitting drink/driving warnings to which we are now all accustomed as part of TV's pre-Christmas routine, it was mild fare. However, one or two girls fainted at the close-ups of blood and carnage and this had a domino effect on others – male and female. Audience casualties exceeded those on the screen and unconscious bodies had to be carried from the hall and laid out in rows on the grass outside.

Very successful college hours created a buzz in college and were recalled long after the event. The same, however, was true of disasters. The sharing of a spectacular failure had a particularly strong bonding effect, rather as communities are united by adversity during times of war. 'The man from the AA' who gave a mind-numbingly boring talk on *The Future of the Motor Car* became a legendary figure and featured in numerous apocryphal stories that survived long after the students who had lived through the reality had left college.

As the college hour programme became increasingly ambitious we sought speakers who were important protagonists in national events. Unfortunately, as I had discovered at Letchworth, those who fell into this category were busy people who required at least six months' notice of a speaking engagement, by which time red-hot issues had often cooled. Sometimes, however, the timing of a visit proved to be even more relevant than when the invitation had been made. Dick Taverne QC, key backroom boy for the 'gang of four' who formed the Social Democrat Party in 1981, spoke on *The Realignment of Political Parties* on the actual day that the new party launched its campaign in the national press.

We had a succession of fortuitous timings in that particular year. It was a period of very fraught employer/union relationships and Joe Gormley, President of the NUM, spoke of how he agonised over the power he had to bring the Government down during a very acrimonious miners' strike. When he arrived I was taken aback by his elderliness and lack of physical presence: he seemed utterly exhausted, a little old man who was almost inaudible in conversation during tutor group lunch. I sensed a non-event approaching. However, once in front of the college, he was a totally different character, speaking with a strength and passion that would have done justice to an outdoor rally of the full NUM membership.

The car workers were striking at much the same time as the miners and Andy Barr, Manufacturing Operations Director of Austin Rover, came to give an employer's angle on the industrial unrest. He looked precisely what he was: a formidable, no-nonsense, hands-on leader who came straight from addressing a shop floor meeting of the workforce at the Cowley Plant in Oxford. I remember his visit particularly well for he was so horrified that I drove a Ford that he offered to sell me a demonstration Austin Princess at a knockdown price. Financial perks being a somewhat rare phenomenon in the teaching profession, I accepted gratefully.

In view of their preoccupation with weightier matters, any one of these speakers would have been fully justified in cancelling his visit, yet they all kept their engagement. I was impressed and encouraged by the willingness of very busy people to give up their time to help the college to further one of its educational ideals. Katherine Whitehorn commented in one of her *Sunday Observer* columns that an invitation to speak in QMC's college hour was a summons that could not be ignored. Not actually true, for I wrote many abortive letters of invitation. But, once an engagement had been accepted, people honoured the commitment, regardless of the pressures they were under on the day.

High profile visitors often came with a member of their staff or companion – a chauffeur, PA, wife, or even a mistress. Cabinet ministers, high court judges and chief constables sometimes had a police escort. Manchester's controversial Chief Constable, James Anderton, visited the college in 1989 shortly after his infamous comments on gays and Aids. His armed bodyguard was particularly punctilious, thoroughly casing the joint and parking the Chief Constable's car on a lawn overlooked by the room where tutor group lunch was held. Five minutes before college hour, a phone caller informed the college office that an explosive device had been placed on the premises. I asked James Anderton if he thought we should evacuate the buildings. 'Your decision,' he replied. My normal policy was, I explained, to ignore such calls. 'Fine,' he said, and we made our way to the hall. My unresponsive attitude towards bomb-planting claimants stemmed from my antipathy to any disruption of the normal life of the college – and the evidence from other educational establishments was that, once you gave in to the hoaxers, they had you turning out several times a week. More to the point, I had concluded that, in the event of a genuine terrorist attack, short-term evacuation would be a spurious safety measure: it would, according to the local police, have taken three days to make absolutely sure that the college's 25 buildings were completely bomb-free.

I had no qualms over bringing controversial public figures to the college, although I did get my fingers burnt over this policy on one occasion. Oddly, it was an invitation to Shirley Williams that caused the problem. I say 'oddly' because Shirley was such a respectable and respected public figure, admired by people of all political persuasions, that she hardly came into the contentious category of visitor. At the time that she agreed to come to the college, she was Secretary of State for Education, but we plotted to keep the visit very low key: she would arrive, not quite incognito, but without prior announcement, so that she would see the college as it was and without the media in attendance. I made one mistake, however: bearing in mind her position, I felt it only courteous to inform the education authority of her visit. The response was immediate. The invitation was to be withdrawn. It would be reinstated at a later date as an invitation from the (Conservative) County Council for Mrs Williams to visit the LEA. This alternative was, of course, never implemented, but an unequivocal letter was sent by the Chief Education Officer to all Hampshire heads and principals to the effect that in no circumstances were they ever to take unilateral action by inviting public figures to their schools and colleges. I kept my head down for a while after this, but then ignored the injunction – as I am afraid I did a number of the Authority's directives.

Powerful speakers inevitably aroused strong feelings in college and few visitors came and went without a complaint from someone that they were too left-wing or too right-wing, too feminist or male chauvinist, too pro this or anti that. Objectors were rarely satisfied by reassurances that, over a term, speakers would represent a balance of views. Evaluation of the college hour programmes showed how widely both staff and students differed over what they considered a successful occasion. It was not uncommon for one person's best event to be recorded as another's worst. The Barrow Poets'

224

programmes of music, poetry and original comic verse were always greatly enjoyed by almost everyone, but after one of their performances I received a strongly-worded protest from a deputation of about 25 students objecting to a piece of doggerel featuring the Angel Gabriel on the telephone. Conversely, an obscenity-filled *Christmas Entertainment in the Workhouse*, by the appropriately-named Incubus company, embarrassed or offended nearly all of us, yet was considered by some to be an excellent production.

The occupational hazards of college hour increased when the college became too large to cram everyone into the hall so that we had to introduce an arrangement whereby three senior tutor groups attended one week and the other three the next. Every effort was made to give the two halves of the college equivalent programmes and some visitors were sufficiently public-spirited to speak or perform on two consecutive weeks. However, it proved impossible to ensure that the two programmes matched precisely and I had to steel myself to resist heart-rending pleas, from both staff and students, for them to attend out of turn, because they had a keen interest in a particular occasion that was not being repeated for their half of the college. This situation led to a request that college hour should be voluntary, people attending the events that appealed to them and not being required to go to those in which they were not interested. I was adamant that this ran counter to the main purpose of the occasion – to introduce students to people, events, ideas and experiences that they would not normally choose to encounter.

It is, of course, important for a school or college to feed its students' interests and to deepen their understanding and expertise in their chosen specialist areas. Such provision will include many different optional extra-curricular activities and events – musical, sporting and dramatic activities; one-off lectures, conferences, debates; extended projects for scientists and engineers; simulation and problem-solving exercises for economists and environmentalists; foreign culture and language days for linguists; craft fairs and exhibitions for artists; clubs and societies catering for all sorts of minority interests. It is also the rôle of educationists to open people's eyes to new experiences, to introduce them to the sheer width of human activity, endeavour and knowledge and the variety of ways in which individuals can enhance their quality of life. The college hour experience helped in a small way to further that aim and to emphasise the college's commitment to general education. I suppose I took part in or attended some 700 events. Combined with the planning, preparation and correspondence entailed, this represented a sizeable commitment of time and effort. I never had cause to regret that investment.

18

A Look on the Face

Non-examined general studies were a feature of most sixth forms in the early seventies, an attempt to leaven the lump of specialist examination work. They often took the form of activities afternoons during which altruistic staff sought to convey their enthusiasm for such middle-aged and middle-class hobbies as photography, birdwatching and archaeology. Wine-making was a popular option. Some schools drew up a more ambitious programme of full-length courses spread throughout the week. Timetabling, however, was usually a problem. Letchworth had an impressive range of general studies on paper, but the reality was that many students found the options they chose inaccessible because they were taught at the same time as some of their exam classes. One of the original arguments in favour of concentrating sixth form provision in 16-19 colleges was that the replication of courses resulting from large student numbers would create timetabling flexibility and more meaningful student choice. This applied to non-exam as well as exam courses and all the sixth form colleges developed a general studies programme. However, the rôle and status of this part of the curriculum varied from college to college, as indicated by the variety of designations employed: additional studies, complementary studies, extension studies, support studies. The QMC variant was Main Studies, the upper case being deliberate.

The name intrigued, puzzled and sometimes annoyed people when they were confronted with it. This was useful, for we were constantly called upon to explain and justify the term, thereby clarifying our curricular thinking and reaffirming our faith in what we were trying to do. The explanation went something like this. Main Studies were central to the college's commitment to a liberal education designed to help young people develop into rounded and generally well-educated adults. They were a challenge to the 'wet Friday afternoon' image of general studies, a serious attempt to broaden the curriculum and counteract the ill effects of what C P Snow, eminent scientist and novelist, called 'the fanatical English belief in educational specialisation'.

There were over 50 Main Study courses, all of them one year in length. Students studied two or three a year, sometimes more. They enabled scientists to maintain contact with the arts, and arts students to continue studying science, a crossing of disciplines that was actively encouraged. The programme included many aspects of human knowledge and experience that were normally sidelined in the sixth form, or excluded altogether – social, political and environmental issues, all kinds of creative and practical work, vocational courses. Students were introduced to new ways of learning, using resource packs, case studies, simulation exercises, projects and business games. More time was spent out of the classroom, taking advantage of the locality as a resource and making contact with its community. When Main Studies were combined with all the other contributions to students' general education – their social and extra-curricular activities, games sessions, tutor time and college hour – the specialist academic studies were no longer seen to dominate the week. Exam classes had miraculously become 'minority time'.

Like most deviant behaviour, the college's upside-down thinking on the rôle of general education attracted a good deal of attention, some of it beneficial, some less so. Delegations descended on the college from Havering to Hobart, Rowley Regis to Reykjavik. A study group from the House of Commons took interminable notes; Japanese educationists took interminable photographs. What developments resulted from these visitations, I don't know, but I did hear that one sixth form college visitor returned to his establishment fired with enthusiasm, only to be told by his boss that Queen Mary's College was an aberration and its principal a nutcase. The first observation was probably correct, but I took exception to the second.

QMC's commitment to Main Studies inevitably led to a reduction in the normal time allocation for each exam course, including all A-levels. Also senior tutors discouraged college applicants from committing themselves to more examination subjects than were absolutely necessary to support their career aims. Some parents of prospective entrants took fright at these policies and put their offspring on a fast train to Winchester, where the county's sixth form provision observed traditional priorities. We lost out on several academic high-fliers in this way, but coincidentally gained a number of interesting replacements from unexpected sources: a mature Marlborough head of house and captain of rugby seeking improved A-level grades for entry to medical school, an Etonian wishing to escape from the shadow of an all-conquering elder brother at the same school, a manifestly able Wykehamist whose extra-mural activities had brought his public school career to a premature end.

Fortunately the college's commitment to general education

229

was no deterrent to gifted job seekers. The notices in the educational press inviting applications for Main Studies teachers attracted large and very able fields. But then we did mention in an aside that, in addition to Main Studies, successful applicants would be expected to teach exam classes up to and including A-level. The staff appointed to lead the college's curricular initiatives included the head of Russian at Manchester Grammar School, a canon from Southwark Cathedral, an engineer with teaching experience in Africa and the East End, and a lecturer in social education from York University. These directors of study set the pace for curricular innovation. They took the Main Studies idea and ran with it. They were ably supported by some inspirational teachers in their teams and succeeded by other impressive leaders when they moved on. But initially it was *their* intellectual firepower that won the educational debate and silenced the doubters.

Main Studies offered exciting opportunities to further more ambitious educational ideals than preparing students for certification. They also created a great deal of work: staff designed the courses, produced the resources and decided on the most appropriate teaching and learning strategies. Exams and qualifications are, of course, the driving force behind the secondary school curriculum. Thus teaching Main Studies entailed inculcating a new set of values and expectations: we were asking students to commit themselves to learning for its own sake, a considerable challenge to teachers' enthusiasm, intelligence and creativity. Staff had to fire on all cylinders, constantly evaluating their work, reacting to student response and feedback, refining course content, producing up-to-date materials, deciding which learning situations worked best.

Some educationists were simply unable to envisage such a significant rôle for the non-examined curriculum at sixth form level. 'How do you know if students are getting anything from a Main Study course, if there's no exam?' asked one sceptic at a conference addressed by Tony Reaney, the Director of the College's Scientific and Technological Studies Area. 'By the look on their face,' was the immediate reply. It wasn't as flip an answer as it might have seemed. Teachers can grind a laborious path through an arid examination syllabus and students will keep going, motivated by the exam and hoping that their suffering will be rewarded by certification. The situation is very different with non-exam courses. If students weren't manifestly enjoying their Main Studies and showing by their day-to-day response that they were finding them intrinsically worthwhile, then they soon began to vote with their feet. I learnt a lot about QMC teachers from whether or not they could maintain the momentum of their Main Study courses and retain students' interest right to the end of the academic year.

Main Studies created a need for a much more diverse staff than was usual in the sixth form. Attending my first meeting of Hampshire college principals I happened to mention that I had appointed a drama teacher to the college: the amazement of my colleagues was probably the beginning of my reputation as a bit of a weirdo. Within a few years we had a drama department with three full-time staff; I believe there are now six, plus two dance specialists. The drama department's Main Study courses – *Improvisation, Drama with Children, Theatre Arts* and *Technical Workshop* – were among the most popular, and the most demanding, of the college courses. There were years when a quarter of the student population studied *Theatre Arts*, which had the same weekly time allocation as an A-level and also required a major evening commitment towards the end of the year when groups prepared their work for public performance. Students scripted their own shows, composed the music, designed the costumes and sets. The course bred a very strong work ethic and group dynamic. I didn't normally have a problem in communicating with students, but a notable exception was an occasion when I attempted to explain to an

231

habitual non-conformist that we had to part company. He was stunned, not by the fact of his expulsion, but by the implications: he simply couldn't leave college, he said, as he was a member of a *Theatre Arts* group preparing for its end-of-year production.

Group loyalty and the desire to pull one's weight in a team effort can be very strong motivators. QMC's *Out of Bounds* Main Study was a problem-solving course in which the group worked together to extend their mental and physical capabilities in unfamiliar situations. It produced something akin to the team spirit that I had experienced many years earlier during military training. One bitter winter's day the *Out of Bounds* students gathered at the start of the paratroopers' notorious assault course in Aldershot. The hoar-frost clung to the tops of the barriers and the ice-veneered water jumps looked particularly uninviting. The sergeant, in an unaccustomed act of compassion, announced a concession for the young ladies – one circuit only (two for the men). There was a straightening of backs in the ranks and the NCO was politely disabused of his male chauvinism: every member of the group completed two circuits.

Exams motivate students to individual achievement. Many Main Studies replaced personal goals with group objectives – a presentation, performance or exhibition, a community project or research group's report, the making of a video. Students learnt the skills and satisfactions of working as a team. The ability to function effectively with other people is a fundamental requirement of adult life, yet few young people are prepared for this by their formal education. Some vocational courses provide opportunities for co-operative group work, but the academic curriculum places the emphasis unequivocally on individual competition and achievement. Anyone who wonders why there are so many divisions in our society, so little understanding or consideration of other people's needs, situations and viewpoint, so many examples of people doing each other down, should perhaps take a hard look at the obsessive self-interest that our educational system fosters in children as they compete daily to outperform their peers.

As the college developed its Main Study expertise, the courses became more ambitious and challenging. One-off projects led to ongoing assignments. Simulation gave way to real business ventures and services to the community. *The Project Technology* group designed equipment for the physically handicapped. The *Queen Mary Enterprise* company, run entirely by students, was a profit-making business with shareholders and a democratically elected management team. Students were responsible for the purchase of raw materials, the manufacturing process and the sale of goods. Another pioneering project, *Grapevine*, which evolved from a Main Study computing course, provided Basingstoke with its first electronic information service. With council funding, the students produced a 10,000-item videotext, available at 12 access points in the town and accessible in the home to those with compatible equipment. Students researched all the information and updated the text daily. It sounds old hat now, but this was in the seventies. Such Main Studies entailed an ongoing commitment with real outcomes, the significance and importance of which were obvious to participating students.

Boosted by the heavy demands of the Main Studies curriculum, the creative studies subject area outgrew the dilapidated army huts in which most of its departments were housed. When a health and safety officers' inspection declared the latter unsafe for use, funds were made available for a building programme. In a rash moment the LEA officer in charge of building development suggested that I might wish to produce some sketches of the kind of accommodation that we would like. Pipedream time. There emerged an elaborate set of scale drawings for a building not dissimilar in its shape and dimensions to the Albert Hall. The focal point was a multi-purpose central hall for performances, lectures and exhibitions, ringed by a plethora of studios and workshops, all with rear access directly into the central space and glass frontages opening out onto attractive patios. Art, photography, pottery, design, music, dance, drama, all were to be generously accommodated and serviced – at least, in my imagination. The reality was rather more modest. And yet still impressive. The circular design was retained and also the central performance area – in the form of a small recital hall/theatre-in-the-round. This was surrounded by teaching spaces and practice rooms for music and drama. Art and pottery studios were added at a later date in an extension that linked the creative studies and science/technology faculties. There were mixed emotions when the 'central studio' opened in 1978 and the music and drama departments said farewell to their makeshift homes, where so much creativity and ingenuity had gone into solving the problems of confined space. The passing of an era was signalled by the departure of the drama hut's ex-cinema lighting equipment, which now resumed its interrupted journey to the local rubbish dump.

Programmed by the music and drama departments, the college's central studio added a new dimension to the region's arts provision, catering specifically for the student age group and a variety of minority interests – early English music, jazz, modern dance, fringe theatre, poetry, performing arts from other cultures. There were master classes for the musicians, workshops for English and drama students, dance residencies for anyone interested. The combination of professional and student performance occupied 100 evenings a year and attracted sponsorship from the local and county councils, industry and the Arts Council. The central studio thrived and paved the way for a much more ambitious college/community co-operative exercise, the 'regional centre', which sought to link all parts of the college curriculum with local interest groups through an extra-mural programme of seminars, talks, conferences, exhibitions, workshops and numerous one-off events.

The central studio was run by teachers and students. They managed the programme and publicity, manned and womanned the box office, provided all the front of house services, ran a small refreshment bar, and agitated for me to apply for an alcohol licence. Two Main Study *Technical Workshop* groups serviced the programme of student recitals, concerts and theatrical productions and also supported numerous extra-curricular clubs and societies. Eventually the growth of the central studio's activities required the appointment of full-time administrative and technical staff. Several of those appointed, both initially and in subsequent years, were ex-*Technical Workshop* students. Similarly, an administrator was appointed to the *Grapevine* project, an ex-student who deferred her university place to take up the post. *Theatre Workshop* and *Grapevine* weren't envisaged as vocational courses, but for some students they certainly fulfilled that purpose.

Academic study and vocational training have always been seen as separate forms of educational activity, but Main Studies enabled QMC students to combine the two. Options such as *Learning with Children, Working in Administration* and *Careers in Social Care* all linked classroom studies to work experience. The *Learning with Children* Main Study course was particularly popular and each year required as many as 80 placements a week in local primary and junior schools. A primary school teacher was seconded to assist with the college-based component of the course which provided students with an opportunity – not offered by my Borough Road course 20 years previously – to analyse and evaluate their classroom experiences in a systematic way. About 50% of the *Learning with Children* students went directly from college into teacher training; many others trained to teach after graduating. A fascinating college hour consisted of a demonstration lesson

235

by a *Learning with Children* student who would, presumably, always remember the unique experience of having her teaching observed by an audience of 600.

Most Main Studies gave students a totally different learning environment and experience from that offered by the examined curriculum. However, there was no lack of opportunity for those who wanted their Main Studies to offer a comparable intellectual challenge and academic rigour to that of A-level, although usually in a different subject area. The social studies faculty, in particular, offered a range of thought-provoking Main Studies in the form of discussion-based options on specific themes such as *Man in Society*, *The Family* and a (disturbingly popular) course in *Crime*. In the early days of the college, all second-year students followed a moral and social education course, *Outlook* (or *Lookout*, as the students called it), which was later replaced by an option on *Understanding Human Behaviour*. Some of these courses owed their existence to work undertaken by a Schools Council project team based at York University, which provided substantial packs of resource material. As these became out-of-date and lost their immediacy, staff produced their own replacements, supported by a fast-developing college resources centre. Main Studies were constantly evolving and our evaluation and monitoring procedures became increasingly rigorous. A 'limited life' rule was introduced so that, no matter how successful a course was, it came off the curriculum after five years. It was very important to keep the options fresh and up-to-date, and to create space for new initiatives.

Main Studies were pivotal to our work in QMC. They concentrated our attention on the key aspects of the educational process: course design, provision of resources, learning and teaching methods. There was constant discussion on the nature of education, what constituted an appropriate curriculum and how best to deliver it. This was what I most missed when I left

QMC: none of the four universities in which I subsequently worked produced anything like the same intellectual level of staff debate.

The Main Studies effort had a major impact upon the rest of our work, sometimes in quite unexpected ways. Perhaps the most significant of these was the effect of the reduced time available for exam courses. Some observers had expected this feature of college to have dire consequences, but there has never been any convincing evidence that students' learning is enhanced in proportion to the amount of time they are taught. Indeed, the QMC experience seemed to suggest that the opposite might well be true. There simply wasn't time for QMC teachers to talk their way through an exam syllabus: they had to focus on quality not quantity, on finding ways to motivate students and showing them how to master the essential processes of their specialisms. In short, there had to be a significant shift from teaching to learning. Students had to assume more responsibility for their academic progress. They had to learn how to think critically, how to access, analyse and use information appropriately, how to hypothesise, synthesise and express themselves. We knew that critics of our approach to learning were waiting to see the college's first set of examination results. We never heard from them. And no-one subsequently had grounds for commenting adversely on the performance of QMC students in public exams.

# 19

## We Shall Keep A-levels

The stimulus given to course design by QMC's Main Study programme sharpened the college's awareness of the inadequacies of the prevailing examined curriculum. We chafed at the restrictive syllabuses, the aridity of so much GCE work and the over-bookish nature of early attempts to provide suitable courses for non-academic students. We shopped around the exam boards for the least unimaginative offerings and sought to be involved in all county and national initiatives to improve 16-19 provision. Where nothing seemed to be happening, we tried to initiate change ourselves.

The designing of a new A-level French syllabus was an early example of the kind of reforms in which the staff were interested. A-level language syllabuses, including those in English, focused not on language but on literature, and of course the literature of the past: candidates studied a country's literary heritage. A questionnaire given to A-level French groups who were halfway through their college course revealed that this approach was relevant to just one of the 28 students: she wanted to go to university to follow the traditional French (literature) degree course for which the various examining boards' A-level French syllabuses were designed as a preparation. Three other students were considering studying French at university, but not in its conventional form. Their interest was in using the French language in their career; two were considering a combined French and business studies degree. The remaining 24 students were either hoping to read one of their other subjects in higher education or intending to go directly from college into employment. A course in spoken French would have given these students a valuable skill for the future, opening up career possibilities or, at least, proving useful when holidaying on the continent. None of the existing A-level syllabuses, however, was concerned with anything so practical. The purists would no doubt argue that a facility to read French classics in the original was intrinsically rewarding, but there seemed little prospect of the questionnaire respondents benefiting in this way: most of them stated that they found no time to read *any* literature for pleasure – English or French, ancient or modern.

The French department devised an A-level course that was relevant to our students. It was a language course with an optional literature module for the 4% for whom this might be relevant. Other colleges became interested and supported the submission of the syllabus to the Schools Council. The first students sat for the new exam, offered by the Southern Universities Examination Board, in 1977. The head of French subsequently joined representatives from other colleges and a number of university departments to draw up proposals for a nationwide reform of sixth form French syllabuses. Within a decade the study of language became an A-level option in all the main European languages, including English. The college pressed, with some success, for greater flexibility and relevance in a range of A-levels: the introduction of open-book exam papers, a greater rôle for coursework and practical assignments, more emphasis on understanding concepts and processes and less on memorising facts. The college's expertise in these areas was acknowledged in the secondment of a number of staff to produce materials for new A-level syllabuses.

A perennial concern for me personally was the fragmented nature of students' programmes of study. The subject approach to education has always troubled me. Its effect is to divorce much of what we do in schools, colleges and universities from real life, where experience comes to us not as 'physics', 'geography' or 'biology', but in practical situations that combine many different influences. We pay a heavy price for the convenience of packaging human knowledge and experience into neatly-labelled containers. The subject approach to teaching and learning creates artificial barriers and divisions. In its pure academic form the subject becomes a 'specialism', cultivating its own language, mystique and aura of exclusivity. Children emerge from being sheep-dipped into these artificial academic experiences with very little understanding of the way they connect with each other or impinge on the actual world in which we all live. They accept the process as part of growing up, but don't find it particularly helpful in clarifying the situations that they encounter every day outside school. Even when A-level combinations appear to offer a coherent educational experience, for example three languages or three sciences, the opportunity for a unified approach is more apparent than real. Students follow discrete, self-contained syllabuses taught by different specialists in classes whose members are taking different combinations of subject, each with its own set of connections and transferences.

QMC tried to address this problem in a number of ways. The faculty system helped to break down barriers between related subjects, staff being encouraged to teach more than one examination subject and, of course, to point up the connections between them. However, in forging strong links between their departments, faculties inevitably built ring fences round certain groups of subjects. These had then to be dismantled and fresh groupings created.

All the new buildings that we acquired were single-storey in order to facilitate communication between closely-related departments. This worked particularly well in the science faculty where physics and chemistry were merged into a physical sciences department. Social studies ran an integratory course to explore the common ground between subjects for all students who took two or more options within the faculty. Main Studies often cut across traditional subject barriers and were generally conceived as a means of teaching transferable skills; many were designed, resourced and taught by teams of staff drawn from different subject areas. These developments, taken together, represented a strong statement on the need for a more unified approach to sixth form teaching and learning.

Most of our curricular initiatives in QMC entailed finding ways round the serious limitations of the GCE A-level system. We were one of many voices clamouring for a complete overhaul of the sixth form curriculum, but, as C P Snow had famously remarked in 1959, although nearly everyone believed that the British educational system was far too specialised and exclusive, it appeared to be beyond the collective will to do anything about it. Snow's condemnation of the system focused on the arts/science split in sixth form studies, which, he argued, created a two-culture society in which scientists and those from an arts background were unable to communicate with each other, a polarisation that reduced our effectiveness as a nation 'practically, creatively and intellectually'. In more recent years educationists have become equally concerned at the sharpness of the academic and vocational divide.

During the last half-century, numerous national surveys, enquiries, consultative exercises and research projects have sought ways of providing a broader and more balanced edu-

241

cational experience for the 16-19 age-group. The most exhaustive – and exhausting – of these was a study undertaken between 1974 and 1979 by the Schools Council which looked at the feasibility of a sixth form examination system in which students would study five rather than three subjects, some of them to a less advanced level. The college was invited to take part in a major simulation exercise as part of this study. Each department provided details of the courses it would wish to offer under the proposed system. All A-level students were issued with a mock prospectus and interviewed by their tutors to ascertain what combination of courses they would have chosen had the proposals been a reality when they were considering their college programme. A timetable based on their decisions was then constructed to indicate the implications for staffing and other resources. In today's more mercenary climate the extra work entailed in this whole exercise would have been recognised in the form of fees for staff or an injection of additional funding for the college, probably both. In the seventies, however, the habitual altruism of the teaching profession was taken for granted and the college's known commitment to curriculum development was considered sufficient justification for the extra demands made on people's time. There were no complaints and the staff would have felt amply rewarded for their efforts had something worthwhile resulted from them. Nothing did, however. The newly-elected Thatcher Government wasn't interested in any change to A-levels, which it perversely regarded as the 'gold standard' of the English educational system.

Other half-hearted attempts at A-level reform followed, but nothing tangible emerged until eight years later, when the Government made a concession to the generalists by reintroducing an idea from pre-A-level days – the additional half subject that had been a feature of the Higher Certificate. The terminology had changed – 'advanced supplementary' (AS-level) replacing

242

'higher subsidiary' – but the 'new' proposal was for a curriculum identical to that which I followed in the RGS sixth form in the 1940s. The intention was that students' subsidiary subjects would broaden the range of their studies, but when the AS was introduced most schools used it to strengthen students' specialist grouping of subjects.

In 1987 a committee was set up by the Secretary of State for Education and Science under the chairmanship of Professor Gordon Higginson, Vice Chancellor of Southampton University and Governor of Queen Mary's College, to recommend the principles that should underpin A-level syllabuses and their assessment. Gordon Higginson and his colleagues spent a year visiting schools and colleges and reading submissions of written evidence that, placed on a shelf, stretched almost the width of his study. The final report gave articulate expression to the consensus for greater breadth in the 16-19 curriculum, both in terms of subjects studied and the nature of the educational experiences they offered. The Higginson Committee made the same recommendation that the Schools Council had previously done – five subjects instead of three – but all subjects would be studied to the same level. This would be made possible by a reduction in course content, the aim being to design 'leaner, tougher syllabuses' with a shift of emphasis from knowledge acquisition to an understanding of processes and concepts. QMC would have liked the Higginson proposals to have gone further, but there was much to welcome in the detail of the Committee's Report.

The Government didn't, however, take the trouble to find this out: before anyone had had a chance to read them, the Higginson proposals were consigned to the waste bin by Secretary of State Kenneth Baker, with Mrs Thatcher breathing heavily down his neck mouthing the usual platitudes about maintaining standards. Anyone seeking the reason for such a peremptory and insulting dismissal of a year's work by a distinguished group of educationists had only to read the foreword to the proposals, in which the Higginson Committee had signed its own death warrant by observing that

'the most fundamental error in the traditional GCE/A-level system was that each stage was designed to be suited for those who were going on to the next. Schoolchildren who were not good enough to go on were regarded as expendable. The other view, which seems to be held in every other advanced country, is that each stage of education should be designed for the main body of those who take it and the following stage has to start from where the previous stage ended.' *Advancing A levels,* HMSO.

The provocative suggestion that the English educational system should abandon its long-cherished nurturing of an academic élite, in favour of a curriculum that met the needs of all children, was not the best way to win friends in the Tory Party. The Higginson debacle was a good example of a familiar political process in which a government sets up an independent committee of professionals to investigate some important issue and then disowns it when its conclusions prove to be unpalatable. Professor Higginson's Committee had been formed immediately after the Thatcher Government's much-trumpeted, but sadly inadequate, attempt to silence critics of the traditional A-level curriculum by resurrecting the Higher Certificate half subject. Its thinly-disguised brief was to applaud the Government initiative and to endorse the policy to retain A-levels in their conventional form. Higginson chose, in the light of the overwhelming support for radical reform of 16-19 education, to ignore this brief and come up with proposals for a new system. The outcome was entirely predictable.

It was Thomas Arnold of Rugby who claimed that 'the first, second and third duty of a schoolmaster is to get rid of

244

unpromising subjects'. Whilst few advocates of educational élitism would put their views as crudely today, Arnold's legacy is still part of this country's political thinking. In 2004 a working group on Reform of 14-19 Education, chaired by Sir Mike Tomlinson, proposed that the secondary school and college exam system should be replaced by a new overarching diploma that did away with the class-ridden practice of separating academic study and vocational training. These recommendations were received by yet another Secretary of State sycophantically obedient to a right-wing Prime Minister. The tone of Tony Blair's and Ruth Kelly's response to the Tomlinson recommendations was noticeably more reasoned and conciliatory than that of their predecessors in similar situations, but the bottom line was the same: 'We will keep A-levels.'

Interested as we were in A-level reform, much of the college's concern over the examined curriculum focused on the inadequate provision for the 'new sixth-former', a term used in the seventies and eighties for those teenagers who would not previously have continued with their education beyond the age of 16. QMC had several hundred students in this category. Most stayed for one year and followed individually-tailored programmes combining traditional GCE O-levels, newly-devised academic alternatives and some vocational work. The majority of their courses made a similar assumption to A-levels: that those following them were capable of university-style independent study. The shortfall between this expectation and the reality was a constant subject of debate in the college and in 1980 featured prominently in a series of joint seminars with the staff of Havant Sixth Form College.

Some of the regular supporters of these occasions became interested in undertaking a practical, classroom-based group research project. The Council for National Academic Awards was approached to see whether such a professional investigation, if successfully completed, would qualify the participants for a higher degree in education. The CNAA responded enthusiastically to the prospect of a sudden boost to its Master of Philosophy enrolments, but the group idea was beyond their comprehension: each person's research had to be undertaken separately and should not be part of a co-operative effort. We were disappointed but not unduly surprised – or deterred.

Having been a prime mover in this initiative, I was under some pressure to set an example. Thus I found myself registered for MPhil research on the subject of *Sixth-formers' organisation and management of independent learning, with particular reference to one-year students*. The project would entail an analysis of students' attitudes and approaches to independent learning and seek ways of improving their study habits and skills. It included a practical experiment with a group of one-year sixth-formers, a piece of 'classroom action research'. I anticipated trouble with the awarding body over this aspect of my plans, but it wasn't until the halfway stage of my work that I ran up against a familiar problem over what constitutes an acceptable research topic. With the support of my two supervisors, I applied to transfer my higher degree registration from MPhil to PhD level. The CNAA's Officers accepted that the size and quality of the project that I was undertaking justified such upgrading, but nevertheless rejected my application on two counts. The first was due to a serious oversight on my part: when registering for the MPhil I had omitted to tick a box in the small print of the registration form that would have indicated that I might, at some future date, be interested in transferring to PhD studies. The second objection, which made the first redundant, was more predictable: there was no precedent for accepting educational research as a means of obtaining a doctorate. The gist of the circumlocutory explanation of this difficulty was that education, as a discipline, lacked the academic respectability to justify its study beyond master's degree level. There would have been no problem with palaeontology, Old Icelandic or a detailed analysis of the contents of rabbit turds.

I am not by nature an awkward customer, but I was, by this stage in my career, more assertive than 20 years previously when I had meekly accepted that my plan to edit Congreve's *Way of the World* had too practical an outcome to qualify as proper research. I challenged the CNAA's decision, and did so repeatedly. Fortunately, I had an ally within the academic community – Dr Silver, the Principal of Bulmershe College in Reading, my sponsoring institution. The two of us were eventually given an audience with the CNAA hierarchy, who finally capitulated and accepted their first PhD (Education) registration. I did, however, think that Dr Silver had blown it when he suggested to our interrogators that the work and effort that had gone into the process of persuading the council to change its mind was itself worthy of an academic award, perhaps even a doctorate.

The first stage of my research sought to establish the attitudes and approaches towards independent learning that 16-year-olds brought with them into the college. Eight hundred and forty-six pupils in three Basingstoke schools completed an extensive questionnaire on their homework experience. The responses were remarkably consistent, showing little variation across different age groups, sexes and schools. Researchers are prone to discovering the obvious and my first finding was that children didn't like homework. No groundbreaking revelations there. But the difference between children's attitude towards school and towards homework was interesting: over half enjoyed school; only 2% admitted to the same feelings about homework. Those that completed their homework – a proportion, of course, simply didn't do reading or learning tasks and copied written assignments from someone else – did so in obedience to the system, to satisfy teachers and parents, and to keep out of trouble: they were not normally motivated by an intrinsic interest in the set tasks or because they saw any purpose or value in the work. They found the whole process of working on their own extremely demanding and were constantly frustrated by an inadequate understanding of their instructions, a lack of appropriate support materials, and a sense of inadequacy when they were unable to complete work satisfactorily. There was virtually no evidence of a developing expertise in the organisation and management of their work: the 16-year-olds felt no more confident or competent in coping with their independent study than pupils several years younger. Most children concealed their difficulties from their teachers and didn't admit the extent to which parents helped them, or actually did the work for them.

One of the most telling arguments against homework was put simply, but effectively, by a 13-year-old respondent to my questionnaire: 'Well, homework's all right, but, you know, there's a whole world out there.' I was reminded of an occasion at Letchworth Grammar School when the homework issue was discussed at a parents' meeting and a number of those present expressed the view that homework interfered with the many more worthwhile activities that their sons and daughters wished to engage in out of school. I was inclined to agree with them, but at the time lacked the courage to mount a challenge to such a well-established feature of the English educational system.

The major part of my research concerned the new sixth-formers' response to independent learning. Initially, I had assumed that I would be helping them to acquire relevant study skills, such as reading for information, selecting and ordering data, taking notes, memorising facts, presenting an effective argument, structuring a report or essay. However, the homework survey revealed a much more basic problem and I decided to tackle it in its extreme form with a group of students for whom independent learning was literally a closed book. The senior tutors took great delight in selecting a group of students for me whose school record showed very little evidence of their being able to motivate themselves, organise their work or manage their lives to accommodate the demands of study.

QMC was proud of the level of individual help and guidance that its students received, both in the classroom and through its personal tutoring system, but my hand-picked 'experimental group' proved largely immune to the standard support procedures. Its members weren't used to seeking help or talking to anyone about their schoolwork. They had never disciplined themselves to do homework or to study on their own, but they were streetwise in their methods of concealing this from their teachers, cobbling something together at the last minute or copying someone else's work in order to keep out of trouble. They even deceived themselves, thinking up elaborate ways of rationalising their inability and unwillingness to study. One member of the group had convinced herself that the noise and disruption from younger siblings prevented her from ever getting any work done at home, whilst a self-diagnosed monophobia made it pointless to look for a place to study on her own. Another young lady admitted that she window-shopped for up to two hours each evening on the way home. 'Home' was a children's home and, if she could occupy the space between college and the evening meal, her domestic chores and responsibilities for younger members of her community would conveniently fill the rest of the evening, thus saving her from having to face up to her homework commitments. We are, of course, all adept at finding excuses for putting off the tasks we have to undertake; the difference with these youngsters was that they had perfected the art.

The research project sought to bring these situations out into the open. The experimental group of 15 students met each week to share experiences with me and with each other, and to discuss and try out ways of overcoming the barriers that we all encounter when we have to study on our own. Regular assignments provided a practical focus for dealing with different aspects of study organisation and management (but proved problematic at times, because they added to the sum total of commitments that the students found so much difficulty in meeting). In addition to the group sessions, students met me several times individually to talk about their response to the study process. One of the defining characteristics of the group was that, although they had chosen, or been persuaded, to enter college to improve their basic qualifications, they felt out of sync with the whole business of studying. 'I sit there sometimes,' said one young man, 'watching the others scribbling away and I think, "What the hell are they all doing?"' Sympathetic nods from the rest of the group.

The research hypothesis was a simple one: that regular guidance on how to overcome problems with independent learning would enable students to make better progress and raise their levels of attainment. A crucial task was to gather the evidence to support or refute the research hypothesis, but first there was the small matter of the literature search, the convention that requires researchers to read all the previous studies that might have a bearing on their field of enquiry. It's an incestuous process to which the academic community attaches great importance, not least because it provides its members with a use for their work. In much the same way the TV fraternity feeds on itself with a plethora of chat, game and 'reality' shows that feature its own 'celebrities' seeking to breathe some life into failing careers. I found little material of direct relevance to my project, but trogged through a mass of data and speculation on homework – mostly originating in the United States and concerned with whether or not homework makes any difference to children's educational progress. The findings were nearly always inconclusive, although occasionally someone came down on one side or the other. I had no idea whether any of this data had been massaged by a budding Burt, but there were one or two worrying mismatches of evidence and conclusions: the strength of some researchers' commitment to their original hypothesis appeared to overcome the inconvenience of evidence that clearly suggested an opposite view.

In order to assess the impact of the weekly organisation and management sessions on the students, their course marks and end-of-year exam results were compared with those of 15 comparable one-year students who, during the same year, received just the normal support from class teachers and personal tutors. This 'control group' was carefully selected to mirror the 'experimental group' in ability, attainment, background and attitudes to study. It would have been somewhat embarrassing had the comparison between these two sets of students shown that those who met the principal for weekly guidance appeared to have gained nothing from that experience. It was, therefore, something of a relief when the experimental group duly outperformed their control group 'twins' in both coursework and exam results. Of course, this may or may not have been connected with my input. In scientific investigations carried out in a laboratory it is possible to exert considerable control over the conditions in which an experiment is conducted. This cannot be done to anything like the same extent when investigating human behaviour. In the kind of comparison that I was making, the similarities between the two groups, no matter how carefully worked out, could only be approximate: a whole range of hidden factors and changing circumstances could have influenced individuals' behaviour and attainment. The benefit of such research lies less in the findings than in the investigations themselves: I learnt a good deal about 'new sixth-formers', independent learning and the limitations of the research process.

The CNAA had the last word in our ongoing debate on

what constituted worthwhile research. When the examiner read my thesis his only comment was that he felt it a bit light on the statistical front. He recommended an addition to the appendices in the form of a few tables based on the application of some Chi square tests to the data on the differences in achievement between the experimental and control groups. Unable to think of an appropriate response, I did as requested, but I was concerned when it was completed that readers would either (a) not have a clue what the additional appendix was about, or (b) have sufficient mathematical knowledge to realise that I didn't either. I was reassured by the recollection that no-one ever reads PhD theses, except the occasional writer of another PhD thesis.

20

## You Can't Be Serious

By the mid-eighties the educational climate of this country was undergoing fundamental change. Education was moving up the political agenda – with disturbing consequences. Politicians' habitual attack on educational idealism and 'progressive' methods developed into an indiscriminate condemnation of teachers, their trainers and advisers. The Government was determined to cut the experts down to size and a key strategy for reducing their influence was the application of market forces to state education. The post-16 colleges were to be the guinea pigs in this move. They would be transformed into corporate bodies – business organisations whose governors would acquire a status and power akin to that of company directors. Responsibility for funding and maintenance would be transferred from local education authorities to central government. Colleges would become increasingly business-led and pragmatic in their priorities, policies and management structures.

It was not until 1992 that these plans were fully implemented, but by the late eighties their effect was manifest in a narrowing of educational objectives, an increase in bureaucratic procedures and a growing preoccupation with income generation and recruitment. Aggressive marketing strategies began to upset the delicate balance that neighbouring sixth form and further education colleges had established between competition and co-operation. The rhetoric of mission statements, strategic plans, quality assurance procedures and glossy holiday-brochure-style prospectuses ran merrily ahead of reality.

The dishwasher manufacturer, the double-glazing supplier, the insurance company all render valuable service to society. Nevertheless, their worlds have entirely different values and rewards from those of education. I had never hankered after a business career and certainly had no desire to make the transition at this stage of my working life. The alternative was to fight a rearguard action in a vain attempt to protect the liberal values that had been established at QMC. A familiar image hove in sight: the grumpy old head becoming increasingly impatient for retirement. In 1986-7 I took a year out, accepting a fellowship at Keble College combined with a teaching and advisory post at the Oxford University Department of Educational Studies.

The OUDES offered an environment where things were moving excitingly forward rather than showing signs of regression. The Department was at the forefront of radical changes to teacher training: to give students much more practical experience and schools a far more significant rôle in the training process. The purpose of my appointment was to help evaluate the changes that were taking place. I taught one of the university-based components of the course to a group of 12 students, and monitored their progress in a local practice school. Using the QMC *Learning with Children* Main Study as a model, I sought to integrate the theoretical and practical elements of teacher training in ways that had not been achieved on my own training course. The year in Oxford showed me that there was life after Queen Mary's College and, by the time that I returned to Basingstoke, I had decided to move on.

In 1989 I left the college for the open road, intending to make my way as a travelling proselytiser impressively equipped with smart new briefcase and overnight travel bag generously supplied by my ex-colleagues. A stray phone call determined the direction of my travels, bringing an offer of another one-year higher education evaluation project, this time at Surrey University where an 'Enterprise in Higher Education' initiative promised involvement in a little bit of forward thinking. The next and final stage of my career was to be spent as a member of a small band of itinerant consultants and reformers advocating and initiating changes in university teaching. From Surrey I moved on to my old university, Birkbeck, then to University College London and finally to an outpost of the University of New York, also in London. Every assignment was different, but typically I was contracted to evaluate some aspect of a university's work, culminating in a report and set of recommendations. I then made for the door – but was invariably waylaid and persuaded to initiate some of the reforms that I had advocated. I thus learnt not to be too ambitious in my suggestions for change. Increasingly, I found myself working as a developer and trainer, running courses and workshops, drawing up guidelines for good practice and designing programmes of inservice training, both institutional and national.

It was a very basic form of pioneering or missionary work, bringing a little light to dark and almost impenetrable parts of the education system. The staff in the universities in which I worked had been appointed as researchers. Teaching was a peripheral task for which they were untrained and unqualified, and often unsuited. Although I had been fully aware of this situation I was, nevertheless, taken aback at just how low a priority most academics attached to the teaching rôle.

255

I had moved from an environment where learning and teaching were the focus of everyone's attention, the principles of good practice constantly debated and discussed, to one in which such matters were hardly ever mentioned. For many university staff, teaching was to research what the condom is to love-making – an irksome encumbrance that hinders one's main preoccupation.

Academics usually think of teaching as lecturing: they talk; students listen, and write down what they say. The concept of teaching as an art, a craft, a profession, this rarely impinges. Managing the learning process – providing a range of effective educational experiences, developing students' understanding of how to learn, differentiating between individual student needs – these are considered to be tasks for schoolteachers, not academics. By the time they arrive in university, students are expected to be motivated, fully aware of how to study and well versed in the subject that they intend to 'read' (significant term). This last, wholly unreasonable expectation hopelessly distorts school curricula and is a major cause of premature specialisation, a scourge of the education system in this country.

I entered the academic world at a time when its managers were beginning to take note of growing criticism of the low standards of teaching in higher education. There was an awareness that, unless universities took some inservice training initiatives for themselves, they might well have to contend with more demanding, externally-imposed measures to improve the quality of undergraduate education that they offered. The obvious starting point was to design an in-house probationary course for new members of staff, a task that came my way in more than one of the places in which I worked. Newly-appointed staff were not unreceptive to this initiative to provide some initial guidance on the teaching process: indeed, many took up their first post with an honourable desire to give their students a more worthwhile learning experience than they had received from their own university lecturers. Established staff were more sceptical. New lecturers were often taken quietly aside and advised that it was not in their interest to devote too much time and energy to the teaching rôle or to concern themselves overmuch with associated staff development schemes. Completion of probation, they were assured, would be a formality if the research function was proceeding satisfactorily.

Attempts to involve the main body of lecturers in staff development activities encountered strong resistance. One dinosaur's yelp of anguish would have done justice to a John McEnroe response to a dubious line call: 'You can't be serious!' There were, however, some notable exceptions and sufficient committed and imaginative teachers to save one from frustration and despair. Charismatic performers, once unearthed, were press-ganged into helping with the running of workshops and courses. In return for this help, I promised not to publicise their participation in activities of which their colleagues might not approve. Senior lecturers aspiring to promotion to reader or professor were particularly anxious not to give anyone cause to question their single-minded preoccupation with research.

'Training' is a dirty word in traditional universities, tainted by its association with non-intellectual activities and low-level occupations. Not something relevant to academics. Teaching is thought to be a matter of common sense. If the process requires the acquisition of certain practical skills – and many academics are not at all sure that it does – then intelligent people can work these out for themselves. The prevalence of this view helps to explain the difficulty that practical and vocational subjects experience in trying to gain acceptance, let alone parity of esteem, in the university setting. The following extract from a letter in the *Oxford Today* magazine indicates what they are up against:

A Master's degree in Creative Writing? At Oxford? In 50 years, a latter-day Gibbon will note this nonsense as a milestone in the Decline and Fall of Oxford. Writing is a craft well within the normal compass of every Oxford student; indeed it is a *sine qua non* of scholarship. The addition of the adjective 'creative' is hogwash, and does nothing to legitimise this programme, unless Oxford also intend to offer a PhD in Non-Creative Writing...It is absurd to argue that writing is a craft worthy of scholarly study and a university degree...These craft degrees debase the credibility of all other degrees and bring the University into disrepute.

Peter Weygang, Michaelmas, 2005.

Early HE training initiatives drew heavily on the experience of the newer universities – previously 'polytechnics' – and on the expertise of staff who had learnt their trade in them. The polys produced a steady supply of good teachers, for the same reason that the post-war secondary modern schools had done: poor teaching wasn't a comfortable option for anyone working in these environments. This source of staff developers and trainers was, of course, no great selling point in the traditional universities: the aristocracy has never felt it had much to learn from the working class. These people came from a totally different culture and spoke of strange and disturbing practices – 'evaluation' and 'course development', 'active learning' and 'student participation', 'simulation exercises' and 'case studies'. ('There won't be any rôle-play, will there?' asked a nervous gentleman hovering in the doorway as one training session got under way.)

My own appointment tended to puzzle rather than offend. Obviously schoolteachers were an even lower form of life than new-university lecturers. However, I didn't fit readily into the staff-developer image of young upstart trying to tell

258

his elders and betters what to do, and I wasn't much into the 'training-speak' that characterised the conversation of this new species. Most importantly, I had a passport to academic acceptability that many of the staff-development crew had carelessly neglected to acquire: I'd done my time as a researcher. I learnt to use the 'Dr' handle to advantage – and to keep quiet about my schoolteaching past. Reprehensible, but effective. In certain other respects I was less circumspect. As an advocate of change, it stood me in good stead that I had never been inclined to kow-tow to people on account of their position or to revere practices simply on grounds of tradition. Deference to seniority and convention is a major cause of university inertia.

Departmental autonomy is another significant hindrance to progress. Initiatives to establish good practice in teaching and tutoring are easily circumvented by the larger and more powerful departments, whose professorial grandees can be more influential than the nominal (unpaid) head of department. One litmus test of a department's commitment to its teaching rôle is the way in which it allocates lecturing and tutoring responsibilities and associated management tasks. Equal workloads are normally the stated policy. The reality, however, can be very different. New and inexperienced staff not infrequently find that they have acquired the heaviest timetables, largest student groups, least popular aspects of the course, most uncongenial timetable slots and the more tedious administrative tasks. You don't find many of the professorial staff teaching elementary maths for economists or English as a second language, late on a Friday afternoon. There are, of course, complaints procedures for victims of truly dirty tricks, but these are notoriously weighted in favour of the status quo and young lecturers aren't keen to risk their careers by taking on the Establishment over workloads. Indeed, they often contribute to their own difficulties by being too ready to assume responsibilities that more seasoned campaigners have learnt to avoid.

Like most schoolteachers, I suppose I'd always assumed that university teaching, with its clientele of highly intelligent and motivated students, was a bit of a doddle. The image persists, but the reality is very different. No-one ever talks about discipline problems, but the young female engineering lecturer trying to control rowdy chauvinists batting inflated condoms around the lecture hall probably wishes that they would. There's an understandable reluctance to play the school-ma'am, but the most successful university teachers aren't afraid to use strong-arm tactics when necessary. There was a department at the University of Surrey whose staff enjoyed particularly good relations with their students, despite being sticklers over attendance and punctuality. One overhung student had a rude awakening one morning when his lecturer appeared in his hostel and tipped him unceremoniously out of bed. One of the more charismatic lecturers at Oxford posted a notice on the door when he was ready to start a lecture, instructing latecomers to go away. When I taught at the Department of Educational Studies it took my class of postgraduates 15 minutes to assemble for their first seminar. I abandoned my prepared material and, without making any reference to the students' dilatoriness, introduced a discussion on principles of classroom practice, beginning with the procedures my group of prospective teachers would wish to establish to ensure that their lessons began on time and were not interrupted by late arrivals. The prompt start that I was usually able to make to subsequent seminars suggested that the message got across.

The opening five minutes of a lesson or lecture are crucial, and tell you much about a teacher's understanding of the learning process. I observed some attention-grabbing starts in the universities, not least by the physiologist who opened a lecture with a short extract from a video-recording of a major operation that he had undergone. I also witnessed impossible situations where lecturers began talking, and inexplicably continued to do so, against a hubbub of chatter and the clatter of late arrivals, a procedure then repeated an hour later when an attempt was made to issue instructions for written work while students packed noisily away and started to head for the exit. A trip down the Great West Road to Isleworth would not have come amiss – to observe the redoubtable Mr Jones instructing his silent army of little craftsmen.

Much of the poor teaching in higher education stems from disastrous appointments. Research reputation is paramount and the universities' desire to acquire nationally and internationally recognised researchers – not to mention the funding that accompanies their projects – has in the past overridden all other considerations. The result is that some caricature eggheads have found their way onto the payroll and lecture rostrum, reclusive boffins whose single-minded application to solitary study in a narrow academic field has left them remote from the real world and sadly lacking in the social and communicative skills required in teaching. They have come from every civilisation and corner of the earth, which gives a university a truly international flavour, but isn't very helpful to students if they are taught by someone who has just arrived in this country with only a smattering of beginner's English.

In a changing culture that was trying to accommodate the concept of accountability one of my tasks as a staff developer was to provide assistance for inadequates whose long-standing incompetence in the lecture theatre could no longer be ignored. The initial exploratory sessions with these people were tricky: having taught for years untroubled by any appraisal or evaluation procedures, they were, not surprisingly, a bit irked at suddenly being told to report for training. Even those who were quite receptive to advice found it difficult to change lifelong habits and to make any more than a token gesture towards improved performance.

A senior lecturer who obviously cared about his lecturing asked to discuss a special assignment, a memorial lecture that he had agreed to give in New Zealand in honour of his father, a distinguished researcher. The address would summarise his father's research findings and suggest ways in which his work might be taken forward. We adjourned to a lecture theatre where he began reading out his carefully-prepared script. The opening paragraphs were domestic reminiscences of his 'dad', which sat rather uneasily within the context of a read paper. I tentatively suggested that this part of his address might have more immediacy and impact delivered less formally, that is, if it were spoken rather than read. The improvement was marked and I was encouraged to advocate his continuing in the same way, which he did to promising effect. He appeared a willing convert and departed to redraft his paper as a skeletal outline to be used as a prompt for a speech. Some weeks later he came to report on the New Zealand trip, which had apparently been a big success. The country's academic élite had mustered in numbers for his lecture and he felt that he had acquitted himself well. He was generous in his appreciation of the help that I had given him. 'No problems then,' I said, 'with the changed format.' Embarrassed silence. 'Well,' he replied, 'I decided in the end that it would be safer to read it.'

Some of the referrals with whom I worked seemed to require character training rather than professional development. One senior member of staff, a head of section in a large department, had undertaken to deliver a weekly lecture in a neighbouring university to boost his income in order to help pay for his children's private school education. Fair enough, if that was his priority. A slight snag, however, was that the timing of this additional lecture overlapped with one of his teaching commitments in his own university, which situation, combined with the short journey between venues, required him either to terminate one lecture half an hour early or to start the other half an hour late. He alternated the groups that received short shrift each week. Students' tolerance of this sort of thing never ceased to amaze me. One professor went AWOL for four weeks before anyone from his only teaching class made an enquiry about the group's non-existent tuition. If student passivity is a factor in situations like this, so too is the willingness of conscientious and concerned staff to cover and compensate for irresponsible colleagues. Lecturers who take a genuine interest in students acquire a reputation, and a queue of supplicants seeking the help they cannot obtain from their own designated teachers and tutors.

One of the areas most in need of improvement in HE is the level of individual support given to students, and several of my evaluation projects focused on this aspect of teaching and learning. My enquiries always began with the students, and their eagerness to discuss their experiences was significant. A recurring theme was the remoteness of staff and the need for more individual help and encouragement. Even the most able, mature and self-sufficient would have liked more interest taken in them and a closer working relationship with staff. The following comments were transcribed immediately after an interview with an ex-student:

'The teaching style meant that you had no contact with staff. You just sat in a lecture hall and listened. Sometimes staff lectured for two hours non-stop. Anyone with any knowledge of how to teach knows the futility of that strategy. I was taught by some 15 different people. Only two, possibly three, knew my name. I don't know how anyone could ever write a reference for me. I didn't know who my personal tutor was. I think they changed every year. I was a self-sufficient person but if staff had been more friendly or accessible there were minor problems that I'd have liked to have shared with someone. I had a lot of pressures in my life while I was at university. I'd have liked someone to have known about these, someone to appreciate my achievement in managing to keep going.'

Insights like this put the tentative staff development initiatives of the last 10 to 15 years into perspective. I worked mainly with a network of enthusiasts, those members of staff who were most interested in the learning and teaching processes. One could easily forget the vast arid tracts that remained unvisited. The recent reforms have been mostly rhetorical: handbooks of good practice that may or may not be read; schemes of initial training that new staff may or may not feel obliged to attend; procedures whereby experienced lecturers can become certificated teachers – if they so wish. It's progress of sorts, but radical change isn't even on the horizon.

The whole concept of higher education has to be re-thought and current priorities turned upside down. I have a recurring dream of universities as centres of student learning, the rôle of the staff being to teach not to research. In this vision, university teaching has become a bona fide profession whose members are trained and qualified before taking up an appointment. The curriculum has been redesigned and courses updated to cover much broader fields of study, all of which include a component on 'the subject within its modern setting'. Research is undertaken in separate institutes, researchers being full-time and not required to teach. Their work focuses not on esoteric and self-indulgent topics, but on areas where it is possible to make an important and demonstrable contribution to human knowledge and understanding. Significant new findings are relayed to university teachers and students by closed-circuit television. Universities no longer control the school curriculum. Premature specialisation is a thing of the past and the secondary school curriculum is relevant to all pupils, not only the academic élite… I must be going doolally.

In my final post – at the University of New York (in London) – one of my tasks was to analyse student assessments of their teachers. American universities take student evaluation of their courses very seriously and students are accustomed to completing detailed questionnaires on all aspects of the education that they receive. They are disconcertingly frank and direct in their comments on staff – to an American, an asshole is an asshole. Weaknesses are spelt out in no uncertain terms, but so too are the qualities of the teachers whom they admire and sometimes disarmingly recommend for renewed contracts and salary increases. Staff can indeed be hired and fired on the basis of these assessments.

About 250 NYU undergraduates come to this country each semester to study in London and to be taught by English teachers. In accordance with the American system, they take a variety of modules, many of which are topical and relevant to their temporary environment – *British Cinema, Modern Drama in Performance, London Architecture, British Art, Contemporary Political Culture of Britain.* American universities believe in general education and are quite happy to accept such components as part of a degree course, whether the student is a potential chemist or economist, philosopher or lawyer.

The staff at New York University in London had a training day at the beginning of each semester at which my conclusions from the student evaluations for the previous three months were discussed and appropriate action agreed. We then engaged in a dialogue with the new intake. In groups of about 10 students and one or two teachers we discussed people's hopes and aspirations for the next three months: students talked of what they wanted from their teachers; staff explained what their expectations were of students. I briefed volunteers from the students on key rôles that they would assume during the day – either chairing the discussions or acting as rapporteurs in a plenary session. Promises were wrung from staff not to dominate discussion. It was always a very good occasion:

265

the American students were much more used to participation than their British counterparts and were highly articulate and entertaining. They chaired the group sessions with aplomb and reported back confidently and stylishly, usually without recourse to notes. One of these occasions proved to be the last task of my final contract. It was a stimulating and rewarding way in which to bring my educational career to a close, interacting with young people, learning whilst teaching.